THE IDENTITY THEFT PROTECTION GUIDE

THE IDENTITY THEFT PROTECTION GUIDE

- SAFEGUARD YOUR FAMILY
- PROTECT YOUR PRIVACY
- RECOVER A STOLEN IDENTITY

Amanda Welsh, Ph.D.

St. Martin's Griffin   New York

To my family

www.stmartins.com

ISBN 0-312-32709-9
EAN 978-0312-32709-5

First Edition: September 2004

10 9 8 7 6 5 4 3 2 1

CONTENTS

ACKNOWLEDGMENTS

I am deeply indebted to the many individuals and organizations who have worked for so many years educating consumers and lobbying government on the issues of information collection and privacy. They do the heavy lifting for the rest of us: EPIC, PRC, ACLU, ID Theft Center, PIRG, Junkbusters, and many more listed at the end of every chapter. While these folks may not agree with everything this book contains, I hope they find that our goals aren't too far apart.

I want to thank my agent, Ted Weinstein, for keeping me focused on the issues that matter and worrying on my behalf about all the ones that don't. My thanks also to the people at St. Martin's Press who put their best into what you see here: especially Sarah Delson for the cover design, Mark Steven Long for production editing, and Art Gatti for copyediting. And to Mark Fowler of Satterlee Stephens Burke & Burke LLP for his courteous, careful scrutiny of any potential missteps. To my editor, Ethan Friedman, who got so excited about the book he actually followed its advice, I am especially thankful. We can *all* thank Ethan for keeping the bad jokes to a minimum. (And the rest of the book coherent.)

Finally, I want to thank my mother and the rest of my family, friends, and colleagues for their enthusiasm and assistance with this project from beginning to end. Here's to all of you who supplied me with countless news clippings, stories from your neighbors, and forwarded e-mails. My husband, whose passions make the world a better place, was the biggest contributor of all. It goes without saying that his support, in all the big and little ways, is what made this whole thing possible. Well, let me say it anyway: Thank you and I love you.

THE IDENTITY THEFT PROTECTION GUIDE

1. IDENTITY, PRIVACY, AND PROTECTION

One day when I was a little girl in the playground, several of the bigger kids began to taunt me. "I can see your epidermis! I can see your epidermis!"

I was horrified and embarrassed. With tears in my eyes, I screamed back, "No you can't!" and ran home as fast as I could. It wasn't until my mother reassured me that epidermis only meant "skin" that I could stop being afraid.

In many ways, the current furor over identity theft and privacy invasions is reminiscent of that playground experience. A few vocal crusaders are shouting to get your attention. But are they asking you to worry about something that is really wrong, or are they telling you that you're exposed in a way that's basically okay? What exactly are the dangers? And are they real?

IDENTITY

Identity theft—when a criminal knowingly uses identifying information about you to commit, aid, or abet any action that is already illegal—seems to be on everyone's mind. You can't pick up a newspaper or watch a newscast without hearing about it. The chances of having your identity stolen are about the same as having an item of personal property stolen—pretty impressive for a crime that was virtually nonexistent just twenty-five years ago.

You take precautions to protect your personal property from being stolen without even thinking about it. Today you must also take steps to protect your identity. But while it's easy to understand what it means to have a car radio or a wallet stolen, it's not so clear to many of us just exactly what identity theft is. What actually is it that gets taken?

When you stop to define it, your identity is a bit bigger than news reports might suggest. It's not just your credit card number. It's more than your driver's license, or your Social Security number, or your computer passwords.

Think of everything that makes you who you are—the things that make you unique. The fact that you like the color blue. That you read the Sunday *Times* and watch CNN. That you graduated from Central High School with a B average and that you like brussels sprouts. That's your identity.

Your identity is the sum of every bit of information about you that there is. It's every action you've ever taken, every preference you've ever expressed. It's everything that's ever happened to you, everything you've ever purchased, everything you've ever written down, and everything other people have written about you.

In short, it's anything at all that anyone can or might use to figure out who you are and how they will treat you as a result— whether they will date you or do business with you or sell you things or throw you in jail or accept your kid into a school.

The issue, you'll quickly discover, is that when it comes to keeping your identity safe, there is more to worry about than you might think.

IDENTITY DAMAGE

Now ask yourself what's worse: having your car stolen or having it totaled in an accident? Not much difference really, is there?

While identity theft has grabbed all the headlines, there is considerably less focus placed on identity *damage*—even though it's a potentially bigger problem. Ten million Americans are victims of identity theft each year, but many more of us are the victims of identity damage. In fact, it's likely that we're all victims to some degree or other—every single one of us.

Identity damage occurs when a piece of information about you is mischaracterized, misinterpreted, or just plain wrong. These mistakes might be inconsequential, but they can also be costly. An incorrect entry in your credit report, for example, could mean you pay a higher mortgage rate than you should. An error in a medical record could deny you insurance coverage or cost you a job.

Identity damage also occurs when a piece of information about you that is absolutely true negatively affects your life or your ability to get something you want. It's possible that you're even doing this kind of damage to yourself without realizing it. Filing too many insurance claims, sending a personal e-mail from work, even being unfriendly to your neighbors can all cause identity damage if you're not careful.

Identity theft, you see, is just the tip of the iceberg.

WHAT HAPPENED TO PRIVACY?

But if these problems are so big, why are we just hearing about them now? Why didn't identity theft and identity damage pose much risk twenty-five years ago? Because back then, we had a pretty effective antidote for identity dangers: privacy. The technology to keep a watchful eye on all your actions just didn't exist. It was impractical to store much information about you, to collate it, and to share it with others. Practically speaking, even the things you did in public were really pretty private.

So, while your local grocer knew of your fondness for brussels sprouts (and who knows, may have even kept a card in a file cabinet that said so), it was doubtful that your banker or the grocer across town or even the brussels sprouts distributor knew anything about it.

But now they do.

Technology has put an end to privacy. Computers allow a lot more information to be organized and stored. These days, information that could fill football stadiums with file cabinets can be stored on computer disks that cost under one hundred dollars and fit in the palm of your hand. The Internet has connected every one of these computers—as well as every cash register, gas pump, and ATM—to form one big readily-accessible pool of data. Miniature devices like cameras or sensors have extended what information about us can be collected. Software can sift though this vast information in the blink of an eye, analyzing, sorting, and detecting patterns. The result: your life is an open book to just about anyone who wants to read it.

Six hundred insurance companies in the United States can access your medical history from a central database. Two thirds of large companies perform background checks on job candidates. Direct marketers determine that four-and-a-half-million tons of junk mail should be delivered to you and your neighbors each year.

Did you know that computers in your car monitor if you're speeding? That software predicts if you're likely to commit a crime? That doctors, banks, hotels, casinos, and apartment owners maintain blacklists? That invisible surveillance cameras photograph you more than seventy-five times each day—sometimes for security and sometimes to catch you in an embarrassing situation for broadcast on Internet Web sites?

Did you know that thirty-five federal agencies have bought information collected on you by large profiling companies to gauge if you're likely to be a terrorist or drug smuggler? And the only way that you're not profiled is if you've never bought anything with credit, don't have a driver's license or a checking account or any kind of insurance, and have never held a job or even filed a change of address with the post office.

Some would have you believe that the key to reducing identity theft and damage is to fight for more privacy, hoping to stem the tide of all this technology. But although most of us value privacy as a concept, when push comes to shove we rarely care about what people know about us. Until a line is crossed—and for most people that line is at the doorway to the bedroom—we're quite happy living in a world where *Big Brother* is a television show and not an Orwellian nightmare.

The key is to forget about trying to keep your identity private.

It's a bit like worrying about showing your epidermis. You need to worry about what really matters.

WHAT REALLY MATTERS

First, the Bad News

Consider what happened to these people:

- A busboy in Manhattan contacted credit reporting agencies and obtained the Social Security numbers of two hundred CEOs and celebrities such as Steven Spielberg, Ted Turner, and Oprah Winfrey. Using their identifying information, he authorized transactions with banks and stock brokers that allowed him to swindle millions of dollars from his famous victims.

- A man in Massachusetts was wrongly classified as an alcoholic by a medical information bureau and was charged higher premiums than he should have been for disability insurance; another woman was denied insurance altogether because her father's record incorrectly indicated that he had a hereditary disease.

- After being turned down for many potential jobs, a man who was unsuccessfully looking for work found out that his Social Security number had been mistakenly assigned to a murder suspect. Another luckless job hunter discovered that he was marked as being wanted in a database of suspected arsonists and shoplifters. Unfortunately, both men were law-abiding citizens whose records got mixed up with those of true criminals. And both men lost their houses and families before the problems were uncovered.

- A kindly grandmother was disturbed to receive phone calls from a prison inmate who made detailed references to her personal situation along with vulgar sexual suggestions. It turned out the inmate had been hired by a mailing list vendor to input information about catalogue purchasers into a master database. He chose the elderly woman at random as a plaything to harass.

- Another woman—this one only nineteen years old—was stalked by a psychotic classmate who used an information tracking agency to find out where she worked. The classmate shot and killed her outside her place of employment.

We've all heard these stories or ones like them before, and most of the time we're shocked and appalled by them. The funny thing is, though, we don't really change anything that we do because of them. The reason we don't is that the people who share these stories with us—reporters and consumer advocates—have generally presented them as invasions of privacy.

But here's the catch. These stories aren't really about privacy at all. These stories are about mistakes and abuse and stalking. Their message isn't to worry if someone knows how often you buy corn flakes. Their message is that, once put into a database, information about you has a life of its own. People you don't expect—and maybe don't even like—can get to it. They can use it to hurt you in surprising ways. Or they may be well-meaning screwups who get your information wrong and make you look like a credit risk or a sucker.

The issue isn't privacy. It's protection.

Now, the Good News

On the face of it, all this information tracking and profiling sounds pretty bad. It certainly can be, but for the most part it's also a very good thing.

Think about buying a new car. For most of us, it's a pretty major investment. We don't usually have the money to pay for it outright, so we turn to the bank for a loan. Before the bank will give us the money, it needs to make sure that we're financially stable and that we'll keep making our monthly payments. Typically, after filling out a few short forms and waiting a couple of minutes—sometimes without even leaving the dealership—we're sitting behind the wheel enjoying that new-car smell.

Now, consider the plight of a poor guy in Beijing looking for his first car. He, too, can't afford to pay outright and needs a loan. And just as with our bank, his bank wants to make sure he's trustworthy and will make his monthly payments.

So how do they do it in China? Loan officers go to his job and interview his boss. They visit his home to see how he lives. They even talk to his neighbors to see what gossip about him is floating about. Pretty embarrassing, don't you think?

Banks in China don't have access to a magic computer file with this guy's credit history to determine whether he's a reasonable risk. The result: getting a loan is a nightmare, and less than 20 percent of car buyers even bother to apply for a loan, compared to 80 percent in the United States.

The existence of consumer reporting means that we don't have to endure such personal invasions to get credit, loans, or insurance. It also means that only data that is actually relevant to the transaction at hand gets considered. A banker doesn't look you up and down and decide that he doesn't like your nose ring. Instead, he gambles that your twenty years of good credit is more important. In an interesting twist, the existence of all this personal information tucked away in computers actually gives you a certain amount of anonymity and privacy protection.

The existence of data collection also means that we get more of what we want. Shops that track what we buy from them frequently reward us with free items. That eighth free cup of coffee tastes pretty good, doesn't it?

And we get what we want faster. Computers can look up information in seconds. Bored clerks in dusty rooms filled with index cards have been known to take weeks. Even though the government says it takes six weeks to get a passport, they can usually turn around applications in a few days now. Request a transcript from your school and it's in the mail the same day.

Computers can also follow information that a human simply wouldn't be able to, like how many cars are on each block in a city at a given point in time. The result is a quicker trip home, because traffic lights can be optimally timed to keep traffic flowing.

Information access helps prevent mistakes. Electronic ID tags on shipping containers used by airlines help eliminate lost luggage. Patients who need many different medications *want* doctors to have access to their entire medical history so that they can avoid becoming one of the 98,000 people killed each year by medical errors.

Many have argued that information is the grease of capitalism. We are better shoppers in a world where we can compare price for products, or access information on whose service isn't quite up to the standard they claim. The United Nations even goes a step further. It thinks information is the key to reducing poverty. In Bangladesh, entrepreneurs have purchased cell phones to rent to rural farmers that otherwise have no contact with the outside world. Farmers have been using these phones to determine crop prices in city markets. By learning what prices are being charged in the cities, rural farmers assure that they don't get taken by unscrupulous middlemen who offer them below-market rates. A UN report indicates that these information-savvy farmers have increased their profits by 10 percent, a big deal when you're living on the edge of survival.

Perhaps most importantly, given the debate in society today about the balance of freedom and security, let's not forget about information and the role of government. If knowledge is power, democratic safeguards that provide us with access to information mean that the government never gets too much power. Free access to government records—both what the Department of Homeland Security is doing as well as what you are doing—was designed to prevent the development of a secret police or an authoritarian state.

THE BOTTOM LINE

Nobody can escape the system. Integrity of and access to information is everybody's business now, every day, whether we like it or not. Just because you don't know how a television works, that doesn't mean you can't enjoy watching it. Just because you don't understand all the gee-whiz technology that runs the Internet or satellites or all the other new stuff, don't think the information they collect and share can't affect you. It's time to wake up and smell that free coffee.

So, if there is a good side and a bad side to information tracking, where do we end up? Is it more dangerous to live in the Information Age, or are we all better off as a result? The answer is "Yes" to both.

It's a little like driving a car. Driving a car is certainly more dangerous than sitting at home, but the benefits of getting swiftly from point A to point B can be great. And while taking commonsense precautions like staying on the right side of the road won't guarantee your safety, they do make it far less likely that you'll be injured. This book shows you where the yellow line in the middle of the road is and gives you tips on how to avoid crossing into oncoming traffic.

This book isn't an exploration of future technology, or even technology that doesn't touch a whole lot of us most of the time. It's not going to suggest that you to move to Montana and live in a bunker. It won't try to indoctrinate you to a political agenda or ask you to change the world. This book is about the basics of everyday protection.

The first topic we will cover is your single biggest vulnerability: identity theft. We will figure out what it is, how it happens and what you can do to prevent it. Then, we'll move on to how information can be used to get you what you want. We'll talk about credit reporting, insurance tracking, and banking and money issues. Next, we'll examine just how big Big Brother has become. After that, we'll talk about lists of every type you can imagine, what they're used for, and how you get off the wrong ones and onto the right ones. We'll talk about the Internet issues you need to be most concerned about: hacking and tracking. And we'll talk about what you need to know in the information age to protect yourself and your family from prying eyes. We will review mobile tracking, and surveillance by law enforcement and crooks. Last but certainly not least in terms of its importance, we'll end up exploring information issues of particular concern to kids, such as Internet stalking and school record-keeping.

Although the book has been arranged with a certain flow in mind, there is no reason that chapters need to be read in order. Feel free to move around as your mood requires. Some chapters on the most mature information tracking—credit reporting, for example—are long and occasionally technical. Others on newer topics, like mobile tracking, may fit the bill when you need something a little lighter. And, of course, if you think a particular issue doesn't affect you, skip that chapter entirely and move on. Just be warned: you may find that if you do read each chapter you will learn things you hadn't expected!

Within each chapter you will read about the general issues, take a checkup to understand where you, personally, are vulnerable, and figure out actions that make sense for your situation. Each chapter ends with a list of the resources that you'll need to get started on your new action items.

And finally, even though we will be talking about the bread-and-butter issues that all of us need to know about, it's important to understand up front that the world is changing very quickly. The Department of Homeland Security has brought the seriousness of both the need to track information and the implications of doing so home to a lot of us. The dramatic increase in identity theft has caught the attention of corporate America, which foots most of the bill for it. The resulting awareness in our society has prompted lawmakers to consider more and more protective legislation and companies to rethink tracking systems with a new sensitivity to privacy issues. Given that so many are working so hard, new developments in information protection are inevitable. Every effort has been made to present you with the most up-to-date information in this book, but for those times where changes have gotten ahead of print, you can follow the latest developments at this book's companion Web site, www.identitytheftprotectionguide.com.

Okay, are you ready? Let's get started.

2. THE BIG WORRY: IDENTITY THEFT

IN THIS CHAPTER:
What identity theft is, how it applies to you, how you can reduce your risk of becoming a victim

The biggest danger you face in the information age is identity theft.

It used to be that a talented con artist might forge a check or make a fake ID—tactics that took some skill. Today, any malicious fiend can simply fill in the preapproved credit card offers you throw away each week. Or steal your name from a database you didn't even know existed. Identity thieves have filed false tax returns to get refunds, bought and sold stocks using somebody else's account, opened new credit card accounts, and leased expensive cars that they never intend to pay for.

You know the old saying: "An ounce of prevention is worth a pound of cure." The likelihood you'll be a victim this year is around 1 in 26, about the same likelihood that some of your physical property will get stolen. Since you probably think it's reasonable to lock the door to your house to prevent someone from breaking in, you ought to think it's reasonable to take basic precautions against identity theft. Precautions to protect against identity theft include understanding your points of vulnerability, gathering key information in one safe location, and establishing a plan for what to do in case of a problem.

WHAT EXACTLY IS IDENTITY THEFT?

That's a difficult question to answer because the definition, and indeed, even the crime is changing.

Basically, identity theft occurs when someone assumes some or all of your identity to engage in criminal behavior. This may be as simple as using your telephone calling card number to place long-distance calls on your account. It may involve getting ahold of information that identifies you, like your Social Security number, and using it to open new credit accounts or to lease a car in your name, and leave you with the bills. It may even mean having someone take on your identity to create a new life in which the thief rents an apartment, applies for government benefits, gets a job, or—if you're really unlucky—commits a crime that gets you sent to jail.

Here are some stories of identity theft that illustrate the range of the potential problems:

- Fresh out of law school, a young woman from San Diego turned up for her first day of her new job, only to be greeted by a police officer who put her in handcuffs and carted her off to jail. Turns out her new boss had contacted the authorities when a routine background check unearthed a warrant for her arrest. Unfortunately, the warrant was for a crime that had been committed by the woman who stole the lawyer's purse, and with it, her identity.

- Gerald Barnbaum didn't much like who he was. So he took on the identity of Dr. Gerald Barnes, an orthopedist from Stockton, California. Barnbaum legally changed his name to Barnes and requested a duplicate of the real Barnes's medical license and diploma, which he used to find work. For twenty years Barnbaum practiced medicine—at one point working for the U.S. government to do physical exams of FBI agents—until he was finally convicted of manslaughter when an unlucky patient died as a result of his misdiagnosis.

Sadly, an identity thief is often a troubled father or sister or ex-spouse taking advantage of a family member.

- A brother and sister struggled with finding out that their father had opened checking accounts in their names and written bad checks to cover his debts. Their father, who was sixty-eight, had a gambling addiction.

- A Baltimore man was dropped by his car insurance company and flooded with medical bills when his brother took to giving his name out to the victims of car accidents the brother caused.

Perhaps the most heartbreaking stories come from those who must deal with the abuse of the identity of a loved one they've lost. Because it takes a few weeks for an individual's death to be reported to companies tracking his or her Social Security number, this kind of abuse is not all that difficult to pull off. The Identity Theft Resource Center relates these stories:

- A young couple who had just endured the death of their toddler had their tax return rejected by the IRS. Someone else had already taken the deceased child's Social Security number and filed a return listing the child as a dependent.

- The widow of a man who died in the World Trade Center collapse discovered that someone had been using his identity. Not only is she coping with becoming the sole provider for her family, but she must deal with the unexpected actions being taken in her spouse's name and keep them from getting tied to *her* financial information.

IS IDENTITY THEFT REALLY A BIG DEAL?

Identity theft has been getting a lot of press in the past few years and the tone of some reports has been, to put it mildly, dramatic. In the face of so much hype, it's worth taking a look at some basic facts.

THE COST OF IDENTITY THEFT

Because federal law limits your liability in a lot of identity theft cases, most victims don't suffer more than a few dollars of loss, mostly in notary fees. The real cost of identity theft is the hassle of cleaning up after the thief has been cut off. The U.S. Public Interest Research Group reports that it takes an average of two to four years to explain away the thief's bad debts. The FTC estimates that 36 percent of victims also experienced problems like being denied credit, a loan, or insurance as a direct result of the theft. Of the people unlucky enough to have an identity thief actually impersonate them—instead of just using their credit card account for an unauthorized shopping spree—14 percent were investigated by the police or thrown in jail.

The truth is that no one can reliably quantify how bad identity theft is, because some crimes—like using your credit card number to make a few bad charges—often don't get reported to the agencies that track it. Past estimates of the number of people affected range from 250,000 to 10 million per year.

Taking the biggest estimate of the problem, the likelihood you'll be a victim this year is around 1 in 26. This number includes someone using your credit card to make some bad charges—a pretty small inconvenience—as well as the more extreme cases of opening fake accounts, renting apartments, leasing cars, and filing false tax returns—a decidedly bigger deal. If you only consider the serious cases, the likelihood that you'll fall prey to an identity thief is more like 1 in 74. Clearly, it is less likely that you will suffer this kind of problem.

Unfortunately, all trends suggest that the numbers are growing— and growing fast. A big study by the Federal Trade Commission (FTC), the government agency that enforces consumer protection laws, reports that ID thefts in 2003 were up 33 percent over the year before. If you just look at fake charges on credit card accounts, the number of problems grew 71 percent. Other studies report growth

THE WILLY SUTTON PRINCIPLE

We all know that companies collect a lot of information about us. Most of the time they do it for the right reasons, such as wanting to give us better service. But in creating a juicy stockpile of data, they create a very attractive target for information thieves. It's just as Willy Sutton, the infamous bank robber, supposedly said when asked why he robbed banks: "Because that's where the money is."

Organized criminal groups wanting long lists of personal information don't waste time breaking into our mailboxes one by one. More and more, they're going for the large corporate databases.

rates that are even higher. Given the current rates, identity theft could well touch 1 out of 9 Americans annually by 2007.

And here's another way to think about it. Even if you are never personally victimized by identity theft, you're definitely a victim in the aggregate. The cost of identity theft is estimated to be about $5 billion for the folks whose identity is stolen. However, for business, which absorbs the majority of the costs, the price tag is closer to $50 billion. Companies don't just pay these kinds of amounts without passing them on to you in the form of higher fees or penalties. Without even realizing it, you're already a victim of identity theft—you're helping to foot the bill for it.

Finally, as you think about identity theft, it's important to consider where the real danger is. You can control some personal risk—we'll talk later about how—but you can't control or often even find out about the risk that the companies you do business with expose you to. And, increasingly, that's where the real action is.

See if you think you could have protected yourself from cases like these: A theft of computer equipment (and the data it contained) from the office of TriWest Healthcare Alliance put the Social Security numbers and other highly personal information of 500,000 servicemen and women at risk. A similar theft of the laptop belonging to a consultant for Wells Fargo Bank posed a risk to the personal information of thousands of bank account holders. An insider at a data processing company sold 30,000 credit files stored on his company's computers to a ring of identity thieves for sixty dollars apiece. An accountant filed thirty-six fake tax returns using information from his company's legitimate clients. A sale of surplus computers owned by the State of Virginia exposed employee evaluations, credit card numbers, and other sensitive data of Virginia citizens, because the hard drives on these computers hadn't been wiped clean before going to auction.

This list is chilling enough, but the really scary thing to consider is that these are only the problems that we've heard about. Because most companies are under no obligation to report security breaches, and because they don't want the bad PR that goes with reporting one, the majority of companies are choosing to keep silent when information is stolen. In a survey conducted by the FBI and the Computer Security Institute, 60 percent of roughly five hundred companies interviewed suffered a computer security breach in the year they studied. Only one third reported the break-ins to law enforcement.

The state government of California knows all about this. In April 2002, hackers stole payroll records for 265,000 of its employees. The company housing the data for the state didn't tell anyone about the break-in—which included theft of names, Social Security numbers, and bank account info for everybody all the way up to the governor—for three weeks. Startled by the lack of disclosure, the state legislature passed the first law in the country that requires companies to inform customers if any of their identifying information is ever stolen from databanks. If you don't live in a state with a law like the one in California, it is almost impossible for you to know just how risky it is to give your information to a company.

Given the explosive growth, the fact that you're at the mercy of the companies you do business with and the fact that you pay for the crime whether you experience it personally or not, the answer to the question "is it really a big deal" is yes. It's worth your time to pay attention to what is going on.

HOW CAN MY IDENTITY BE STOLEN?

If you ever are victimized by identity theft, chances are reasonably good that you will never know how your information was stolen. Victims have no idea when or how the theft occurred in almost half of the cases.

Still, we can learn from the remaining half and recognize at least some of the times we may be vulnerable. A little more than a fifth of ID theft victims are able to trace the problem back to a loss or theft of something like a wallet, credit card, or checkbook. Another 4 percent noticed something missing from the mailbox.

Experts and counselors who work with victims note that identity thieves steal what they need by grabbing bills and credit card offers from unlocked mailboxes, sifting through papers that have been thrown away (also called dumpster diving), or looking over your shoulder at ATMs or anytime you have to swipe a card and punch in a password (also called shoulder surfing). They may also con you into giving personal information to them directly. By posing as a customer-support person needing your account information to take care of a quick problem, or a government official investigating a situation, identity thieves can trick you into helping them steal from you.

The rest of the time, the weak link is probably one of the many companies you buy things from and the agencies that follow those purchases.

WHAT MAKES ME A GOOD TARGET FOR IDENTITY THEFT?

Your behavior helps determine your risk, but, as with most crimes, having a relationship with someone who is trouble, or living in a place where a lot of criminals also live, definitely makes you a more likely target.

According to an FTC survey, a stunning one tenth of all identity theft is committed by a family member. Once you add in dubious friends, neighbors and coworkers, simply being involved with troubled people accounts for roughly a fifth of the ID theft cases.

The six states with the highest instances of theft per hundred thousand citizens made up approximately half of the cases reported to the FTC consumer hotline between 1999 and 2003. These states—California, Arizona, Nevada, Texas, Florida, and New York—are more dangerous to live in than the other forty-four. Along those same lines, the cities with the highest number of complaints were New York City, Orange County, San Bernardino, Los Angeles, Houston, Miami, Oakland, San Francisco, Las Vegas, Phoenix, Washington D.C., San Diego, Dallas, and Atlanta. In other words, identity thieves tend to operate in big cities. You're not totally safe if you live elsewhere. Cyberspace knows few geographical boundaries. But given past trends, you are more at risk if you live in San Francisco than in Des Moines.

WHEN SHOULD I SUSPECT IDENTITY THEFT?

Unfortunately, the answer is "Always." You can't take a breath in today's world without being tracked somewhere. That means that you are always exposed and always a candidate to become one of the unlucky ones.

Generally, your first indication that you have become a victim is when you notice something awry on a bill or account statement. Fifty-two percent of problems are caught this way. In 24 percent of cases, a call from your credit company or a bill collector gives you the tip. This call may simply ask you about suspicious activity. In other cases, vendor companies duped by your thief—or their bill collection agencies—come to you for payment. Much less frequently, a routine traffic stop takes on an ominous tone if you find out then that someone has been committing crimes in your name.

Other indications of identity theft are the sudden absence of correspondence, like bills, that may indicate that someone has filed a fake address forwarding request, or questionable information showing up on your credit report, such as addresses you've never lived at or accounts you have never heard of.

IS SOME IDENTITY THEFT WORSE THAN OTHERS?

There are basically two reasons to commit identity theft: to commit fraud (consumer theft) or to impersonate you, generally to commit a crime (criminal theft). Of the two types, consumer theft is the lesser of two evils and accounts for the vast majority of all identity theft cases. Probably because it affects so many people, there are a handful of laws that protect us from the bad outcomes.

In the world of consumer fraud, credit card fraud is the most common kind of identity theft and the one that you have the most protection from. It generally involves either an account takeover—someone makes bad charges on your account—or account creation. In the latter case, the criminal sets up a new account with a fake address. They ignore all of the bills that go to that address, and you generally find out about what is going on when the bill collectors get involved.

Assuming that you report any loss of your credit card—say your wallet is stolen—within a timely fashion, federal law limits your liability for any resulting fraudulent activity to fifty dollars. Most banks won't even charge you that. If an identity thief steals your card number but not your physical card, you have no liability whatsoever. This makes sense when you think about it. Because you have no way of knowing that your number has been stolen until a problem occurs, there is no reasonable way you could have prevented the fraud. More information on liability limits can be found on the Federal Trade Commission Web site (www.ftc.gov).

By far the worst type of identity theft is criminal theft. The consequences to you, like getting arrested, are potentially more serious than in consumer ID theft, and your ability to clean up the problem on your own is much more difficult. Because every criminal has some sort of excuse, law enforcement agencies are naturally suspicious when you say that someone else must be posing as you. Even when you convince the police that they've got the wrong guy, law enforcement needs to keep track of the fact that the crook might use your name again. Your name is inextricably attached to the actual criminal's wrongdoings. You are now an "alias."

The good news is that this kind of worst case scenario is fairly uncommon, accounting for only 4 percent of the reported cases of identity theft. And despite being somewhat torturous, there are legal actions that you can take to clear your name. More advice on this very thorny issue can be found at Privacy Rights Clearinghouse (www.privacyrights.org).

WHY IS MY SOCIAL SECURITY NUMBER SPECIAL?

It all began with the depression. In 1935, Franklin Delano Roosevelt signed the Social Security Act, creating a state-sponsored pension program for all workers. Beginning with the first day of 1937, workers were given a unique identifying number to track earnings for participation in the Social Security retirement program.

Since that time the number has been used to track federal tax returns (starting in 1961), state and local tax returns, Medicare, Medicaid, welfare programs, and driver's license and motor vehicle registration (since 1976). It is now also used by the government for military ID cards and immigration papers, and as a way to hunt down deadbeat dads. Most health insurance is linked to this number. Colleges and companies put it on ID badges. In other words, as the need for a unique identifying number came up, our Social Security numbers provided a convenient system to co-opt.

The result is that this one number is the key to a fairly complete digital history on you. With knowledge of that number, a thief has no difficulty taking over your identity to add new pieces to the puzzle. Does he want a loan? He simply puts your Social Security number on an application and uses your very good credit history to convince the bank to give him as much as he needs.

Government is slowly beginning to catch on to the fact that it may have created a monster. Several initiatives at the state and federal levels are under way to restrict or forbid the use of the Social Security number as a means of identifying us. The federal Privacy Act of 1974 was an important early step in this process, and it still has force today. This law requires all government agencies (federal, state, and local) to tell you if you are required to provide your Social

Security number, what gives them authority to request that number, and what the number will be used for.

With a few exceptions, such as being involved in a transaction that requires notification of the IRS, no private entity can legally require a Social Security number. However, no company is required to give you service if you refuse to provide your number, either. The unfortunate reality is that it's difficult to get companies to change their policies of using a Social Security number as a customer identification number, and sometimes the service we seek is something we can't really do without. Faced with the choice of making your Social Security number public information and not getting health coverage, for example, the vast majority of us have opted for the coverage.

What is truly amazing—given how easy it is to get ahold of Social Security numbers—is that credit card companies and banks rely so consistently on this single number to verify your eligibility for a new shiny plastic card or the right to drive off in a red convertible. The balance for them has been that it's more lucrative to sell a lot of credit services and write off a few bad apples than to try to avoid the problems. Given that thefts of information used to commit fraud is growing in leaps and bounds, it's reasonable to predict that the balance is now changing and that companies, with their own interests at heart, will start offering you more protection.

IS IDENTITY THEFT AGAINST THE LAW?

Sort of. Way back in October 1998, Congress passed the Identity Theft and Assumption Deterrence Act (Identity Theft Act). This law basically made it a federal crime to knowingly use identifying information about a person to commit, aid, or abet any action that is already illegal.

In other words, you can't be convicted of identity theft unless you're involved in some other crime. The law doesn't make pretending to be someone else at a party a crime. However, if you then go on to use another person's ID to swindle money from someone you met at that party, this act allows the FTC, the U.S. Secret Service, the

FBI, and the U.S. Postal Inspection Service to get involved. The law further requires the FTC to coordinate identity theft information and to track the latest trends and issues relating to identity theft.

The law also addresses another problem. For years, the person whose identity was stolen often didn't get recognized as the victim and had no rights. This meant that only the credit card company who lost money was given information about an identity theft case. The person whose credit was ruined, who was getting turned down for jobs, and who was fielding calls from bill collectors was left in the dark. The Identity Theft Act gives the individual who is impersonated some power, but there are still reports of police departments who won't take identity theft complaints or companies who won't share information with the victims. Another more recent law, the Fair and Accurate Credit Transactions Act (FACTA) takes on this last problem directly. We'll talk more about FACTA in chapter 3.

In the past few years, individual states have also been creating legislation to address identity theft. A list of specific laws broken down by state can be found on the FTC Web site (http://www. consumer.gov/idtheft/federallaws.html#criminalstate) or you can contact your state's Attorney General.

CHECKUP

Now that you're an expert on what identity theft is, it's time to see just how vulnerable you are to it. The following checkups help you to evaluate your own situation to see where you stand.

Can You Pass the Wallet Test?

There is one point of vulnerability to identity theft that you have *absolute* control over: your wallet. Are you prepared for what happens when your wallet gets stolen? Here's the test. Don't take out your wallet. Just close your eyes and try to remember everything you have in it. You probably have at least one credit card. And a driver's license. There's also probably something with your address.

And your signature. What about your bank account number? Scribbled phone numbers? Business cards? Is there anything with your Social Security number? You haven't written down any PINs or passwords and stashed them in your wallet, have you?

If someone stole your wallet right now, this is all the information about you that they would have. And it's also all the information that you now need to change, to prevent them from pretending to be you and taking advantage of everything you've ever worked for. Okay, now take out your wallet and look at what it contains. How well did you do?

If you remembered everything perfectly, if you have memorized the numbers on all the cards in your wallet, and the phone numbers to report problems to, give yourself a perfect score. If you're like the rest of us, give yourself a "5" and read the first part of the Taking Action section carefully.

Weigh the Risks

The following set of questions will help you find any special risk areas that deserve your attention. For each question, put a check next to any answer that applies to you. When you are finished, circle the score in the box below that corresponds to the number of check-marks. If you score higher than a 3 on the scale for any given question, your risk is too high in that area.

Risk Area #1. How many of the following contain your Social Security number?

____ Health insurance

____ School/company ID

____ Health club membership

____ Phone card

____ Driver's license

____ Pilot, boating, or any other license

____ Any other document besides your Social Security card

1	2	3	4	5
Just one	Two	Three	Four	More than four

Risk Area #2. How many of the following are true about you?

____ You do not have a locked mailbox.

____ You put bills out for the mail carrier to pick up.

____ You do not shred documents that have personal information.

____ You receive preapproved credit offers at least once a week.

____ You provide information to companies without considering why they need it.

____ You have more than three credit card accounts.

____ You write your driver's license number on your check when a merchant requests it, or you have the number preprinted on your checks.

1	2	3	4	5
Just one	Two	Three	Four	More than four

Risk Area #3. How many of the following are true about your situation?

____ You live in Washington, D.C., California, Arizona, Nevada, Texas, Florida, or New York State.

____ You have relatives living in Washington, D.C., California, Arizona, Nevada, Texas, Florida, or New York State.

____ You went to school in Washington, D.C., California, Arizona, Nevada, Texas, Florida, or New York State.

____ You live in New York City, Orange County, San Bernadino, Los Angeles, Oakland, Houston, Miami, Oakland, San Francisco, Las Vegas, Phoenix, San Diego, Dallas, or Atlanta.

____ You have elderly relatives in your care.

____ You have relations or acquaintances that have problems with drugs.

____ You have relations or acquaintances that have problems with alcohol.

____ You have relations or acquaintances that have problems with gambling.

1	2	3	4	5
Just one	Two	Three	Four	More than four

Risk Area #4. How many of the following are true about the companies you do business with?

____ You have made a purchase from a small online shopping site that does not also have a real world store.

___ You often shop online at sites of companies that are also large chains with real world stores.

___ You have used online auction sites.

___ You have bought from a catalogue—even just one time.

___ You are a member of more than one frequent-buyer club.

___ You do business with companies that routinely offer contests or surveys with prizes.

___ You do business with companies that try to put you on an electronic mailing list.

1	2	3	4	5
Just one	Two	Three	Four	More than four

Risk Area #5. How many of the following are true of your employer?

___ Your Social Security number is your employee number.

___ Your Social Security number is on your employee ID badge.

___ Your Social Security number is your ID for your employer-sponsored health plan.

___ Your company does not have (or has not told you about) a stated privacy policy about how the information you supply (or is in your employee file) is shared or not.

___ Your company does not conduct background checks on employees that handle sensitive data.

___ Your company does not limit access to areas containing sensitive data.

1	2	3	4	5
Just one	Two	Three	Four	More than four

It's time to look at the numbers. How did you score? The second section under Taking Action tells you what you can do to reduce your risk in any problem areas that you've identified.

TAKING ACTION

Armed with an understanding of your own particular problem areas, you are now ready to take action. This section tells you how to prepare for identity theft and how to lower your risk of it happening in the first place. It also contains information on what to do should your wallet get stolen, or if you discover that the worst has already happened.

Build an Identity Emergency Kit

The best way to prepare for the fallout from identity theft is to assemble an identity emergency kit. This kit contains all the items that you will need if your wallet or purse is lost or stolen or if you ever find that your identity has been damaged. Of course, you'll want to keep your identity kit in a secure place. You might even consider keeping it in a safety deposit box at your bank. It not only keeps your information safe from theft, but if your house is ever destroyed or damaged by fire or flood, you'll have a head start on picking up the pieces.

Document Yourself

To begin, pull together copies of all the important documents in your life that identify you. For documents that you don't carry around on a regular basis like your passport, birth certificates, or marriage licenses, simply putting them in the kit is enough. For documents that you use regularly, like a driver's license or your bank or credit card, you need to make a photocopy of the front and back of each one. The easiest way to make this happen is simply to copy the entire contents of your wallet. Store the photocopies in your kit.

You also want to photocopy or include sample bills or statements for your bank accounts and credit cards. Since most companies will want to verify your knowledge of account activity prior to any problem you report, having these bills handy will save a lot of time and explanation.

You may also want to download and print the Identity Theft Affidavit available from the FTC Web sites (http://www.consumer. gov/idtheft/). This affidavit can be used to supply information to the various agencies who will want to know about your case.

Your Password Plan

The second part of your first aid kit is a policy and password plan. Start by gathering together all the policy documents and statements from your credit cards, loans, and banks. Read through them to understand where companies will assume liability and where they will try to push it off onto you. When you're in the midst of a problem, having all these documents in one place will make it much easier to figure out who to contact first and what you have to tell them.

After you get the liability issues sorted out, you need to organize your passwords. If you're like the average person, you have made up anywhere from ten to thirty passwords. And you probably can barely remember what all of them are for. Most people have two sorts of passwords . . . important ones that they try to make somewhat difficult to figure out, and unimportant ones that are often their name.

After talking to a lot of people about how they manage their passwords, my recommendation is to go to the drug store and buy a ninety-nine-cent notebook. In this notebook, write down all the passwords that you've created (that you can remember).

Don't be tempted to enter your passwords into a spreadsheet, word processor, or other program on your computer. The beauty of an old-fashioned paper notebook is that no one can hack into it. When you upgrade to a new computer, you haven't given the full list to the next person to boot your old hard drive. It's not in your PDA when *that* gets lost or stolen. And if you ever get into trouble and a loved one needs to help you out, the technology involved in opening a notebook is something that just about anyone can handle.

Of course, this notebook, too, must be kept locked in a secure place. Many security experts would argue with me about the wisdom of writing down your passwords at all. But most security experts don't seem to have trouble remembering thirty passwords. Good for them. For the rest of us, this notebook will be incredibly useful if you find that someone is taking over your accounts. You can quickly identify all the passwords you care about and change

THE GOLDEN RULE OF PASSWORDS

When making up passwords, remember the following golden rule: *Never* use the last four digits of your Social Security number, your middle name, pet's name, birth date, consecutive numbers, or any word that is obvious when thinking of you.

For that matter, don't use any word at all. Password cracking programs begin by checking your password against every entry in the *dictionary*. Think your pet name "pandabear" is safe? Think again. Although only two people in the whole world would think to associate that name with you, it's in a dictionary. Even the simplest password-cracking programs can do a lookup of every dictionary word there is. And they can do it in about two minutes.

Take "pandabear" and change just one character to something from the top line of the keyboard—say "p@ndabear"—and you increase security without having to memorize meaningless gibberish just to get to your e-mail account. Add a number and a mix of capital and lowercase letters— like "p@ndAb3Ar"—and your password now takes an extra couple hundred or so years to break. The best part is that it's still close enough to your pet name to be easy to remember.

them. It's a protective action that can give you great peace of mind. Otherwise, when bad things happen, you can be left with the nagging feeling that you've left some window of opportunity standing wide open for the bad guys. Note that if you have special family issues to be wary of, you don't want to publicize the existence of your notebook.

For the first month or so, when you stumble across another Web site or account that you made up a password for, write that in your notebook. After you've gotten a pretty reliable list, store the notebook with your identity first aid kit.

Next, every six months, open your notebook and look at your passwords. Are there any accounts that you haven't used and you can close? Having open, unused accounts is something of an invitation for a thief. Are there passwords that you should change? Sensitive passwords should be changed periodically. My suggestion is to make up a bunch of passwords for each account and simply rotate between them. Just as you replace the battery in your smoke detector when we "spring forward" or "fall back," you should replace your passwords.

While you're at it, it's a good idea to log into all your accounts periodically to see if there's any unusual activity or transactions you don't recognize.

Storing and Maintaining Your Kit

Once you've built your first aid kit, you still have two more jobs. The first is to let a trusted family member or friend know about it. In cases where you need help but are unable to get to the kit yourself, your hard work will still pay off.

The second is to make a note of when you have to update your kit. You'd be amazed at the things that change in a year. You get a new credit card, you pay off a loan, your insurance carrier changes its policy, or much more likely, new legislation passes that changes your responsibilities and protections. It is very important that you continue to review your kit on an annual basis to make sure that its contents are up-to-date. Having access to outdated information on your accounts is about as good as not having it in the first place. An easy strategy to keep current is to make sure that you review your kit once a year when you do your taxes. If you want to be really good about it, you can check your entire kit every time you change your passwords.

Minimize Your Risk

Now that you're prepared for identity theft, your next action is to lower your risk of it happening at all. To do this, you need to understand where you are most vulnerable to attack and to minimize your exposure specifically in this area. By taking the "Weigh the Risks" test on the previous pages, you now know if your risk is too great in any of the five following areas: excessive use of your Social

Security number, your personal habits, your situation, the companies you do business with, and your employment. Each of the actions below addresses one of the five problem areas. It is a good idea to read through them all, but be sure to pay careful attention to the section that corresponds to your own high-risk area.

Risk Area #1: Limit Unnecessary Use of Your Personal Info

Your Social Security number (SSN) is used by the government to track how much money you are due upon your retirement and how much money you should be paying in taxes each year. It is used by companies to report to the IRS all income paid to you. Period. Anyone else who says they need to know your number is doing so for *their* convenience, not your protection.

- Take stock of what documents use your Social Security number as a way to identify you. And take steps to get that number taken off of them. It is important to recognize that there is value in being circumspect in cases where the service doesn't really require personal data. Your video rental club doesn't pay you money that the IRS needs to track, nor do they offer you retirement benefits. They do *not* need to know your Social Security number. By not giving it to them, you make that one less computer an identity thief can steal your data from.

- If you live in one of the handful of states that still use your SSN as your driver's license, changing the number is as simple as asking your Department of Motor Vehicles to do so. As we talked about earlier, government is beginning to understand that it is part of the problem here. In fact, ever since a case where a popular actress was hunted down using information in her DMV file and murdered by a deranged stalker, DMV's have been much more sensitive to the need to protect information they store about you. Contact your state's Department of Motor Vehicles or Department of Licensing for info on how to do this.

- Other companies will probably be much less sympathetic. After all, you are asking them to do something that messes up a system that works perfectly fine for *them*. Your only real option may be to leave those documents showing your Social Security number in a safe place.

• Health insurance companies are the absolute worst. When it comes right down to it, there is no good reason for them to use your SSN as an identifier, but we're usually hard-pressed to turn down health coverage simply because they insist on using it.

   If you're lucky enough to control what company you contract with, you should speak to an insurance broker to learn about companies that don't require a Social Security number to write a policy. If, like most of us, you don't have the option of choosing your insurance company, or if you can't find an appropriate choice that doesn't track you by Social Security number, here is a simple remedy. First, memorize your SSN. Second, take the health insurance card that you need to keep in your wallet, photocopy the front and back, and black out the Social Security number on it. Put the original card in a safe place and carry the photocopy in your wallet. When you visit the doctor, you simply take your real card. In an emergency, or when you can't plan ahead, show your photocopy and tell your number directly to anyone who needs to know. (Good thing you memorized it!). The admitting personnel may not be too happy with your strategy at first, but a quick call to the insurer to verify coverage will clear things right up.

   Some states have passed or are considering legislation to prohibit health insurers from using SSNs as identifiers. We'll have to wait and see what happens with this.

Risk Area #2: Restrict Your Digital and Paper Trail to Protect Against Local ID Thieves

There are a few simple actions that you can take, or habits to develop, that will go a long way to closing off opportunities to thieves who might try to steal your information directly from you.

- Consider investing in a locked mailbox or using a post office box. This is especially important if you live in a high risk area. And try not to rely on leaving your bills for your mail carrier to pick up. It's not that difficult to find a mailbox on a street corner.

- Shred—or at least rip up—unnecessary documents and personalized junk mail (especially preapproved credit offers) before tossing them, to thwart "dumpster divers." While you're at it, call this number to put your name on the "opt out" list for those "preapproved" credit offers: 1-888-5OPTOUT. An added benefit to doing this is that you will get a lot less junk mail.

- Clean out your wallet. Don't carry stuff you don't have to.

- Treat checks with a lot of respect. Stolen checks are much more difficult to recover from than a few bad charges on your credit card. Leave your checkbook at home whenever you can. In a world where credit cards and ATM/debit cards can be used just about anywhere, it simply doesn't make as much sense as it once did to keep checks with you "just in case." If you live in a high risk area, pick up your checks from the bank instead of having them mailed to you. Order checks with your initials instead of your first name. Before you write checks to pay a bill, ask the vendor if it's okay to write only the last four digits of your account number on it.

- Don't overexpose yourself to credit card fraud any more than you have to. Only keep the credit cards you need—don't keep inactive accounts open.

Risk Area #3: Be More Aware (Because You Have To Be)

If you scored above a 3 on the third question, you are at greater risk for identity theft simply because of where you live or who you live with. The truth is you just have to pay more attention than other people do. If your risk level is high because of the people in your life, particularly if any of them have drug, alcohol, or gambling problems, you probably already know what you need to do.

- Keep sensitive information in a protected place. Don't share details of financial dealings. And certainly don't share access to financial accounts when you don't have to.

- Probably the most important thing you can do, however, is decide for yourself how you will handle a problem if one arises. Will you report the perpetrator to the police, or try to resolve the situation yourself? Having a plan makes dealing with the situation that much less stressful. It is also possible, but by no means certain, that your determination in handling the matter will lead your potential thief to reconsider his actions or at least look elsewhere to make trouble.

If your risk level is high because of where you live, you just need to be a little more aware of what is going on around you.

- One of the great things about city living is that you're always among other people. That also means, however, that there are always people around to watch you. Be wary of "shoulder surfing" at ATM booths or when you use a calling card at a phone booth.

- You also need to keep an eye out for mail theft. If a bill that you're expecting magically doesn't show up one month, don't fool yourself into believing that you got lucky and the creditor just forgot. If bills or any other expected mail goes undelivered, find out why.

- Check your credit reports at least once a year, perhaps even twice a year. Although everyone should do this, you need to pay extra attention to two things: personal information that doesn't make sense, such as a home address for some place you've never lived, and unknown accounts that might have been opened by someone else in your name. For more information on how to order, read, and correct credit reports, see chapter 3.

- Check your Social Security earnings report. Recent legislation requires the government to mail one to you automatically each year (if you're over twenty-five). Everyone should be checking it to make sure that the government is correctly tracking their earnings so that they will get everything they're due on retirement. Because you have an extra sensitivity to ID theft issues, you're going to look for two other things at the same time.

First, you want to make sure that you get the report each year. It is mailed out three months before your birthday to the address on your last tax return submitted to the IRS. If you don't get the report, one reason may be that someone has filed a fake return in your name using a different address. Since the ID thief wants the refund check he has inevitably requested to go to him and not you, he put his address and not yours on the return.

Second, you need to read the earnings report to make sure that there isn't any income you don't recognize. Unknown income appearing under your name could be an indication that someone has used your Social Security number to get a job. In this case, chances are good they are using your Social Security number to get other things too.

If you suspect identity theft and don't want to wait until your next birthday for a form, you can request a free earnings report at anytime. Contact your local Social Security office for info, or download a request form and instructions at www.ssa.gov/online/ssa-7004.pdf.

Risk Area #4: Ask Questions of the Companies You're Supporting

You're at risk whenever you give information to companies who may or may not protect your information as well as they should. You have two options to reduce risk: one is to be very selective about companies you give information to. If you wouldn't give them the keys to your car, don't give them the key to your identity. The other is to lobby companies to put better systems in place. Your legislators may also be persuaded to play a role in shaping policy as well.

- A good basic rule to live by is *never* give out personal info over the phone or by e-mail unless you initiated the contact. No reputable company needs to ask you for information—like your account number—that they already have.

- When you are submitting applications or purchasing by check or doing any of the other many things in which companies ask for information from you, you should evaluate their need for the information. If they can't explain to you why they need to know your date of birth or if you have children, don't tell them. Most of the time, that will be the end of it.

- You also want to question a company's ability to protect your information once you entrust it to them. You want to ask about what happens to your applications once they are processed, whether the company trains its employees how to handle sensitive information, and who the information will be shared with.

    Consider this: You fill out a form to apply for a credit card. You mail it in to a processing center. One of thousands of typists enters your data into a computer and then throws your application into a trash can. The contents of that trash can end up in a Dumpster outside the building . . . along with all of the other applications thrown into all of the other typists' trash cans. By diving into that one Dumpster (remember the Sutton principle), an identity thief could score a whole lot of potential dupes for his or her credit schemes. Sadly, it is amazing how a simple question like "Will you shred my application after you process it?" can flummox most clerks you ask.

- We know that identity theft is becoming a favorite crime of organized gangs who want big scores. And we know that the favorite targets of these gangs are corporate databases. Given this new reality, it makes sense to take into consideration the fact that every time you allow your information to be entered into a database you increase your risk of becoming a victim. If your information is going to be stored for any period of time (a 99 percent certainty), see if someone can tell you about employee access limitations and security software that will protect you.

• Aside from obvious companies like banks and credit card issuers, companies like utilities and landlords often request information from you to determine if they want to offer you service or let you live in their building. Most often, they will request your Social Security number to run a credit check on you. It doesn't hurt to try to offer alternate information. The people who run these companies hear about ID theft in the news just as much as you do, and a lot more companies are sympathetic to your concerns than you might think. If you can get away with getting the service you want without supplying the really sensitive information about yourself, like your mother's maiden name, your driver's license, or your Social Security number, you win. The data that goes into the database and is available to steal is a little bit less sensitive than it otherwise might be.

• And finally, the really important question to ask is what options you have to limit the spread of your information. Some industries, like the financial industry, are required by law to allow you to opt out of information sharing. Some companies will agree not to sell your name, out of a desire to preserve their relationship with you.

In most situations, unless you ask about opt-out options, the information you give a company becomes something that company can sell if it wants to. You may have done terrific due diligence before deciding that entrusting your information to a company in exchange for the service it provides was a reasonable risk. But if it sells your information to a less-careful company down the street, you might as well have never been so diligent in the first place.

It's difficult to get into the habit of asking these kinds of questions. We don't want to appear impolite, we've gotten used to giving out this information since it's asked for so often, or we don't want to jeopardize getting something we want. But it's a habit that is worth adopting. Always ask about how you can limit your exposure, no matter what.

Risk Area #5: Talk to Your Employer

Depending on the size of the company you work for and the nature of your relationship with your boss, this can be an easy or difficult area in which to reduce your risk. You are at the mercy of the policies of your company.

- To reduce your risk, you first need to fully understand what the company policies are. You will probably find a lot of information in an employee handbook (if there is one), or you can contact your human resources (HR) department and ask to interview them. You will probably find a very sympathetic hearing with your HR rep.

- Your second task is to speak with your boss about those policies that put you at risk. Putting your Social Security number on your ID badge is a good example. The key is to know what you're concerned about and why. It may help you to get other employees involved. As always, you have to be practical and, of course, you don't want to put yourself in danger of losing your ability to put food on the table. But the questions are at least worth asking.

A couple additional points of consideration:

- First, know that resumes are generally handled with incredible disrespect. They get put in files, left in piles, and thrown away in unlocked dumpsters. While the contents of resumes generally are helpful only to criminals who want to impersonate or stalk you, it is an easy step to make sure they don't contain anything that will help an ID thief intent on fraud. A resume is *not* the place for your Social Security number. Does this sound familiar, yet?

- Second, be aware that your biggest threat from most companies comes from the inside. It is more likely that someone inside the organization is going to collude with a gang of ID thieves than that a random theft will rob a company of its employee data. You would be well served to pay close attention to the screening and training of anyone who could access information about you.

If you find that your company isn't doing a great job on this front, there are information sources you can supply to your head of HR or your CEO. The Electronic Privacy Information Center offers an excellent starting point for this and other privacy related issues (http://www.epic.org/privacy/workplace/). Company management should understand liability issues very well. It may be that they simply haven't addressed this problem because it hasn't been brought to their attention. If you present your concerns as "hey, there is this growing problem and, hey, I've come across the fact that we may be exposed," you can look like a team player helping out the company, not a whiner who is creating more, and unnecessary, work.

What To Do If Your Wallet, Purse, PDA, or Identity Is Stolen

If your wallet, purse, or PDA is stolen, you will need to contact a lot of people to warn them of potential problems: banks, credit card companies, the police, etc. If you think you've become a victim of identity theft, you will need to contact the same set of people to get them to fix problems that already exist.

One of the most important things you can do is place a fraud alert on your major credit accounts. According to a 2003 law, initiating an alert with one nationwide credit reporting agency will require them to share the alert information with other nationwide agencies. For ninety days if you call, or seven years if you file a written report, your file must identify you as a victim of fraud and state that you do not authorize additional granting of credit. Calling to place an "initial" alert assures that any credit grantor needs to take "reasonable" steps to verify that you are who you say you are before granting you additional credit. Initiating an extended fraud alert by filing a written report requires credit grantors to contact you for the next seven years (typically by phone) to make sure that everything is on the up-and-up before allowing you to get further into debt.

Once you've safeguarded your basic digital identity, you will have to begin the tedious and inevitable process of telling and retelling your story to just about everyone you deal with. As you do, here are few general guidelines to keep in mind:

- Whenever possible, speak to a fraud investigator and *not* a customer service rep. One is trained to handle identity theft problems and can make decisions, the other can't. If possible, have the conversation face-to-face. Establishing a more personal relationship with the manager at your local bank can help a lot in the long run.

- Log any phone conversations and *get names*. Follow up with a written request.

- NEVER use the word "dispute." To most companies, disputing something means that you accept the bill but want to contest particulars about it which gives them the right to send collection information to the big credit reporting agencies. Instead, state that you are a victim of fraud or identity theft and have become aware of information or transactions that are a result of that.

- Once you get over the initial reporting of any problem, know that you've only taken the first step. You will need to be a little extra vigilant for the next year. Identity theft experts counsel that you request your credit report every three months for the first year following a wallet, purse, or PDA theft. Some also warn you to prepare yourself for the emotions associated with the sense of invasion that you may feel.

Step-by-step guides on what to do in the event of identity theft can be found at the following Web sites:

- Federal Trade Commission (http://www.consumer.gov/idtheft/)
- Privacy Rights Clearinghouse (http://www.privacyrights.org/fs/fs17a.htm)
- Identity Theft Center (http://www.idtheftcenter.org/vguides.shtml)
- Call for Action (http://callforaction.org/publications/id theft/victim.asp)

Thanks to underwriting from Visa, you can also speak to a trained counselor at Call for Action, an international, nonprofit network of consumer hotlines, by phoning 1-866-ID-HOTLINE.

Finally, Citibank offers a program to help its customers who have been victims of identity theft. Talk to your local banker to find out if you qualify for this.

LOOKING AHEAD

Whew! You made it. Congratulations on taking the first and most important step to protect yourself in the modern world. As we've been talking about, identity theft is growing dramatically. As a result, it is getting a lot of attention from companies and lawmakers. You can and should expect that things will change a lot in the next few years. The following list identifies some of the key groups that track identity theft issues. The FTC in particular is a terrific resource of information. The Privacy Rights Clearinghouse and the Identity Theft Resource Center offer individual assistance, as well as counseling and referrals for more thorny problems. The U.S. Public Interest Research Group (started by Ralph Nader) and the Electronic Privacy Information Center can keep you up-to-date with legislative issues concerning identity theft. You can and should check them periodically to stay on top of the latest scams, as well as your rights.

- Federal Trade Commission (www.consumer.gov/idtheft)
- Privacy Rights Clearinghouse (www.privacyrights.org)
- Identity Theft Resource Center (www.idtheftcenter.org)
- U.S. PIRG (www.uspirg.org)
- Electronic Privacy Information Center (www.epic.org)

3. Your Key to Getting Just About Anything: Credit Reporting

IN THIS CHAPTER:
How credit reporting works, what credit agencies track, how you can request, read, and correct your reports

This chapter is all about making you more attractive. No, you won't find tips on hair and makeup. It's about making you more *financially* attractive—making you a more appealing consumer to companies that you want to do business with. It's also the start of keeping your identity damage-free.

This isn't about vanity. The more financially attractive you are to a bank, an insurer, or a car dealer, the more likely they are to offer you better rates and prices. This is about saving you money. And in some cases, *big* money. It's possible to pay hundreds of thousands of dollars over the life of a thirty-year mortgage than you have to, simply because you're not as financially attractive as you could be.

It all starts with your credit report. This one report serves as the measure of your attractiveness as a consumer to countless companies. Indeed, now that computers have made sharing information so easy, more and more companies are turning to them to inform decisions. If you worry about how computers are increasing the importance of credit reports, consider this: easy access to accurate information has eliminated a lot of the discrimination and inflexibility that tarnished the credit process for decades. Easy access to accurate information has made it possible for the average person to buy a home and a car.

The key word, however, is *accurate*. Many people might believe that computers have increased accuracy by eliminating human error. But guess what? Some studies suggest as many as seven out of ten reports still have a mistake in them.

It is almost certain that your credit report—the one that determines if you can buy a house, drive a car, or use a cell phone—contains some mistake or piece of outdated information. And since just about everybody wants to see your credit report, this can be a pretty big issue. This chapter tells you what you need to know about the credit rating system, gives you the scoop on mistakes, and spells out what you can do about it.

WHAT ARE CREDIT REPORTS?

Credit reports are exactly what they sound like they should be: reports of your credit activity. They usually contain a list of every credit account you have ever opened—even if the account is now closed or paid off. They include every credit card, department store charge card, car loan, home mortgage, student loan—you name it. If you've borrowed money, it's been reported.

Credit reports include information about things such as how much you owe on each account and how good you were at making your payments on time. They include other information such as your employer, a list of recent addresses, and any other names or aliases you may have used. They also provide a score that paints a general picture of your financial situation.

Credit reports do *not* include information about your hobbies, your lifestyle, your religion, your race or color, your marital status, or your politics. This is a numbers-only game.

The basic purpose of a credit report is to give someone who is considering extending you credit an idea of how big a risk you are and how likely you are to pay them back on time. Also, as computers have gotten more powerful, credit card companies are beginning to analyze report data on a regular—sometimes monthly—basis to adjust your card's interest rates. If you carry credit cards from any one of the 75 percent of credit companies that do this, then the more you owe, the more borrowing more money is going to cost you.

Companies who grant you credit report on your spending and payment habits to more than a thousand local and regional credit bureaus around the country. These smaller bureaus, in turn, submit the information to one of three large national consumer reporting agencies (also called CRAs) that aggregate all of your data into an exhaustive profile.

Because each of the large agencies may rely on a slightly different network of report sources, the net result is that you don't have just one credit report. You have at least three, and counting the smaller agencies selling their piece of the puzzle wherever they can, probably more. Because most lenders will use data from one of the three national agencies, Equifax, TransUnion and Experian, we'll focus on the information contained in these three reports.

WHY SHOULD I CARE ABOUT MY CREDIT REPORTS?

Some people care about credit reports because they don't like the idea of information about them being collected in one place. They think it's intrusive or unfair. One such man in California pushed his credit card to its spending limit and was late in making payments on the bill. When another credit card company found out about his actions and raised the rates on his second card, he got upset. He had always been careful to make timely payments and never pushed the limit on the second card. So he felt that one shouldn't affect the other, and that the very nature of credit reporting was wrong.

Let's change the story slightly. Imagine this same guy gets a speeding ticket while driving his Toyota. Should he expect that his auto insurance company would only raise his rates for the times he drives the Toyota and not when he drives his wife's Honda? Was it him or the car that was speeding?

When you think of it this way, credit reporting doesn't appear so outrageous. A company that doesn't know you is willing to give you money. The purchasing power of your card or loan is nothing more than money that someone else agrees to front you. Your part of the deal is that you promise to pay the money back. In that light, don't the lenders have a right to judge how good your word is?

Since we no longer live in villages where everyone knows everyone else, businesses want something to base their decisions on. They turn to a few big companies who make it their business to collect information about you and create a profile of who you appear to be. This profile isn't the sum total of who you are, but it's enough for people who don't know you to make decisions about you.

The existence of a profile and the fact that businesses make decisions based upon it means that—like it or not—you have to deal with it. The bottom line is that you should care about your credit reports because the people you borrow money from care about them. Unless you want to join a commune in the wilds somewhere, you have no choice but to care.

What you should care about is that the reports are accurate and that they are used appropriately. Unfortunately, a number of sources suggest that unless you've been vigilant, the chances that your credit report will be complete and correct are pretty small indeed.

HOW LIKELY IS IT THAT MY CREDIT REPORTS ARE WRONG?

At least one of your credit reports *is* wrong. I can almost guarantee that some CRA lists you with a funny address or an incomplete birth date or an old job title or some other issue.

The Credit Data Industry Association estimates that two billion pieces of information are entered into consumer credit files each month. That's twenty-four billion opportunities a year to make a mistake. You figure the odds that one of your reports contains one.

According to a survey conducted a few years ago by the U.S. Public Interest Research Group, 70 percent of the credit reports they examined contained mistakes. Close to one out of three credit reports contained errors that were big enough to cause a rejection of credit that really should have been granted.

In another study, *Consumer Reports* found that the number of mistakes was even higher. More than half of all credit reports would have incorrectly resulted in a denial of credit or overcharging. Bad reports contain things like accounts that are incorrectly listed as delinquent, closed accounts that are listed as open, credit limits that are reported as amounts due (or overdue!), and major accounts that were missing that would demonstrate a consumer's good credit.

Still another study, by the Consumer Federation of America, corroborates the last point. This study found that as many as eight out of ten incorrect files miss a piece of good news—a mortgage or account that you consistently pay on time—that can materially affect your credit rating. One in ten bad files neglected to mention that a bankruptcy had been resolved!

Another big problem that comes up again and again in studies and individual stories is that information from one person gets incorrectly reported as belonging to someone else. This problem is a direct result of how the reporting system has been designed. When lenders want to see your credit profile, they really aren't doing anything more than inputting your identifying data into a search engine. That engine looks through all the files in its massive databases and returns information on anyone who looks like they might be you.

But here's the problem: information is really kind of messy. Some of your accounts may be listed under the name "Kathy"; others under "Katherine"; maybe even others under "K. Susan." Or perhaps the person typing in your information makes a mistake and transposes two of the digits in your Social Security number. In all of these cases, a search on "Kathy" with this Social Security number might miss some of the information that rightfully describes your financial behavior. The answer to this problem is that the search functions programmed by the reporting agencies don't require the match to your name or Social Security number to be exact, just close.

The result is that information from someone you've never met but whose name or Social Security number is similar to yours might also get included in your report. The Consumer Federation of America found that 10 percent of files they requested for a large study of credit reports contained at least one—and sometimes three—additional reports. The three big agencies, each competing for lenders' business, tend to lean toward reporting too much data instead of too little. It makes them look like they're doing a better job and offers them a better competitive position. And because each agency writes its own "smart" search software, the report from each one may be wrong in different ways.

No one has yet quantified the impact of errors from the loose matching system on the accuracy of the reporting—or on the price that you ultimately pay. But understanding that the system makes these problems more, rather than less, likely is an important first step in making sure that you're being shown in your best light to the companies with the checkbooks.

WHAT CAN GO WRONG BECAUSE OF WRONG INFORMATION IN MY CREDIT REPORTS?

A lot of mistakes in your credit reports—things like bad addresses or old job titles—really don't hurt you in any meaningful way. But some of the mistakes can keep you from getting mortgages, car loans, or jobs, or put you in a situation where you have to pay more than you reasonably ought to. And because you probably find out about the problems at the time that you need credit of some kind, they can cause you a lot of hassle just when you don't want it.

Here are a few stories you don't want to experience firsthand:

- An elderly woman from California allowed her bank to foreclose on a mortgage she could no longer afford. Unfortunately, the bank was charging her a higher interest rate than they otherwise would because an error in her credit report made her seem like a greater risk to the lender than she really was. If the report and the rate had been correct, she might not have found herself on the street.

- If another man's credit report had been correct, the happiest day of his life wouldn't have become his worst. While he and his wife were living overseas, she gave birth to their first child. Unfortunately, when the hospital requested payment, the man's credit card was refused. Unbeknownst to him, his credit rating was in the basement and his limit had been lowered along with it. The reason: unpaid student loans. The problem: this guy had never taken out any student loans. It turns out that his credit history had mistakenly been tied to two additional Social Security numbers, and those other folks weren't as conscientious as he was about paying bills. The unfortunate dad was forced to sort through the situation at a time when he really wanted to be cooing at his newborn.

• In what is now an infamous case in credit circles, TRW (now Experian) admitted in 1991 to incorrectly reporting that each and every one of the three thousand residents of Norwich, Vermont, had failed to pay property taxes. After the Vermont State Attorney General got involved, the problem was cleared up. But the experience for the three thousand suspected "deadbeats" wasn't pretty. One year later, Equifax did the same thing to residents of Cambridge, Massachusetts.

HOW ARE CREDIT REPORTS DIFFERENT FROM CREDIT SCORES?

In addition to collecting data about how you pay your bills, the CRAs also analyze what they know about you and assign a score that supposedly quantifies your creditworthiness.

There are two major differences between a credit score and a credit report. First, your credit report is a collection of verifiable facts. Your credit score is the result of someone's interpretation of those facts. It's someone's best guess as to your creditworthiness.

Each of the three credit reporting agencies bases its guess on slightly different information—which is a nice way of saying there is a bit of voodoo in them. In its credit report study, the Consumer Federation of America also examined credit scores for half a million files. It found that there were variations—big ones—in the scores assigned from one CRA to another about a third of the time.

Who's Keeping Score?

From the way privacy is talked about in the news, you'd think that the credit reporting agencies just opened their doors in the past few years. The truth is actually a bit different.

Equifax, which started as the Retail Credit Company in 1899, has been tracking credit activity and building profiles for more than a hundred years. Today, Equifax's database has grown to over 205 million records.

TransUnion, the second of the big three agencies, was created in 1968 to assess credit risks for the Union Tank Car Company, a railcar leasing operation. It acquired the Credit Bureau of Cook County, whose employees maintained index card files in four hundred seven-drawer cabinets—all by hand! Now the company has computers that store two hundred million records.

Experian, a subsidiary of a British company that is linked to the Burberry Brand, is the biggest and newest of the three, starting operations only about thirty years ago. Despite its late start, Experian now employs thirteen thousand people and makes $2.2 billion a year. In other words, the sale of your information makes the company more money than a lot of Third World countries have in their entire treasury.

All told these three agencies supply an army of lenders with somewhere around two million reports every *day*.

The second difference between your score and your credit report is that access to your credit report is free by law, but access to your score is not. For a long time these companies wouldn't admit that a score existed or show it to you when you asked to see it. In 2001 the CRAs, bowing to pressure from Congress and consumer advocate groups, determined that they could fend off legal action *and* make more money by charging consumers for a peek at their scores. As a result, Equifax, Experian, and TransUnion began to admit publicly that such calculations did exist. Now you can see your credit score in addition to your credit report—but you have to pay.

HOW DOES CREDIT SCORING WORK?

The big thing to understand about credit scores is that they are not at all static. You don't get assigned one score forever. In fact, your score doesn't even exist until someone asks what it is. When someone wants to know your score, it is calculated on the spot, based on what is in your report at that exact moment in time. According to Fair Isaac, the company that supplies software to the big reporting agencies, the score calculated for you will go up and down, based upon what you do from day to day.

The range of possible scores typically runs from 500 to 850; average is between 700 and 750. Although different lenders have different cutoffs for how they categorize potential customers, anyone with a score above 750 would generally be considered financially attractive—a prime borrower. Anyone with a score below 700 probably would not.

About 40 percent of borrowers fall into this lower category. The difference between having a score of 550 and one of 720 doesn't necessarily mean you won't be given credit—but it almost always means you'll be hit with higher interest rates. According to Fair Isaac, a low-scoring consumer could pay almost $131,000 more than the one with the higher score over the life of a thirty year fixed mortgage for $150,000. That's a big deal, especially considering that according to a major mortgage lender, anywhere from 10–15 percent of consumers—or thirty million people—are incorrectly offered rates that are lower than prime.

Fair Isaac claims that the calculation of your score only uses information that is found in your credit reports—a very good reason to check out what the reports say. For anyone without special consideration (like being too young to have a long credit history), the information considered, in order of priority, includes your payment history, how much you owe, the length of time you've had any kind of credit, types of credit that you have, and how much of your credit is new. Your profile is compared to thousands of profiles of other people. Based on what happened with those folks—whether or not they paid their bills—you are as-

> ## A Score by Any Other Name . . .
>
> Don't be confused if you see a few different names for your credit score. Even though each agency has trademarked its own name (BEACON from Equifax; EMPIRICA from Trans Union; Experian/Fair Isaac from Experian), most people refer to credit scores generically as a FICO score. FICO comes from the first letters of the name of the firm, the Fair Isaac Company, that writes the underlying analysis program for the three big CRAs.
>
> The word "fair" in Fair Isaac Company isn't there to advertise the fact that it is impartial or unbiased. It's the last name of Bill Fair, who founded the company with Earl Isaac in the 1950s. Like TransUnion and Equifax, Bob and Earl's company has been scoring all of us for a long time.

signed a number that indicates how much of a nonpayment risk you represent.

The good news is that lenders typically look at scores from all three CRAs when evaluating you as a potential customer. The bad news is that that still doesn't always mean a perfectly happy ending. A twenty-seven-year-old buying his first townhouse in Southern California found that the three big CRAs had assigned widely varying credit scores to him. Unbeknownst to him, the lender used the middle number to determine the young man's mortgage rates. Unfortunately, this number put the man into the high-risk category, costing him an extra $3,450 for the first two years of his mortgage (he refinanced after that). Had he been aware of what was happening up front, he might have been able to request a review of his files and a rescoring of them to negotiate a better deal.

The moral of this story is that it's worth talking with any potential lender about your credit scores and how they are used.

HOW DO THE CREDIT REPORTING AGENCIES KNOW THINGS ABOUT ME?

Whenever you apply for credit, some person at the credit company or bank looks at your application, types your Social Security number into a computer, and pulls up any file on you from the CRA databases. If no name comes up—incredibly unlikely if you're over twenty—that person will type your information into an input screen, click on a button, and *Wham*, you've become a twenty-first-century citizen with an electronic file.

If a previous file does come up it is evaluated, and if credit or a loan or whatever is offered to you, the details of that new relationship are entered into the database. In either case, someone in the modern equivalent of the steno pool now has your financial future in his or her hands. If this person makes a typo, you've got a problem.

Once you are using a credit card or have begun making payments on your loan, the same companies that granted you credit will report on your payment activity to the CRAs. This is often nothing more than a regular transfer of information from one database to another, but to give you a feel for the scope of this whole endeavor, one of the big CRAs estimates that it receives 30 to 40 million bits of new information every day.

The worry is that some companies are better at regular reporting than others. While most major companies regularly share information with all three CRAs, smaller companies may not share data or may only report to one bureau. In other words, some of those nagging debts that you finally cleared up may never be reported as resolved. And as with creating your credit profile, let's just hope that the fact that you paid was entered correctly into the first company's database, or else you'll pay the price as the bad info gets passed first to the CRA and then to everyone else with an interest in you.

Other information comes from collection agencies or is culled from public records by companies who make it their business to do this for the CRAs. The government also gets in the act. It informs the CRAs directly about overdue support payments, overpaid unemployment benefits, and those pesky unpaid parking tickets.

DO I HAVE ANY PROTECTION?

Your right to see your credit report, and a lot of the other reports that we'll discuss in the coming chapters, was established by the

Fair Credit Reporting Act (FCRA) and recently expanded by the Fair and Accurate Credit Transactions Act (FACTA).

In 1970 Congress enacted the FRCA to allow bureaus to sell credit reports to any business with a "credit, insurance, employment, or other business need" without first asking your permission. At the same time, however, it also specified basic consumer rights that protect you from abuse by any agency that gathers information about you. There were tales that the unregulated companies in the sixties had quotas for "rejections" and stretched to fill files with gossip and other negative information whenever they possibly could. Since oversight is the best cure for this kind of abuse, the most important right created by the FCRA is your right to see any information a consumer reporting agency has on you.

In 2003, reacting to increasing accounts of identity theft and problems created by inaccuracies in credit files, Congress passed FACTA to address these issues more carefully. Perhaps the biggest change has been the requirement that certain consumer reporting agencies must provide you with a free credit report each year (but only if you ask—more on how in the Taking Action section).

In addition, the FCRA and FACTA require that:

- You must be told by a decision maker if the information in your file is used against you—for example, to deny you credit, or an apartment, or the lowest rate.

- You must be told by a company reporting negative information to a national consumer reporting agency that it is doing so.

- Companies reporting information to the national bureaus cannot forward information that they "believe" is inaccurate or that you have told them is the result of identity theft.

- You can challenge information in your file directly with the company reporting the information or with the major bureaus who sell it to others; if you do contact the bureaus, they must investigate and correct any errors, in most cases, in thirty days.

- Access to information in the report is limited to those who need to know. Unfortunately, that need is pretty broadly defined, so don't expect too much from this provision. Your consent is required for the release of medical information.

- There are time limits on how long most (but not all) *negative* information can be kept—generally seven years, ten years for bankruptcies. There is no time limit on *positive* info.

- You can request that the last five digits of your Social Security number be blocked out on your credit reports.

- If you believe that you have been the victim of identity theft, you can place a fraud alert on your account, which identifies you as a victim of fraud and states that you do not authorize additional granting of credit.

You also have some protection via other federal laws, like the Fair Credit Billing Act and the Equal Credit Opportunity Act, but the bulk of what you need to care about is covered by the FCRA and FACTA. Since none of us wants to study law simply to get a mortgage, we will only consider those two for now.

CHECKUP

Now for the important part: requesting, reading, and checking your credit reports. The first two sections help with getting the report and deciphering it. The last lets you score how well the CRAs are doing at scoring you. It will also help you identify any errors in your reports that you may want to be concerned about.

Find Out If Your Credit Reflects How Good You've Been

Given that thousands of people you've never met can access your credit report, how can you see it, too? In the past few years, as the result of increased publicity about the CRAs, extensions to the FCRA and a few lawsuits, it is easier than ever to see what everyone

---

INFORMATION WITH NO TIME LIMIT

Despite the time limits, you should be aware that negative information is *always* available to a potential employer if the job that you're applying for has a salary over a certain amount (currently $75,000). It is also *always* available to an insurance company if you are applying for a life insurance policy worth more than $150,000. In other words, the law allows businesses seeking to engage in a significant and noncollateralized financial relationship with you to know the good and the bad in its entirety. You should also know that information about unpaid tax liens (some states provide exceptions) and criminal convictions may be reported to anyone without any time limitation.

---

else can see. Among your options you can request a report directly or through an intermediary often called a credit management agency.

Using a Credit Management Agency

Credit management agencies are the ones that send you junk mail or buy ad banners on Web sites proclaiming a "free" credit report or an instant credit check. The benefits of using one of these companies are that you may really get your first credit report for "free" and that you may get a combined report with information from all three CRAs with one request.

The downside with these agencies is that they still need to make money somehow. In some cases, you may find out that, while you do get a free report, you get charged for access to your credit score. In other cases, requesting your first report signs you up for an ongoing service as part of the free "trial." The second report that gets "automatically" ordered for you almost certainly costs more than doing it yourself. Some services charge up to $80 a year. And I've known some folks who have had problems when they tried to cancel a subscription following the free trial.

What's worse, a lot of the free credit reports are really being offered by the big CRAs themselves. It's just a new way to package the data they already sell. Not only do they get to charge for what the law requires them to provide for free, they get your name on a list of potential suckers—which they can sell too, if they want to.

None of this is to say that all credit management agencies should be avoided. But, like credit repair companies, they do have a bad rep in some circles. There are a lot of bad companies out there and a lot of just plain bad deals. Most experts agree that you're better off taking responsibility for monitoring your credit profile yourself.

Requesting a Report Directly from the CRAs

If you choose to request a report directly from the CRAs, you can take advantage of your new right to a free annual report under the Fair and Accurate Credit Transaction Act (FACTA). This law required the FTC to set up a one-stop request mechanism to allow consumers to submit a single request and receive one free report each year from each of the main CRAs. Because the system is still relatively new, you should visit the FTC Web site for the most up-to-date information on what you have to do to get your free reports (www.ftc.gov).

If you find yourself needing to contact the CRAs directly for a report—say you want to see your credit score, which is not required to be free under FACTA, you can do so using the Internet, by letter, or by phone. All three of the big names offer a combined three-in-one report, if you want to do less work and you want to buy your score at the same time. It's a great deal, but just be careful that you're ordering the "tribureau" report and that you're not signing up for any credit management service like the ones described in the previous section.

Generally speaking, if you have no special circumstances, it's okay to start with a report online. Ordering a report by phone is the best idea if there is something special about your request—you suspect identity theft, you were turned down for something, you are unemployed—because the procedures for special requests seem to change periodically. If you talk to an actual person, you avoid back-and-forth about what you need to do. In every case, do make sure that any other correspondence—particularly about problems—is in writing.

When you request a report, the CRA will want certain information from you. This is to help them locate the record and to verify that you are requesting your own and not someone else's report. If you order online or over the phone, the CRA will generally verify your identity by asking you questions about yourself drawn from your credit record (the amount of your monthly mortgage payment seems to be a popular question). If you are ordering the report by mail, you will probably be asked to include two to three items that show your address, such as a photocopy of your driver's license, a utility bill, or an insurance statement.

If you don't use the system established by the FTC, you will probably pay to get each report, but the fee depends on your situation and your state of residence. The FCRA stipulates that the CRA cannot charge you a fee if you . . .

- Have been turned down for credit, insurance, employment, or an apartment in past sixty days because of information on a report from that CRA
- Are unemployed and intend to seek work in next sixty days
- Are on welfare
- Are a victim of credit fraud

If you don't fall into any of these categories, the FCRA sets a basic fee that the CRAs are allowed to charge. However, some states have passed their own laws regulating report fees, so the actual amount you will have to pay varies widely from state to state and by CRA. (the FTC maintains a handy summary chart of costs by state at http://www.consumer.gov/idtheft/recovering_idt.html#10).

The bottom line, no matter where you live, is that the cost to get reports from all three of the national CRAs will be somewhere less than thirty dollars a year, and that's a lot cheaper than watching your credit card rates rise through the roof or paying over $100,000 more on a mortgage.

Here's where to go to request a report.

FTC clearinghouse for free annual reports
www.ftc.gov

Experian
888-397-3742
http://www.experian.com/consumer/index.html

Equifax
800-685-1111
https://www.econsumer.equifax.com

TransUnion
800-916-8800 (customer relations) or 800-888-4213 (automated order line)
http://www.transunion.com

Now, *Really* Read the Reports

Once you receive the report, your next challenge will be to decipher the information it contains. Although this task is a lot easier than it used to be, don't expect to glance quickly at the pages and be done. Reading a credit report will require some concentration. The layout for the reports seems to change periodically, but the reports themselves always include the same basic facts, typically organized into four or five sections.

The first section of the report shows what identifying information the agency has on you. This information includes your name and any other names you've ever used, current and previous addresses, Social Security number, date of birth, driver's license number, spouse's name, and employer.

The second section will offer a summary of the report contents, including how many of each type of account you have. If there is any bad news—things like late payments or accounts sent to collection agencies—it will be listed in the summary section. Sometimes reports include information taken from public records in this summary; other times public records about bankruptcies, etc. are reported in a separate section.

The next section will contain an exhaustive listing of your credit accounts. The account reports may contain a credit history of up to twenty-four months of balances, changes to your credit limit, and the highest balance you've ever carried or the original loan amount.

The final section shows all of the requests for your credit file within a set time period. This information is separated into two categories: requests that anyone can see when they access your file and requests that only you can see. Anyone can see inquiries initiated by a collection agency that has taken over your account, as well as inquiries that you have initiated by giving permission for your credit to be checked as part of a credit or loan application. Only you can see who has been asking for your credit report when it is by a potential employer, companies wanting to see if you're a good candidate for a promotion, your creditors just checking in to see that all is okay, or a potential purchaser of your account seeking to assess the level of risk you represent—loans get bought and sold all the time.

Score the CRAs

Essentially, when reading your credit reports, you want to verify that the information it contains is accurate. Your real objective is to determine if you are part of the 70 percent of folks that have an error in their report, or possibly one of the 29 to 50 percent with a serious error.

The other thing you want to check is that the information is up-to-date. As noted earlier, most companies are very good at adding to your file when you open an account, but some companies are not as good about keeping your file updated with payment information or even account cancellation. You don't want old stuff crowding out the important stuff and you want your report to say as much *good* stuff about you as it can. When you've successfully paid off a loan, for example, you want potential creditors to know.

To make the whole process of reviewing your credit reports a little more fun, let's turn the tables for a while. Even once you accept that credit reporting is the key to a lot of opportunity, you would only be human if you found it a little annoying, too. Instead of quietly suffering the indignity of having some large reporting agency track what you do, it's your turn to score *them* on how they well *they* do on reporting.

Here's how the scoring works: for each report, start with 100 and subtract the suggested number of points for each problem that you identify on it. If some issue makes you particularly angry, you have my permission to double the suggested points for that problem.

When you're done, the resulting number will tell you how the agency providing that report rates. Score of 90 to 99 can be considered benignly irritating; 80 to 89 means they're pushing it; 79 or below is definitely over the line. Don't worry about the outcome; it's not meant to be fair! Got your pencil?

Personal Info Errors (Subtract 1 Point For Each Error)

- Name—small discrepancies in your name may not matter, because even with misspellings the loose matching algorithms will generally find your information. On the other hand, if the file shows you as your father (i.e., you're a "III" and you're listed as a "II"), or "Junior," this could be a problem. A bank may not want to give a thirty-year mortgage to someone in their nineties!

- Social Security number—if more than one is listed on the report, this is a big red flag that suggests you may already be a victim of identity theft. It's a myth, by the way, that getting a new Social Security number gets you a new credit report—the old report is typically linked to your new number.

- Date of birth—again, you may not care if the reporting agencies have listed you with a slightly incorrect date of birth. But when your date of birth is used to verify your identity, an incorrect date on your credit report may become a problem. By all means, do make sure that your credit report isn't telling your potential banker that you're a minor!

- Bad addresses—if one of the addresses listed for you doesn't ring a bell, this is another red flag for potential fraud. In particular, someone may be applying for new credit accounts in your name.

- Employment—wrong employment information is not a major problem because it is very common. The only time that the CRAs receive data on where you work is when you supply that information to a credit card company or loan company as part of an application. If you've switched jobs since the last time you applied for new credit, you will not have given the CRA any way to find out about your new job. Unless you have special circumstances that warrant attention to accuracy here, it's not crucial to keep your employer information up-to-date on your credit report. Most creditors will verify your employment separately and not rely on CRA information.

Errors From Info Found in Public Records (Subtract 20 Points For Each Error)

- Public records that aren't yours—make sure that records such as a court judgment belonging to someone else with a similar name haven't been listed as yours. Remember the basic technology that compiles your profile is designed to favor creating this kind of problem over missing something important about you.

Errors about the Accounts You Have (Subtract 10 Points for Each Error)

- Accounts in good standing—are all the accounts you want reflected there? Sometimes no information about you is more damning than so-so information. If you're building credit, it does you no good not to have the good accounts listed!

- Delinquent accounts—are any accounts incorrectly listed as delinquent?

- Unknown accounts—do you see any accounts that don't belong to you? Before you get concerned about identity theft, make a quick phone call to the CRA. Oftentimes, your credit report will contain a history of a relationship with a bank or credit company that you've never heard of. Information about special financing offered by appliance and computer stores, for example, is reported by the parent bank that has offered you the credit. Since you think you are dealing with ABC Electronics, it's unlikely that you will have ever heard the parent bank's name. The reporting agency will often be able to supply you with the information that fills in that piece of the puzzle. If the account is genuinely unknown to you, then you should get very concerned indeed.

- Closed accounts—according to one study, 26 percent of all reports contain closed accounts that are still listed as active. Check to see that any loans that you took out and paid off are shown as paid in full. Loans that still show a balance—even if it isn't delinquent—may affect whether or not you get a new loan down the road, because a lender will look at the total of outstanding liabilities vs. your income when making the offer decision (the rule of thumb is no more than 20 percent of your income can be leveraged).

- Multiple accounts—are accounts listed multiple times? First, make sure that it's not just a history of an account being sold from one creditor to another, but if you think that an account is incorrectly listed more than once, clean this up. In addition to a current liability calculation, lenders evaluate your potential credit liability when determining how safe a risk you are.

- Forgotten accounts—this is a big one. Are there any credit cards you've forgotten about that are still open? This often happens with instant credit retail cards. You open an account to get a 10 percent discount on some purchase and then forget you have the card. Unfortunately, having too many credit accounts may negatively affect your credit score, and open, unused accounts can always be stolen by someone else.

- Credit limits—are all your credit limits listed and are they correct? Credit limits play a role in calculating your credit score, and not having that information in your file could hurt you. The Federal Reserve suggests that as many as 33 percent of all credit reports fail to show any credit limits. And since they also found the problem occurs most often to borrowers with bad credit, the oversight is especially damning. Also check to see that any limit increases have been reported. If not, it may look like you're over the limit on a given account or that you don't have enough credit to take on additional debt. Finally, read the report carefully to make sure that your potential credit (i.e., limit) is not listed as "maximum borrowed." This is less of a problem since the CRAs simplified the way information is presented in their reports but the two items used to be easily confused—with negative effects on you.

- Up-to-date information—is the information on your accounts current? Check on the date of the last report from each creditor. As with having all the good accounts shown, you want the fact that you use credit responsibly *and* often to reflect positively on you.

Who, Besides You, Is Asking to See Your Credit Report (No Point Score for This Section—How Would You Ever Know If They Got This Right?)

- Unknown inquiries—review all the requests to see your credit report listed in the section titled: "Requests viewed by others." This section contains inquiries from creditors that have accessed your credit report to process an application. If you do not recognize the credit grantor accessing your report, that may be an indication of fraudulent activity.

- Too many inquiries—this is often cited as the reason for a lowered credit score. Fair Isaac reports that people with six inquiries or more are eight times more likely to declare bankruptcy. You need to make sure that companies you've contacted just to see what kind of lower mortgage rate you qualify for aren't running credit reports. Until you're serious about a loan, it's best not to let companies start the formal process. Fair Isaac does say that they try to eliminate the influence of multiple inquiries when you're rate shopping by ignoring any inquiry that occurred less than thirty days prior to the date a score is requested.

Negative Info (Subtract 40 Points For Each Error)

- Negative information removal—liens, delinquent accounts, and judgments generally should be removed from your file after seven years. Bankruptcy information may be reported for ten years. As with the inclusion of public records or the reports of your account activity, the timing of negative information removal is dependent upon someone correctly typing a date into a database field. Think of how easy it would be for someone to make a mistake after typing in hundreds of records before yours.

- Special cases—there are some special cases that you might need to consider regarding the removal of negative information. Some states have passed laws that shorten the seven and ten year time frames. New York State allows paid judgments to be shown for only five years, as an example. In any state, the time frame for information about a lawsuit or an unpaid judgment against you can be reported until the statute of limitations runs out. If this is longer than seven years, negative information may legitimately stay in your file for longer than seven years.

If there is anything that isn't clear to you on your credit report, you will find an 800 telephone number on the first page for customer service. Customer service reps may be able to supply a little more information about the identity of a creditor or explain the meaning of various terms used to describe your accounts. Don't hesitate to take advantage of this service. The CRAs make a lot of money off of you, and you have a legal right to make sure that they are doing their job correctly.

And if the customer service person is helpful, you might consider adding back five points to that CRA's final score.

TAKING ACTION

Now that you've done your basic homework on your credit reports, you're ready to take the steps to make sure that you get and remain as attractive as possible to potential lenders. The first action is to clean up any errors that you uncovered in your checkup; the next is to develop a plan to stay on top of your credit reports; and the last is to forget about your credit score (really).

What You Can Do If There Is a Problem

There are basically two reasons you will want to follow up on your credit report: if your report is correct but contains information that should be explained to potential credit grantors *or* if your report is incorrect. Regardless of why you need to contact the reporting bureaus, keep a log of all communication with them. If you contact them by phone, get first and last names of anyone you talk to. Write down what they promised, by when, and make sure you repeat what you're writing back to them.

Adding an Explanation

If the information in your credit report is correct but there's an explanation that would make things look better for you, you are entitled under the FCRA to add a one-hundred-word statement. Whether or not you want to add an explanation, however, is a tricky decision. A statement remains part of your report for two years and is displayed to anyone who reviews your report.

It may be in your best interest to explain your specific circumstances only to the individual bank or company with whom you apply for credit. For example, suppose a former spouse ran up debt on a joint account. Because you are both legally responsible for the debt, adding an explanation will gain you nothing. You are better off including your spouse's plans for paying the debt in settlement papers and showing that information directly to any banker you are dealing with.

On the other hand, a case where you probably would want to add an explanation might be a genuine and unresolved billing dispute.

Correcting an Error

If the information on your report is incorrect, you should consider getting it fixed. Mistakes in your personal information can be corrected by writing directly to the address listed on your report.

If your report contains a problem with account information supplied by one of your creditors, you would do best to try to resolve the error with the creditor directly and then send confirmation of the resolution to the CRAs. Your creditor has a vested interest in retaining you as a customer, so you have more leverage with them than you do with the CRAs. Once the CRA has verified the correction with the creditor, they should update your report and mail you a copy so that you can be sure all is well. Under the FCRA, they must resolve your situation within thirty days.

It's definitely worth stating that, although I've just made correcting problems sound simple enough, horror stories of frustrated consumers abound. The truth is that handling errors generally falls to overworked phone clerks motivated by quotas not customer service. Sometimes problems never get referred to a human being at all. In either case, your beautifully written letter to a creditor or CRA is probably reduced to a numerical code that translates to some very basic three-word explanation.

This is what happened to Luis Jarmillo. Upon checking his Trans-Union file, he found that it listed several accounts that didn't belong to him, including one that was opened when he was only eleven years old! Luis informed TransUnion, which translated his explanation into a computer code along the lines of "account not mine" and submitted it to the bank in question. The computer at the bank searched its files, found Luis's name and reported back that he was indeed on record as the owner of the account. The computer told the truth: the bank had this info. But the whole transaction did nothing to resolve the fact that the information was *wrong*. Luis found himself caught in a logical loop reminiscent of a "Who's on First" routine.

Unfortunately, writing directly to the bank might not have helped Luis all that much either. One major lender, as an example, is on record as saying that it does assign an actual person to dispute resolution, but it admits that it doesn't even talk to the consumer reporting the problem as part of its investigation. As with solving problems created by identity theft, finding decision makers, not front-line employees, and arranging for face-to-face interviews can make a big difference.

If you do find yourself caught in one of these Catch-22 situations, you will probably need to turn to professional help to get the muscle you need. Consumer reporters for local news stations can make a surprising amount happen. Attorneys specializing in credit disputes are becoming easier to find. And if you're feeling really feisty, you can always try to get a government official—who might affect legislation—interested in your case. Some names to get you started are listed in Resources at the end of the chapter.

Pat Yourself on the Back—And Check Your Reports Again Next Year

Now that you've gotten the credit part of your identity in order, it's time to give some thought to keeping it that way. Right now, decide that you're going to order your credit report the same time next year (or every time you do your taxes, if you prefer). The point is that you should check your credit report with each of the three big agencies each year. Just because it's so important, I'll say it again: You should check your credit report with each of the three big agencies each year.

You should check with each agency because, despite all the technology hysteria, the world of information is still a messy place and each one will have different information on you. And you should check each year, because these reports are constantly being updated with new activity, which means that there are frequent opportunities to input bad data.

You should also check your reports—and your score—a few months before a big financial event in your life. It is far better to find and correct a problem before you go house hunting than when you're worried about losing your dream home because the mortgage is held up. Or remember the guy who found out about a mistake as his wife was holding their brand new baby in a hospital in another country?

If you're one of those more litigious types, another reason to check your report annually is that the protection you get from laws like the FCRA and FACTA have time limits. You get five years from the time a problem occurs (and two years after you find out about it) to sue somebody over it. I'm not a big advocate of this, but, that said, there are sometimes legitimate problems that the court system must address. Don't become a victim twice over by finding out about these problems when it's too late to have your day in court.

And if you don't have enough of them already, still another good reason to check your reports annually is that there have been times when consumers have found a problem in a report, worked diligently and successfully with the big three to clear it up, and were frustrated to find the problem reappearing the next time the offending creditor again reported the wrong information to the CRA. Since FACTA, you have more legal protection from this, but mistakes still happen.

Don't Worry About Your Credit Scores

When you're considering a big financial event like buying a house or a car, it is worth a check of your scores to see how you are classified and how solidly you fall into your rate category. If your scores put you on the edge of being forced into higher rates, the time and expense to track them can be worthwhile. On its Web site, Fair Isaac offers an interactive tool that calculates a score (based on

Equifax profile data) and lets you test out what you can do to improve it.

Other than that, forget about your scores. Although it can be intensely irritating to know that you're being scored, you do *not* need to check them on a regular basis. Remember that the scores are calculated with up-to-the-minute information. Checking your scores on March 1 offers no assurance that you will know the numbers on April 1. In addition, scores only identify what broad category of borrower you fall into. If you fall solidly into one of the prime or subprime categories, any variation from day to day or from CRA to CRA probably won't affect you in any real way. So why make yourself angry? Let the big companies crunch their numbers. You have more interesting things to do.

RESOURCES

As with identity theft, credit reporting is getting a lot of attention from legislators at both the federal and state level. You can keep up-to-date with local legislation that affects you by going to the Web site for your state's attorney general. The watchdog groups listed below also tend to follow the national news pretty carefully.

If you have a problem that needs resolution, your bookstore should have a full shelf of books on cleaning up credit reports. You can also submit a complaint to the FTC, or try to contact one of the consumer advocate groups for a referral to a reputable attorney who specializes in these matters. The general wisdom is to avoid private "credit repair" agencies like the plague. Now that you know your rights, you can do it without them.

- National Association of Attorneys General (www.naag.org)
- Federal Trade Commission (www.ftc.gov)
- You can also submit FCRA complaints online: www.ftc.gov/complaints
- U.S. PIRG (www.uspirg.org)
- Electronic Privacy Center (www.epic.org)
- National Consumers League (http://www.nclnet.org)

- Consumers Union (www.consumersunion.org)
- Consumer Federation of America (www.consumerfed.org)
- Call For Action, Inc. (www.callforaction.org)
- Consumer Action (www.consumer-action.org, or e-mail hotline@consumer-action.org)

4. Your Key to Protecting What You Have: Insurance

IN THIS CHAPTER:
How insurance works, what insurers track to make underwriting decisions, how you can affect and monitor what they know

While most people are aware that their credit history is tracked, many are surprised to learn that their insurance history is tracked, too. Every claim you've ever filed—car insurance, home insurance, even some medical insurance—is compiled in a database.

Insurance companies, just like banks and credit card companies, prefer to do business with people who are "attractive"—which in their world means "low risk." They offer more coverage at lower rates to individuals they determine are low risk. And they try to avoid or raise rates on those people who—from their perspective—are "high risk."

Insurance underwriters have used information to figure out how much risk you represent since policies were written with quill pens. Modern technology has simply allowed them to get a lot more personal. Whether or not you can get auto, home, and medical coverage may depend on what your individual files say about you. How much you pay may also depend on a score calculated from your credit report.

The good news is that you have some say in the matter. You have a right to know about the tracking, and you can be smart about what you do. The bad news is that insurance companies may not always be evaluating risk as advertised. Your claims history, which is fine in good times, may lose you coverage when the economy slows. Simple mistakes can cost you dearly. If you don't check, you may never know that you're too big a risk until it's too late. So check. Here's how . . .

HOW DOES INSURANCE WORK?

Before talking about what tracking the insurance industry does and how it can affect you, it may help to go over the basics of how insurers set rates and evaluate customers. If you're not quite clear on the details, don't worry. Many people don't understand insurance. Here's the nickel tour.

The basic idea behind insurance is that companies collect premiums from a lot of people and anticipate that only some portion of them will file claims for whatever the insurance covers. And so, the obvious way insurance companies make money is by collecting more in premiums than they pay out in claims.

But there's another way they make money. Insurance companies, after all, must make sure that there's enough money in the "pool" to cover all potential claims. Out of necessity they find themselves sitting on a pile of money. It makes sense to invest this money rather than stuffing it in a mattress (albeit a very large mattress). And while you might be tempted to criticize insurers for "double-dipping," the fact that they make money through investments is actually a good thing for us consumers because it keeps our insurance premiums down.

Part of this strategy, of course, requires that they do, in fact, take in more money than they pay out in claims. The lower the risk of a payout to an individual, the more money the insurance company keeps and the more "attractive" that customer is to the insurance company. The more attractive the customer, the more likely they are to be offered coverage at reasonable rates. People who are less desirable—those high-risk individuals who are more likely to cost the insurance company more money in claims than they pay in—are usually denied coverage or hit with expensive premiums.

During the boom years of the 1990s, this basic reality got turned on its head. Insurance companies were making far more money buying Enron stock with premium payments than they paid out for claims—no matter how big the claims seemed to be. They were quite happy to write policies for just about anybody.

Suddenly, that all changed.

First, the stock market bubble of the 1990s burst. Then, insurance companies were hit with major claims. The attacks of 9/11 lead to almost $40 *billion* in insurance claims for that one event alone. To make matters worse, there were some big settlements for water damage to homes that resulted in mold infestations. One notorious ruling required a Texas insurer to pay a mold damage claim of $32 million. Companies selling homeowners' insurance still fear the cost of mold claims across the country could total another $18 *billion*.

Once times got tighter, the insurance companies were paying out roughly $1.20 for every $1 they were taking in. Not surprisingly, many companies began looking for ways to save money. That's where you come in.

HOW DOES THIS AFFECT ME?

Insurance is an industry that is highly regulated by government. Regulation of insurance happens at the state level, and specific rules imposed on insurance companies vary from state to state. Sometimes this regulation can create unanticipated problems.

Consider the skewed incentives created by a system called "prior approval." In a state that regulates insurance using a prior approval system, insurers must submit rate charts for approval. After they receive approval on their menu of prices, they can't really change them. However, they can change who is eligible for what prices. If they find that an insurance product at a certain price doesn't make money for them, they have to seek to minimize the loss. Because they are limited in how much they can change the price to better reflect the market, they focus on saving money by not selling the unprofitable product any longer.

FIND OUT ABOUT INSURANCE IN YOUR STATE

Remember that insurance regulation happens at the state level and that there is wide variation in the systems that each state has set up. The problems created by prior approval may not apply to you, but there may be other benefits or issues that you should know about. To get a quick heads-up on what the scoop is for your state, simply go to the Web site for your state's insurance commissioner or contact the National Association of Insurance Commissioners (www.naic.org).

And here's how it can affect you: On the recommendation of his insurance agent, a fellow who lived near a golf course spent an extra $35 a year on his homeowner's insurance for coverage of broken glass. When a bad hit sent a golf ball through his window, the homeowner filed a claim. When it happened a second time, the homeowner filed a second claim. The total for both claims, his only ones in fifteen years, was $330. The real cost, however, was that when his policy came up for renewal, the insurance company, looking to sell fewer property policies, now had an excuse to drop the homeowner.

Of course, in states that exercise less control over rates charged by insurers, unattractive customers can still feel the pain of bad times. Many have found themselves hit with rate increases of 200 to 300 percent—which is pretty much the same thing as being dropped altogether.

HOW DOES MY INSURANCE COMPANY DECIDE THAT IT WANTS TO DROP ME?

If your company is looking to drop or raise rates on unprofitable customers and it wants to determine if you fit the bill, it's got a lot of information about you to consider.

Your driving record is part of the rate calculation for your individual auto insurance. Your love of skydiving or your case of asthma figures into whether or not you can get life insurance. A record of how many claims you've filed in the past three to five years measures you against the rule of thumb used by most properly and casualty insurance companies: two claims in three years is too many.

Last but certainly not least, a copy of your credit report is used to generate still another score—this one to determine the risk that you will file a claim and, consequently, your appeal as a customer. Since most of us buy insurance in six-month or one-year terms, we're vulnerable each time our policy comes up for renewal.

This is why technology that tracks you becomes something you need to know about.

HOW DO INSURANCE COMPANIES KNOW THING ABOUT ME?

ChoicePoint, a spin-off from one of the big credit reporting agencies, collects data in a system that it calls the Comprehensive Loss Underwriting Exchange (C.L.U.E.). This exchange is available to insurance companies for a subscription fee.

ZIP CODE PROFILING

In addition to learning everything they can about your individual behavior, insurers have long looked at the trends of large groups to predict what will happen to any particular individual. Actuarial science, the statistics of predicting longevity, is one component of your life insurance premium.

Another piece of aggregate information that gets considered is your zip code. Based upon your home address, insurers know roughly what your income and style of living is. The result is that, in some states, zip codes are used to help set rates. A driver living in a poor neighborhood may pay four or five times the rates offered to another driver with an absolutely identical record but an address in a more affluent section of town. Drivers in more rural areas also often tend to get hit with higher rates.

C.L.U.E. Property includes info on you, your mortgage, and both you and your house's claim history. That's right—they track not only *your* claims history but also those of previous owners of your house as part of *your* record. If you're unlucky enough to buy a house whose previous owners filed a lot of claims, you might find yourself being denied coverage.

C.L.U.E. Auto provides access to identifying info about you as well as historical info about your insurance coverage, your driving record, and claims history. Both the auto and property exchanges seem to do a pretty good job of tracking. ChoicePoint claims that their data was used to make one hundred million underwriting decisions last year.

Another big player is The Insurance Services Office (ISO). They have created the Automobile-Property Loss Underwriting Service (A-PLUS), a collection of three to five years of claims information on all losses that have been filed. Each month, nearly seven hundred insurance companies, writing roughly 85 percent of the premiums collected for personal auto policies, update the ISO information on hundreds of millions of individual policies. The property data is contributed by twelve hundred insurance companies accounting for almost 90 percent of the premium volume written for property holders. At any one time, ISO's computers store some 9.3 billion records. In other words, if you've made a property or auto insurance claim of any kind, chances are very good that A-PLUS has recorded it.

You have a right by law, our old friend the FCRA, to read any of these reports on you car or your home. We'll go over just when you might want to, and how, in a little bit.

WHAT KINDS OF PROBLEMS MIGHT I HAVE WITH REPORTING?

Now that you've gotten this far in the book, you can probably figure out for yourself that insurance profiling not only quantifies your risk for a company, it also exposes you to risk.

First, as with credit reporting, there is the familiar issue of errors. Since information about you is reviewed to determine how much of a risk you represent, and because the riskier you look the more you'll have to pay for insurance, errors can cost you money.

Note the case of a man in Massachusetts who unwittingly paid exorbitant rates for his disability insurance because someone somewhere along the line had incorrectly classified him as an alcoholic. Mistakes may even lose you coverage altogether. In fairness, the reports of problems for property, auto, and medical reporting generally range from less than one to 3 percent of files, a far cry from the 60 to 70 percent cited in credit reporting.

Another problem is the ubiquitous issue of identity theft and exposure to violent criminals. One major insurance company had its online access to the California Department of Motor Vehicles (DMV) records revoked because it failed to protect the information it was accessing. The DMV sent undercover agents to branch locations and discovered multiple instances where employees had engaged in "file browsing" and improperly requested information for friends and relatives. While no employees got caught selling client data to ID theft rings, it isn't inconceivable that something like this occurred. It is documented that a client of the insurance company believed that a confidential address had been released as the result of such "file browsing," which resulted in threats to that customer.

Finally, there is increasing evidence that underwriters, when trying to eliminate expensive customers in bad times, make links between a piece of information and the risk of a claim that are, to put it kindly, dubious. Don't get me wrong. An insurance company has a legitimate reason to know about you in order to evaluate risk. If you have a terrible disease, you do represent a different life insurance risk than if you're a healthy twenty-five-year-old.

And they have the right to use that information to make sure that you are upholding your end of the bargain you made with them. A little more than ten years ago, Bonnie McCaslin purchased seventy-eight life insurance policies worth $11 million on her ex-husband. She then reported that he died in an earthquake in Mexico and filed claims for compensation. Later, the unwitting ex-husband was discovered alive and well in California working as—get this—an insurance agent! This somewhat notorious case is an example of why the life insurance industry began tracking applications for coverage to red flag anyone who is stocking up on policies. Similar tracking has been put in place to limit workers' compensation and disability fraud.

Studies suggest that Bonnie is not alone in her shenanigans. A survey by the Insurance Research Council indicates that one out of three Americans has made a false or exaggerated insurance claim. The National Insurance Crime Bureau estimates that paying out these unfair claims adds about $30 billion to the cost of insuring us all, which translates into an extra $200 to $300 per year per household for insurance premiums. We should applaud tracking as a tool to stop this fraud.

But here's the rub. Although meant to uncover fraud or better evaluate risk, tracking can be used. There are also stories that suggest that, in bad times for the insurance business, a line can genuinely get crossed.

A young couple found their dream home and put in an offer for it. It was accepted. They then sold their existing home and waited eagerly for the closing date. As the day approached and their financing was falling into place, they took the final step of seeking homeowner's insurance to meet the requirements of their mortgage company. Unfortunately, when the couple tried to get coverage they learned that the current owners of their dream house had filed two insurance claims in the past three years—one for a broken tree limb and one for a break-in. The property was deemed excessively risky to insure—regardless of who was living there—and the couple was turned down by company after company.

Another homeowner filed a claim for a broken water pipe. His insurance company sent its own authorized plumber to do repairs. This plumber didn't do a very good job. The homeowner brought in his own plumber to do the job correctly and submitted a second claim. At renewal time, his policy was cancelled. Why? He'd had two claims in three years. Despite the fact that the second claim was only made necessary by the first plumber's incompetence, the insurance company refused to make an exception.

Yet another homeowner with one claim on her record was told

that a second claim she wanted to make wouldn't be covered. Even though the company only paid out for one claim, she had attempted to make a second claim and it was entered into her profile. She was treated as if both had cost the company money and her coverage was dropped.

And perhaps most egregiously, a homeowner filed a claim for water damage. A few years later she called her agent to check if her policy covered a leak from her dishwasher. She didn't say that she had a problem. She merely wanted to know if something like this would be covered. Unbeknownst to her, the agent listed her question as a claim. It was reported to the tracking companies and the next thing she knew her policy, too, was being cancelled.

Given the potential for aggressive interpretation of claims losses by insurance companies when they want to limit underwriting or raise rates, it is well worth checking out what they know.

AND WHAT'S THIS ABOUT AN INSURANCE SCORE?

That's right, scoring doesn't stop with credit. Fair Isaac has helped the major credit bureaus and ChoicePoint develop scores based on your credit reports, which they sell to property and auto insurers. The ISO has its own score based on your TransUnion credit report.

It is important to note that the way this score is calculated is completely different from the financial score we discussed in the previous chapter. This score doesn't try to predict whether or not you have the financial wherewithal to sustain the standard of living you've adopted. Instead it tries to predict how likely it is that you'll file a claim during the term of the insurance.

The argument in the industry for the use of scores is that there is a demonstrable correlation between your financial behavior and the likelihood that you will file an insurance claim. If you have a lot of extended credit, you may live a little less cautiously than your more parsimonious neighbor. That means that you may also be a risk taker who drives a little faster and has more accidents.

One insurance company also claims that being stretched financially makes you more stressed out—which means that you're more likely to get into an accident. Regardless of the explanation, it appears to be the case that drivers with the lowest scores are 60 percent more likely to file a claim than drivers with better credit.

Unfortunately, there have been consumer horror stories where scores have played a bigger role in determining insurability than the actual claims history. Drivers with absolutely no moving violations or accidents have had their rates raised or were denied coverage based on the score derived from their credit history. Given this overinterpretation, several states have pushed back on allowing insurance companies to consider scores when underwriting policies. It's worth checking to see where your state stands on this. The National Association of Mutual Insurance Companies, a trade group for the insurance industry, maintains a Web page with a summary of state laws (www.namic.org/scorecard/03 insscoring.asp).

As with credit scoring, you can buy your insurance score along with your report if you're curious.

WHAT DOES MY INSURANCE REPORT ACTUALLY CONTAIN?

The primary report used by underwriters is technically called a claim history report. This name gives you a good indication of what is really of interest to your insurance company.

For auto insurance, the report will list information about you, your car, any past claims you've made, and who else has been asking about your claim history (generally a red flag for fraud if there are a lot of inquiries).

Insurance companies may supplement this data with reports on your particular motor vehicle (a VIN report), your coverage history, and guesses at who else you may let drive your car. This last bit of information is generally derived from DMV data that lists the names of other licensed drivers who live at your address.

For house and property insurance, the report will list the same type of information about you and the house in question. Additional reports may also include information on the property itself, gathered from public records—things like previous sale prices, the physical location—or information prepared by the ISO from analyzing past events in your area—how well your local fire department is outfitted, or the occurrence of fire, flood, or windstorms.

HOW IS DMV INFORMATION USED IN INSURANCE TRACKING?

The Department of Motor Vehicles (DMV) collects a lot of information. For most of us, our driver's license—which includes a picture

WHO ELSE CAN SEE DMV RECORDS?

In case you're wondering who besides the hundreds of thousands of insurance agents, brokers, and government officials can see your DMV file, there is finally a bit of relief.

Following a high-profile murder case in which an actress was stalked using information obtained from the DMV, Congress passed the Federal Driver's Privacy Protection Act to limit the release of personal information from motor vehicle records. This act regulates how the DMV releases your record (i.e., they can share reports only with others who have permissible use, and they must keep a record of sharing for five years). Personal info is defined as information that identifies an individual, including a driver identification number, name, address (but not the five-digit zip code), and telephone number. It also includes your photograph or image, Social Security number, and medical information. This information may not be shared unless you explicitly agree to allow it, except in certain cases that have to do with the government wanting to find you, say to collect child support or taxes.

Once upon a time, lists of licensed drivers were sold to anyone who wanted to buy them. Thanks to the DPPA, states that used to top off their coffers by selling your DMV records to marketers have generally stopped doing so. But be warned: at least one state, Florida, has been caught going around the restriction. The next time you have a reason to contact your DMV, it's worth asking about their policy on access to your records and about any opt-out provisions to keep your name from being sold to commercial list vendors.

and increasingly a thumbprint—is a key form of identification. In states with motor-voter laws, it also keeps us registered to vote. But probably the biggest impact that our DMV records have on us is that every vehicular indiscretion, big and small, is on record for insurance companies to see. For insurance purposes, most states report information on car accidents and driving violations for the past three years. Some unlucky citizens live in states that report for the past five years or more. Your DMV can tell you the policy in your state, if you're curious.

WHAT REPORTING EXISTS FOR MEDICAL INSURANCE?

Medical insurance is different from car and home insurance in a couple of very important ways. First, most of us get coverage as a group instead of as an individual. Since certain risk can be expected

---

HEALTH CARE CLEARINGHOUSES

We've been discussing how information tracking affects your ability to get insurance. We have not been talking about the privacy of your information. That's because, as with everything else, it's long gone. Your very personal chat with your doctor is now in a file that gets tracked by an industry that has built up around paying for the problem you were talking with him or her about.

Medical records are routinely shared with companies called clearinghouses whose sole function is to facilitate the process of getting payment. These companies, staffed by lawyers and accountants as well as data entry clerks, all see your records before they share them with the insurers, health plans, HMOs, and government agencies who end up paying for it.

One privacy consultant estimates that by the time you account for laboratories, x-ray facilities, and pharmacies playing their part, hospitalization for a treatment that is paid by a third party routinely allows between one and ten thousand people access to your "confidential" medical information.

to be present in every large group, there is no need to determine who personally represents each risk. By applying as a group, you've all agreed to bear the others' cost. Because of this, individual tracking is used less by medical insurers, and we are less likely to be affected by it.

Next, the one company that warehouses information for medical insurance providers is a nonprofit trade association called the Medical Insurance Bureau (MIB). Unlike commercial enterprises such as Equifax or ChoicePoint, the MIB has no competition and no profit motive that encourages very aggressive reporting.

Finally, the medical information that is tracked is, by and large, gathered directly from you. Instead of relying on regular reports by third parties, insurers ask each of us what they want to know about. The function of the MIB is really to retain information that you give one company and compare it to what you tell the next one on the insurance application.

Here's how medical reporting works: The six hundred insurance providers that belong to the MIB association agree to share information with one another using the MIB as a central repository. If you've ever submitted an individual or small-group application for any kind of medical insurance, the insurance company probably translated key pieces of information about conditions that affect your health or longevity into numerical codes. They transmitted those codes to the MIB database. The next time you apply for coverage, your new insurance company will send a query to the MIB database to verify that the information you're submitting is in line with what you've told other insurance companies in the past.

And before you get too excited about all this, bear in mind that this method of fraud protection for the medical insurance industry has been in place since 1902.

Despite its long tradition, we can only assume that computers have made the MIB more efficient at tracking. Curiously, they are still quite modest in their goals. According to the MIB, out of every one hundred life insurance applications, only about fifteen to twenty result in an MIB record. This is despite the fact that 95 percent of life insurance business is handled by the MIB members.

WHAT IS IN AN MIB REPORT?

First, an MIB report will contain the inevitable identifying information like your name, your date and place of birth, your address, and any other names you might have used in the past. In a truly refreshing break with most medical insurance practices, it is optional for an insurance company to submit your Social Security number. This information may actually not be in an MIB report on you!

The other information contained in your report is a series of codes that correspond to any medical conditions or hazardous activities that might affect your health or longevity. There are approximately two hundred and thirty codes that the MIB system uses. While most are for medical conditions, a handful do capture so-called dangerous hobbies, one exists to note the fact that you have a bad driving record, and two indicate family history (one for cardiac problems; the other for any kind of hereditary disease).

It's difficult to say which conditions are considered important enough to report to the MIB. There appears to be some bit of discretion afforded each insurer about what they deem worth storing in the database. From your perspective, you should probably consider anything you've disclosed on an insurance application or allowed a doctor to tell the insurance company in the past seven years as fair game. The time limit on most information is seven years from the time it gets communicated to the MIB. If an application reports that a condition is still going on, the date of that report resets the seven-year clock. In other words, a condition that started ten years ago but that you *still* have today is still listed.

The final bit of information contained in an MIB report is how many times an insurance company has requested your record in the past two years. These days, asking for information has become almost as important as the information itself.

WHAT LEGAL PROTECTIONS DO I HAVE?

All of the companies that we've been discussing are consumer-reporting agencies and are regulated by the Fair Credit Reporting Act. That means that you have the right to know if they have a file on you and what that file contains. It also means that your neighbor does *not* have the right—without being able to demonstrate a reasonable business relationship—to order an insurance report on you.

When it comes to medical information, there are a few additional safeguards. The FCRA explicitly restricts dissemination of any medical data on you without your written permission. The only problem with this is that the fine print of absolutely every insurance application I've ever read includes waiver language that not only gives the insurance company the right to see your report, but do everything up to interviewing your grade school principal if they feel like it.

More recently, a law has come into effect that even further restricts what can be done with medical information. This law, the Health Insurance Portability and Accountability Act (HIPAA), was designed to provide federal-level privacy restrictions on medical information collected by health care providers, pharmacists, and insurers. Although many states had effected protective legislation, this was the first time the issue was addressed at the federal level.

In a nutshell, HIPAA requires that you be able to see, copy, and add to any of your medical records and that you be informed of the privacy practices adopted by your health care provider. Surprising as it sounds, you had no legal right in some states to see your own medical records before HIPAA.

HIPAA also limits the use of your medical information. Before a doctor, pharmacist, hospital or insurer can release any medical information to companies that aren't directly involved in offering you health care, such as a life insurer, a bank, or a marketing firm, they have to get your signed permission.

CHECKUP

Unlike with credit reporting, it isn't really necessary to request copies of your claims history reports on an annual basis. The following checkups offer two easy tests: one to assess the insurance climate and the other to identify special circumstances to help you figure out those times when it does make sense for you to take a look at your report.

What Is the Insurance Climate?

As we've noted, the use of tracking in the insurance industry is gaining momentum, but having a clean insurance profile is still less of a cornerstone for successful modern life than having a clean credit report. Whereas you and I buy stuff all the time, the average person files a property claim once every ten years. The sheer bulk of data about you that gets moved from place to place simply is smaller, and the potential for common data entry errors is lower.

What's more, insurance companies only access claims history reports at three clearly identifiable points in your relationship with them: when they want to assess a claim you've just made for potential fraud, when they analyze your rates at renewal time, or when they set rates for a new policy. Since most companies renew policies annually, the potential effect of a claims report can be traced back relatively easily. This is in striking contrast to the use of credit reports that are pulled by countless different companies seemingly on a daily basis.

The result of the differences is that—unlike with credit reports—it's quite possible that you don't need to worry about insurance claims reporting at all. The ISO estimates that 70 to 75 percent of inquiries for property reports and 50 percent of inquiries for auto reports fail to uncover anything worth paying attention to. Here's one way to determine if you should bother requesting your claims history reports.

For one week, read the paper every day and watch your local news, especially the stuff about consumer reports. Look for reports on the state of the insurance industry. Listen for stories about people having trouble finding or keeping coverage. Talk to your friends about *their* insurance. Ask them about any real estate transactions they've heard of—any horror stories concerning insurance come up? Take a quick trip to www.consumerreports.org. Any striking headlines on insurance there?

Use this awareness to assess the current insurance climate. If times are tight, we all need to be more careful and each of us should go through the exercise of talking to our broker and ordering our reports.

If times are good, you can rest easy—unless you happen to be a special case.

Special Cases

To determine if any special circumstances have or will arouse suspicion that you represent a higher-than-usual risk to an insurance company, take a look at the statements below. If any of them describe you, you probably need to check on that report.

Auto Claims/DMV Report

- You have been in an accident that got reported to the DMV (whether it was your fault or not) in the past five years.
- You have been arrested for a moving violation in the past five years.
- You have ever had an arrest or conviction for drunk driving.
- You have ever had your license suspended or revoked.
- You have bought a used car in the past thirty days.
- You are considering buying a used car.
- You have recently been denied auto insurance.
- Your auto insurance rates have risen more than 10 percent in the past year.
- Your have ever had your identity stolen or you suspect that it might have been stolen.

Property Claims Report

- You own a house that you are thinking of selling.
- You have just bought or are thinking of buying a new house.
- You have made a property insurance claim in the past five years.
- You have recently completed major maintenance on your house, like replacing your roof.
- You have recently been denied homeowners' or other property insurance.
- Your homeowners or other property insurance rates have risen more than 10 percent in the past year.
- You have ever had your identity stolen or you suspect that it might have been stolen.

Medical Insurance Report

- You have ever applied for life, health, disability, or long-term insurance as an individual or as part of a group of less than ten people.
- You applied for life, health, disability, or long-term insurance as part of a larger group, but you requested higher coverage than the rest.
- You have recently been denied any kind of medical insurance.
- Your medical insurance rates have risen more than 10 percent in the past year.
- You have ever had your identity stolen or you suspect that it might have been stolen.

Bonus Question: Have you filled out more than one medical insurance application in the last seven years?

TAKING ACTION

In order to assure that you can get ongoing insurance coverage at prices that make sense for you, you may want to investigate your property for its insurability. Depending on your results from the checkups about the economic climate or your own special circumstances, you may also need to request, review, and possibly correct one or more insurance claims reports.

Investigating Insurance

One way to protect yourself from insurance gaps is to do some investigating before you buy a car or house. It's a given that if you own a car, you will be required by law to insure it (at least for liability). If you buy a house and have a mortgage, you can bet your lender will require you to buy coverage.

As our young couple discovered when they purchased their dream home, it would be terrible to discover too late that you can't get insurance for a property or car because of *its* history. If you're buying a house at a time when insurers are being more careful, you would do well to request a report from the seller as part of your prepurchase inspections.

Car reports are much easier to get your hands on. One company, Carfax, compiles individual vehicle histories from over four thousand sources of information, which they then sell to consumers and car dealers. Reports like these will alert you to title and registration problems, odometer readings that are off, and whether or not the car was in a major accident, a fire, a flood, or was ever stolen. Carfax.com is easy to find online; a search on the phrase "car history reports" should bring up other companies as well.

Auto Insurance/DMV Reporting

If you determined that any of the statements in the auto section of the Special Cases checkup applied to you, you need to do a little due diligence with either the DMV or your insurance broker. The first four statements may have identified potential information on your DMV report that could reflect negatively on you. You will want to make sure that this information is as full and accurate as it needs to be. Some states' DMVs, for example, will report your involvement in an accident regardless of who was at fault. If that

HOW LONG IS LONG ENOUGH?

The policy on how long negative information is retained on your driving record varies from state to state. To use New York State as a fairly typical example, you can expect the following lifespan for problems.

- A moving violation conviction or accident remains on your record during the year of the conviction or accident and for three years thereafter. On January 1 of the fourth year after an incident, it no longer appears on your record or abstract. For example, if you had a traffic accident or conviction anytime during 2002, it would remain on your record from 2003 through 2005. It would no longer appear on your record beginning January 1, 2006.

- A suspension or revocation of your license that has been cleared or is over remains on your record during the year it is cleared or finishes and the following three years. If the problem has not been cleared or officially ended, it remains on your record indefinitely.

- Alcohol- and drug-related convictions remain on your record for exactly ten years, because higher penalties may be imposed for repeat violations within that time.

happens to you and you know that your insurer will see it, be proactive about telling your side of the story.

The fifth and sixth statements may have identified an instance where you want to check on a vehicle that someone is selling you to make sure that it isn't a lemon. Reread the last section about vehicle history reports. The last three statements suggest that something may be amiss with your claims history report.

The DMV Report

Requesting a report from your state's DMV is actually quite simple. It's also something I'd recommend you do for yourself. Since most states have programs to withhold certain minor infractions from insurance companies if you go to traffic school, this is not the time to ask your insurance agent or broker directly if he knows that you've been bad. There is a time to talk to your agent or broker, and we'll get there in a minute.

As a matter of routine, I'd also suggest getting a copy of your DMV report every time you renew your license. Just call it a reasonable precaution. All that you need to do is fill out a form readily available from your DMV, provide proof of identity, and pay a fee.

The things to look out for are essentially that all of the information included in the report is correct, that there aren't any fines that someone else has been racking up in your name, and that information about license suspensions, revocations, or driving violations isn't listed when it should have been removed.

If you find a small problem with your DMV report, you will need to ask the DMV for the appropriate government form to fill out. It will be bureaucratic but doable. If the problem is related to false charges, be forewarned that this is a big problem that is best handled with expert advice. Start with a local attorney.

The Auto Claims Report(s)

If you think that something is awry with your car insurance rates, you will want to look at the claims history report that your broker sees. The best way to do this is to ask your agent or broker to get it for you. It's cheaper and doesn't waste your time tracking down information that simply isn't used by the company you do business with. Most major insurers access both the C.L.U.E. and A-PLUS databases, but not all of them do. Also, if you're a long-term customer of an insurance company, they have their *own* database of claims you've filed while you've been with them. They don't need to go to a centralized source.

If your agent can't get it for you, or for whatever reason you simply want to contact the CRAs yourself, the procedure is relatively straightforward. Because you are once again operating under the Fair Credit Reporting Act (FCRA), you are entitled to a free report if you have reason to believe that the report from ChoicePoint or the ISO was used in a decision to deny you coverage. Otherwise, you will have to pay some fee set by your state. Remember that some states require free reports for their residents, while others set fees slightly below the basic rate stipulated by the FCRA.

According to FACTA, you also have the right to a free report once a year. The FTC will spell out how this should happen by March 2005. Here's where to go to request a report:

FTC
For information on how to order free reports visit the FTC Web site at www.ftc.gov.

ChoicePoint
ChoicePoint has made all of its reports available online. Their Web site, www.choicetrust.com, actually goes out of its way to make selling you your own information as easy and compelling as they can. If you want immediate, online access to your reports, you will need to create an account. If you order online, you must pay the full basic fee set by the FCRA. If you live in a state that set lower fees for reports, or you are entitled to a free report, you will not be able to take advantage of the lower cost. If you want to pay the lower fees or are entitled to a free report, you can order a report over the phone by calling 888-497-0011. Once you give them information to find the file, they will mail a report to the address that they have in their records.

You can also download a written request form from www. choicetrust.com. Mail that form with payment to:

ChoicePoint Insurance Consumer Center
P.O. Box 105108
Atlanta, GA 30348-5108

ISO
The ISO isn't engaging in a consumer outreach campaign the way that ChoicePoint is. They do make the reports available under the terms of the FCRA, but aren't overly concerned with whether or not

you order it. Simply call 800-709-8842 to ask for a "request for disclosure" form.

ISO will mail you a report. They will also agree to fax your report to you if you want it quickly. Be prepared to pay an extra handling fee if you choose this option.

What You Should Look For on Claims Reports

Once you get the claims history report, you will need to review the five or six sections of information it contains. Following a listing of information the insurance company uses to identify you, there is a summary of any claims you've filed in the past three years. There is also a summary of claims filed on your car by other people (including previous owners) and of claims filed by anyone who also lives at your address (because it is presumed that they will also drive your car on occasion). The report typically concludes with a list of insurance companies who have recently ordered your report.

The things to look for in a report have to do with incorrect information, the time frame of reported claims, and anything that deserves comment or further investigation.

- Incorrect personal ID info: Wrong info may pull up the wrong credit file or claims you've never heard of.

- Claims that you don't recognize: did you actually file them? Check to make sure that there aren't cases where you'd only made an inquiry and had that reported as a claim. If a claim is attributed to a former owner or resident of your house, check with them to make sure the details are accurate.

- Claims without proper resolution: Are all claims correctly shown as resolved and are payment amounts correct?

- Old claims still listed: Are all claims made within the last five years or less? For example, if you order a report in 2005, only losses occurring between 2000 and 2005 should be reported.

- Additional drivers: If you've never heard of someone who is identified as a potential driver of your car, this could well indicate some kind of ID theft. Alternatively, someone listed as a possible additional driver may no longer be a factor. You broke up with your reckless driver of a boyfriend and he moved out, for example. If that person has a poor history as far as the insurance industry is concerned, it may make sense to update your files to get his name off of them.

- Unusual inquiries: Any unusual insurance requests or ones that you don't recognize? Be alert for someone using your name to commit insurance fraud.

Correcting a Claims Report

If there is an issue with any of your auto claims reports, you need to follow the same procedure you did for credit reports. If information is correct but needs explanation, think carefully about whether adding an explanation won't have side effects that are less than desirable. It's good to bear in mind that information about claims is only reported for three to five years. Although information about you and your coverage history remains, problems particular to claims may simply go away.

Property Reports

If you determined that the first two statements under property reports described you, you are thinking about or actually in the process of a real estate transaction that may go more smoothly if you order the appropriate claims history reports. ChoicePoint is making a big deal of suggesting that you review claims reports on your house before putting it on the market or that you ask a current seller for the report on his house as part of your due diligence before buying. Some Realtors' associations are jumping on the bandwagon and beginning to recommend it, too. If you're a seller, you may want to be prepared for the request from a potential buyer.

If the remaining statements described you, you should double-check your property claim history report to make sure that the information it contains is accurate and up-to-date.

The means of getting and correcting a C.L.U.E. or A-PLUS property report will be the same as that of a C.L.U.E. or A-PLUS auto report. The content and layout of both reports will also be similar to the auto reports. The only significant difference is that the property reports don't include guesses on possible related claims or additional drivers.

You will look for similar kinds of problems in property as in auto reports. There is only one additional issue to look out for: claims that might benefit from an explanation. Are there any claims with extenuating circumstances, or changed circumstances, where an explanation might help? The biggest one, according to the ISO, is that you filed a claim because your dog bit your neighbor, but you no longer own that or any dog. The second biggest one is that you filed a claim for damage from a leak in your roof but you replaced the roof last year. Major maintenance on a home should be added in an explanation for any claims that are now unlikely to recur.

Medical Reports

Because of the way medical insurance is offered, MIB reports won't affect too many of us. That said, you really do need to request a report search if any of the statements in the medical section of the Special Cases checkup described your situation. In other words, you have applied for insurance individually or you have some cause to suspect that something is up.

If you only answered "Yes" to the bonus question, you don't need to order a report, but I do have a helpful hint for you. From here on in, keep copies of any insurance applications that you submit. You do it often enough that you can't predict when you will switch from a group to an individual plan, and you need to be aware of information about you that you have made available for tracking. Besides, it makes filling out the next application so much easier!

Ordering Your MIB Report

If you decide that you do want to check for an MIB report, you must submit your report request in writing because of the extra sensitivity of medical information. You can get the request form online at www.mib.com. The information you need to provide is breathtakingly simple: name, date of birth, and state of birth. The MIB does ask for other information but indicates that it's optional. This is because they will verify your contact information with your current insurer before releasing your report to you. The final part of the form consists of directions for how you'd like the information sent to you.

Just as with all of the other information trackers, the MIB is subject to the FCRA and FACTA. This means that they will ask for a fee for the record search, but that fee may be waived if you can prove that an MIB report was used in a decision to deny you insurance, or lowered if you live in a state that requires this. After March 2005, you will also be able to request a free report once a year (check the FTC Web site for info on this).

The written request form with a check should be mailed to:

MIB, Inc.
P.O. Box 105
Essex Station
Boston, MA 02112

If you have any questions about the process you can call the MIB at 617-426-3660.

How to Read the MIB Report

If the MIB doesn't have a file on you, they will send you a simple letter saying so. If they do have a file, you will really need your decoder ring. The MIB reports have probably the most "interesting" format of all the reports we will discuss. Unlike other reports, these try to protect your private information. They have actually been designed to be difficult to read so that a clerk can't tell you've got a heart condition from a quick glance.

The report from MIB will include:

- The names of the MIB member companies that reported information to the MIB.
- The names of the MIB member companies that have requested a copy of your MIB record in the past.
- The type of information that MIB has on you, i.e., files from MIB (life), DIRS (Disability Insurance Record System), and HCI (Health Claims)
- And the contents of your record itself, containing your name, your date of birth, your occupation, and a list of the codes that have been submitted about you.

When you get your report, you will also receive a plain English description of the codes that apply to you. You'll need it. A sample code taken from an MIB example looks like this:

301GZN

And it breaks down like this:

- The first three numbers represent a condition code.
- The first letter indicates the degree of severity.
- The second letter identifies the info source.
- The final letter denotes the time of condition (i.e., within one year of the application).

Easy, right?

What to Look For in Your MIB Report

Errors crop up because of typos—looking at the bizarre code above, you can imagine how easy this must be. They also happen when labs mix up test results. And they can happen because sometimes even well-trained and well-meaning doctors don't get the diagnosis right. If a doctor made a judgment call that exaggerated a problem or perhaps missed the mark entirely, that information might still be sitting in your file, even though you got it sorted out years ago. Remember the (non)alcoholic man mentioned earlier?

Correcting Your MIB Report

If you find anything wrong with your MIB file, there is a little more to consider. Honest errors need to be corrected.

But if the error is because your file is out of date, don't waste time trying to update it. According to the MIB, if you raced cars in 2003, and this was reported, the information that you raced cars in 2003 is correct. Remember that condition codes come with dates attached to them. Even if you give up car racing in 2004, they will not remove this info from your file, because the report that you raced cars in 2003 is correct. Since there is no code for "doesn't race cars anymore," there is no way to add to your file to indicate that you once did something that might affect your longevity but that you don't do it anymore. If you submit an application to an insurance company and don't mention that you race cars, the insurance company will either assume that you no longer race cars or ask you about it. If they don't, your best defense is to be aware that an incomplete record exists and to make sure that the vendors using it are using it appropriately.

If you don't plan on applying for insurance in the near term, there really isn't a need to do anything. It may be better to wait. If the information in your record is close to seven years old, your entire file will soon be expunged as a matter of course. The MIB is pretty careful about keeping around any information that can't be justified.

RESOURCES

Aside from medical privacy, there is less legislation changing insurance than other topics we've discussed so far. However, new problems may pop up when the economy forces companies to get creative. If you think you've got a problem with your insurance coverage and want some extra help, the place to begin any further investigation is with your state's insurance commissioner. To find the address and telephone number of the insurance commissioner in your state, look in the blue pages of your local phone book or on the Web site of the National Association of Insurance Commissioners.

You can also file complaints about insurers with the same association. If you have any problems with your C.L.U.E. or A-PLUS report, you should consider contacting the Federal Trade Commission.

The Department of Health and Human Services is tasked with regulating the use (and misuse) of medical information. Issues of significant concern can be taken up with them. Consumer groups that help with credit reporting issues can also address insurance reporting. In addition, there are consumer rights groups who provide information and support on what is happening specifically with access to medical information and insurance fraud.

- National Association of Insurance Commissioners (www.naic.org)
- U.S. Department of Health and Human Services (www.dhhs.gov)
- American Health Information Management Association (www.ahima.org)
- Health Privacy Project (www.healthprivacy.org)
- Coalition Against Insurance Fraud (www.insurancefraud.org)

5. MONEY TROUBLES: BANKING AND FINANCIAL SERVICES

IN THIS CHAPTER:

How electronic payment works, what financial organizations track, how you can protect yourself from fraud and reduce what companies know

In a world of information, money is no longer just a shiny coin or a piece of paper. More and more, we are turning to plastic cards and computer networks to manage our finances. Credit cards, debit cards, online bill payment, direct deposit—all ways to get and spend money without ever physically touching it.

The last time it counted, the Federal Reserve Bank figured out that 30 billion electronic payments were being made a year. The Electronic Payments Association (NACHA), says that more than $27.4 trillion is shuttled about electronically.

The convenience of electronic transfer of funds is obvious. You might be surprised to learn that electronic payments also offer more protection than paper checks. In fact, by the end of this chapter I'll be surprised if you ever write another check.

On the other hand, electronic payments don't offer the same anonymity as using cash. And now it's possible to steal your money in countless new ways without even meeting you. As with so much else in today's world, technology brings both benefits and burdens.

Let's see how it affects you.

HOW DO ELECTRONIC PAYMENTS WORK?

Electronic payments are made through a dizzying progression from one bank to another. Since we're talking about someone having their electronic hand in your wallet, it's probably worth knowing whose hand it is.

Intermediary banks called clearinghouses negotiate the transactions needed to get funds from one account (yours) into another (like the grocer's). The Federal Reserve acts as one of these intermediaries, but so, too, do a number of private competitors. The network of intermediaries, also called The Automated Clearing House Network (ACH), has been in use for thirty years. It serves 20,000 banks and financial institutions and 3.5 million businesses. According to NACHA, 135 million of us have our money touched by an ACH, whether we know it or not.

Suppose you get cash from an ATM at a convenience store. You go to the machine, insert your ATM card, type in your password, and make a request for $20. Then you wait a few seconds. While to you it seems that nothing is happening, in fact, there is a whole lot going on.

In those few seconds, the ATM contacts a computer at its owner bank (quite probably an intermediary bank you've never heard of) who contacts your bank. The computer at your bank verifies your account info and the amount of money you have available. The ATM's bank initiates a transfer of $20 from your bank to its own account, plus $2 or so in transaction fees. It then tells the machine to spit out a twenty into your waiting hands.

As you walk away with money in hand, the ATM's bank now transfers $20 into still another bank account—the one belonging to the convenience store owner who has to physically put another $20 bill into the ATM to keep it full of cash for the next person. Simple.

DO I HAVE TO WORRY ABOUT ELECTRONIC PAYMENTS?

Not really. Although studies show that a lot of people are quite concerned about the dangers of ATM/debit cards, online banking, and

CREDIT VERSUS DEBIT

Although your credit card and your ATM card—which is officially called a "debit" card—look an awful lot alike (they're often indistinguishable) and seem to work in much the same way, they are actually two very different beasts.

The most obvious difference, one you're surely aware of, is that when you use a credit card to make a purchase, you're borrowing the money, which eventually must be paid back to the credit card issuer. When you use a debit card, the money is coming right out of your bank account in one immediate electronic payment.

other electronic payment schemes, the truth of the matter is that they are really quite safe. Not perfectly safe. But then, neither is having cash in your wallet.

One reason why electronic payments are safe is that we have protection in the event something bad happens. While most people are aware of the limited liability for unauthorized credit card use, fewer folks know about liability protection for systems that move money around electronically. If you become the victim of unauthorized use of your ATM/debit card, or if someone uses your password to break into your bank accounts online, the amount of money you can lose is determined by the Electronic Funds Transfer Act (EFTA). According to this act the amount of protection you enjoy depends on when you notice and report the problem.

If you report an ATM/debit card missing before it's used without your permission (say your wallet is stolen and you get to the bank right away), the EFTA says the card issuer cannot hold you responsible for any unauthorized transfers—zero money lost. If you report a loss within two days of discovering it, don't expect to pay more than $50. If for some unfathomable reason it takes you longer than two days to check with the bank after you discover money disappearing from your account, the amount you won't see again may go up to $500.

The kicker is that if you still haven't called the bank sixty days after a statement listing the fraudulent transaction is sent to you, you are on the hook for everything the thief takes until you take action. You could lose all the money in your bank account and have to pay any portion of your line of credit established for overdrafts. Happily, once you've reported the loss of your ATM/debit card, you cannot be held liable for additional unauthorized transfers that occur after that time.

Online banking follows the same rules, except that your degree of exposure is directly connected to how quickly you report a theft or loss of your password. What's more, a lot of banks are very careful to offer assurances about the safety of online banking and promise even more protection than required by the EFTA. The end result is that, as long as you're paying a little bit of attention, the liability for unauthorized transfer of funds using a debit or ATM card or online banking system is pretty much like that of a credit card.

A second component of electronic fund safety is your password. Just about every electronic payment scheme requires two bits of information to be pieced together to gain access to your money. Consider your ATM/debit card. First, there is all of the data on the magnetic stripe of the card, such as your account number, the name of your bank, and the routing number for the bank. Without the physical card, faking this information is difficult (but not impossible—more on this later).

Second, there is your secret password or PIN. Passwords are generally treated with great care in computer systems. They may be stored in a separate database from other information, usually in an encrypted form, and surrounded by many layers of security. Hacking a bank's computers to gain this data would take a fair bit of work.

The result is that there appears to be considerably less interest among thieves in hacking computers to commit debit fraud than, say, hacking systems to steal credit card numbers—which only require one piece of data, the number, to do damage. The danger of unauthorized access to your bank account exists on a much more personal—and therefore controllable—level. By far, the most common method of gaining access to your bank account is by stealing information from you directly.

In some cases, a lucky thief steals your wallet and finds in it both the card and the PIN written down on a piece of paper. If you haven't been kind enough to provide the password directly, the thief has to watch as you input your PIN at an ATM machine before he picks your pocket for the card. Other cases have involved sales clerks who first swipe the card in the legitimate reader, then surreptitiously swipe it a second time in a second reader that he or she controls. The data grabbed by the second reader, combined with watching you input your PIN, is all the thief needs.

Still other methods begin to sound even more like they belong in a James Bond movie. Thieves have used devices to cause your card to jam in the ATM machine. They then pose as friendly strangers who try to help you retrieve your card. In the process of doing so, they ask for your PIN. Once you give up and leave to report the problem to the bank, the thief unjams your card and walks away with everything he or she can.

My favorite trick, however, is setting up a fake ATM machine. The fake machine looks completely real but in fact only exists to grab data, just like the second-reader trick. Once you've entered your PIN, the ATM skims your data and either doles out money or, more likely, flashes an out-of-money notice. You depart, none the wiser. One notorious case involved crooks setting up a fake ATM in a local grocery in New York City. They collected account numbers and PINs for weeks before someone thought to connect a growing number of fraudulent bank withdrawals to the rogue ATM!

The fact that people were willing to use an unfamiliar ATM and that the grocery store owner took so long to question the dubious machine highlights the key element of all of these tactics to gain access to your bank accounts. They exploit the weak link in the chain. And the weak link is not the computer system. It's you.

AREN'T CHECKS SAFER THAN ELECTRONIC PAYMENTS?

Although fewer paper checks are being written each year, they are still the most popular form of noncash payment. Approximately 60 percent of payments processed by the Federal Reserve in 2000 were made by check. That's roughly 116 million checks being written each day.

Despite what most people on the street might think, paper checks are *far, far* more dangerous than electronic fund transfers. The American Banker Association puts the loss due to debit card fraud at around $50 million. The cost of check fraud was on the order of $14 billion or about 275 times more.

We've talked about a thief getting a hold of your debit card info. They had to work pretty hard to do it—setting up fake scanners, hacking into multiple databases, figuring out your individual password. Now let's consider a check.

First, think about what appears on it. It has your name and address printed at the top. It has your bank's name and routing information, as well as your account number. It even has your signature. If you provided extra information at a merchant's request, it may also have your driver's license number or your Social Security number. If someone wanted to steal money from your account, they easily have everything they need from just one check.

Now think about what happens to a check when you use it, say, to pay for groceries. You write a check and hand it to the person running the cash register. From there it goes to a manager or accountant who reconciles cash register transactions at the end of the day. It may go to a central accounting location if the grocery store is part of a chain. Next, it gets put into a bag and loaded onto a truck where a driver takes your check to the store's bank where it is unloaded by someone else.

Once unloaded, the check is read by a teller who processes the request for payment and forwards it to someone to pack the check up for shipment to an intermediary bank. At this point it goes back onto a truck, driven by another driver, and is taken to the intermediary bank where it is again unloaded by still another person. Yet another teller uses the check to figure out what bank is going to be asked to honor the request for payment. That teller then packs up your check for another truck driver to transport it to your bank. The check is unloaded by yet another person and processed by yet another teller who debits your account and credits the intermediary bank, which then credits the grocery store's account at their bank. Your check is photocopied for bank records by someone else and finally put into an envelope by still another person to be mailed back to you.

Starting to get the picture?

Conservatively speaking, the clerk, the manager, the accountant, three truck drivers, three delivery people, three tellers, two administrative assistants, and a handful of postal employees—seventeen

---

CHECK TRUNCATION

The truly amazing thing, in a world of computers and networks, is that paper checks are still trucked and flown all around the country as part of processing them. Indeed, unless electronic payment agreements are in place, one bank is legally obliged to physically present a check to another bank in order to get its money. No wonder checks take a few days to clear. The marvel is that they don't take longer.

The twist that the information age has brought to this system is called check truncation. Check truncation is the process of creating an electronic image of a check and keeping the original at the original place of deposit or somewhere else in the processing chain. Once truncated, the electronic image can zip from bank to bank quickly, using far less gas than the current system. As more and more truncation agreements are put into place, consumer advocates worry about how this will change your ability to resolve errors or recover losses from forgeries. Privacy advocates are concerned that yet another digital record of your daily activity will be created. Time will tell how pressing these concerns turn out to be.

people at a bare-bones minimum—all have access to enough information to empty your bank account. And the only skill they need to possess to rip you off is to be able to read. If I told you it was okay to hand your ATM card with your password written on it to seventeen strangers, you'd think I was completely crazy.

Now here's the really interesting part. While you have limited liability for credit card fraud and electronic payment fraud, there is currently *no* federal legislation to limit your liability for forged checks. In practice, most banks won't stick you with the bill for a bad check, but in some states this may be more an act of goodwill than a requirement by law. And because technically (if not in reality) the bulk of the liability falls on you and the people accepting your checks, not a central company facilitating the transaction, getting the mess of bad checks cleaned up can be incredibly difficult.

The point to understand here is that when you write a check, you are more exposed to more people and have more liability in case the worst happens. Given that just about anyone who wants money from you *wants* you to use electronic payment (it's much cheaper for them) and that it's actually *better* for you, why would anyone in their right mind use checks?

IS MY USE OF CHECKS OR MY ATM CARD TRACKED?

You bet. More than 1.2 million checks totaling around $50 million bounce every day. Having just about one out of a hundred checks turn out to be worthless adds up to a big problem for retailers. In 1964, after determining that they had all been duped into accepting a bad check by the same person, a group of businessmen in Honolulu, Hawaii decided to start keeping a list of the offenders. Since that day, a truly impressive—and not always friendly—system of tracking to combat check fraud has grown up.

Retailers use check verification companies, like EXPRESS-CHEX (using the National Check Network) and SCAN (the Shared Check Authorization Network) to see if you have bounced checks in the past. If you have a bad history, that retailer probably will not

THE DEBITBUREAU

In addition to tracking bad checks and bank account abuse, the parent company of SCAN and ChexSystems has recently consolidated its data and added a scoring system (not again!) to develop profiles on the banking activities of consumers.

The DebitBureau database, containing more than 3 billion records of checking and savings account openings and closings, checking account collections, overdraft histories, and check order histories, is billed as a good means of evaluating consumers with limited credit histories. When a lender asks for a report on a consumer's credit and gets little information back (a "thin file" in the industry lingo), he is now able to turn to the DebitBureau database to learn what he needs to know from that consumer's bank accounts.

accept a check from you. Some merchants may go a step further and verify your check with a company that not only reports if you have bounced checks in the past but who will guarantee the purchase amount for the retailers. Check guarantee companies include Telecheck (the company started by the Hawaiian businessmen) and CrossCheck.

While some check verification and check guarantee companies get their info from collection agencies, two of the biggest tracking sources consolidate reports directly from merchants. In exchange for learning if you're not to be trusted, over 71,000 stores representing the 500 largest retailers and supermarkets report the details and status of returned checks to the SCAN database. Telecheck collects data from over 352,000 retail locations and uses it to sign off on more than 3.6 billion transactions worth more than $182 billion dollars annually.

Of course, retailers aren't the only ones who suffer when someone writes a bad check. Banks often end up fighting the problem, too. A second, related type of tracking offered by SCAN's sister network, ChexSystems, is bank account abuse and fraud. Before a bank will let you open an account of just about any kind, they will check your profile with ChexSystems to see if any other bank has had a problem with you. ChexSystems provides info to and gets info from 90,000 bank and credit union locations.

WHAT DO DEBIT TRACKING COMPANIES ACTUALLY TRACK?

Retailers report any bad check activity when you bounce a check with them. A record of any inquiry on you is also noted. This helps retailers identify risky check writers and understand when some-one has previously written a number of good checks.

Banks report info for accounts with reports of lost or stolen checks, accounts they close for cause (generally fraud or a negative balance for a period of time) and new account applications. This helps them track bad account numbers, bad account holders, and keep an eye out for check-cashing or check-kiting schemes.

It's a reasonable assumption that we've all been in the SCAN/ ChexSystem database at one time or another. If you're an honest soul opening an account for all the right reasons, your record of the account opening will be kept on record for somewhere around three years. Other information about your check-writing history may be retained by Telecheck and SCAN/ChexSystems for anywhere from five to seven years. If you're the unhappy victim of an identity thief who forges checks in your name, information about any ID used to support a bad check, such as your driver's license, might also remain listed for up to seven years as bad news for merchants.

WHAT ELSE DO BANKS TRACK?

In addition to working with businesses to help identify fraud, banks report activity to the government that might help stop criminals. Whether you use cash, a check, or a debit card, just about everyone who handles your money for you routinely tracks what you're doing and tells the government if they think something fishy is going on.

Back in the 1970s, in an attempt to combat money laundering and the use of secret foreign bank accounts by drug traffickers and tax evaders, Congress passed the Bank Secrecy Act (BSA). Essen-

THINGS THAT MIGHT TRIGGER A SAR

- A transaction that is unusually large for a customer
- An increased frequency in transactions for a customer
- Use of false ID
- Changing a transaction when asked for ID
- Breaking large transactions into smaller ones to fall below the $10,000 reporting threshold, especially by using multiple names, people, or locations to do it.

tially, the BSA established reporting designed to force the creation of paper trail for large financial transactions. In 1990, authorized by the BSA, the U.S. Treasury set up an agency whose mission was to put all of this information in a database, analyze it, and make it available to a broad network of law enforcement officials. This agency is known as FinCEN, the Financial Crimes Enforcement Network.

FinCEN has partnered with the IRS to keep track of two types of reports filed by banks and other financial institutions. The first set of reports calls for routine notification of any cash transaction over $10,000. Banks, casinos, and businesses are all required to inform the government if you give them or they give you large sums of cash for anything. Foreign banks file a similar report on you if you have an account with them that exceeds $10,000. And anytime you transport more than $10,000 in cash out of the country, you are expected to file a report on yourself. Look closely at your customs form the next time you cross the border.

Just in case you are already starting to brainstorm about ways to avoid any government reporting, consider two additional bits of info. Banks in certain high-risk geographical areas may be required to report transactions that are less than $10,000. The areas and amounts are dictated by the Treasury Department.

And FinCEN not only follows money movement by the num-

REPORTS THAT BANKS AND OTHER MONEY SERVICE BUSINESSES ARE
REQUIRED TO KEEP ON YOU

- Purchase of money orders or traveler's checks over $3,000
- Money transfers over $3,000
- Currency exchanges of more than $1,000

They are required to keep these records for five years from the date of
the transaction.

---

bers, they also want banks to tell them when customers just look
funny. This second report, known as a Suspicious Activity Report
(SAR), is more subjective than the currency transaction reports
and more secret. Every bank teller in the United States is required
to file a SAR whenever she becomes "suspicious" about transactions
totaling $2,000 or more. And she is prevented by law from telling
you that she's doing so.

More recently, the USA PATRIOT Act amended the BSA to extend the definition of who must report on financial transactions.
Now any "money service business," defined basically as anyone involved in money exchange in an amount over $1,000, is keeping an
eye on you. The USA PATRIOT Act, reinforcing a series of antidrug
and anti–money laundering laws passed in the eighties and nineties
also requires money service businesses to keep more extensive records on its nonsuspicious customers and to make those records
available upon short notice to law enforcement.

In addition to watching transactions of existing customers, the
USA PATRIOT Act has made a particular point of requiring banks
and other money service businesses to do more exhaustive checking on you before opening an account for you. They must verify
your identification, double-check that you're not on a list of potential terrorists, and keep a record of who you are for five years after
you close your account. This ruling created a bit of a firestorm in

the banking community because it involved a level of tracking that went beyond what banks felt they could handle. Want to know how it's been resolved? The company that brings you DebitBureau, ChexSystems, and SCAN now offers a customer-identification database to banks.

We'll talk a lot more about how the government uses information to find bad guys later. The point here is that the increase in electronic payments and in computers to move information about money—instead of people to move paper—hasn't necessarily given the government any more information about you. They were doing pretty well as it was.

ARE THERE ANY LIMITS ON HOW ALL THIS DATA GETS SHARED?

We've talked about convenience. We've talked about fraud and money laundering. The one topic that we haven't really addressed is how much electronic payment or virtual money has changed the average person's ability to be anonymous. Once your every transaction starts getting recorded in humongous databases, there is the potential for a lot of data about you to be available to too many people.

Federal legislation has made sharing financial information both easier and more difficult. A few years ago, Congress repealed long-standing prohibitions on mixing banking with securities and insurance businesses. This allowed various financial institutions to merge, creating what is now called "financial supermarkets."

One effect of these mergers is that information about you collected by an insurance company is now easily available to its sister bank. Put together, a large corporation could build a fairly complete picture of your entire financial situation and behavior. Not surprisingly, that complete picture is of great interest to a lot of different companies, and Congress felt that restricting how it could be used was a necessary component of easing up the restrictions on mergers.

They required that privacy notices be sent out annually by

banks, insurers, brokers, and credit unions to keep you informed of three things:

- You must be told what kind of info is collected and how it is used.
- Your right to opt out of having this info shared with unaffiliated third parties must be explained.
- You must be informed of how the company safeguards your information.

Of course, industry lobbying had its effect and there are some important loopholes in the requirements. The opt-out only applies to financial information. Your name and any publicly available information, like your telephone number, can still be sold to absolutely anybody. Even worse, Congress didn't restrict sharing potentially sensitive information with other companies that your company has a "joint marketing" agreement with. A classic example of a joint marketing agreement would be a bank offering your data to a company that wants to sell you insurance against losses on your credit card. The stuff these joint marketers can legally learn about you? Data can include "experience and transaction" information, like the checks you write, the credit card charges you make, your deposits, withdrawals, wire transfers, and on and on.

Finally, under this new law, there are no restrictions on sharing any and all information among sister companies in the gigantic corporation. Happily, our old pals the FCRA and the FACTA help a little with this. The FCRA allows you to opt-out of having creditworthiness information, like how much you're worth, shared among affiliates for marketing purposes. FACTA extends that to include transaction information as well.

At the end of the day, although electronic payment offers convenience and liability protection, the fact that the record of what you do can be legally shared with so many people definitely increases the junk mail that you're likely to get.

CHECKUP

Now it's time to figure out how firm your electronic financial foundation is. The following quizzes will help you assess how vulnerable you are to unauthorized electronic fund transfers, to excessive marketing from financial supermarkets, and if you need to worry about blacklisting by the financial industry.

Are You Safe from Account-Grabbing Techniques?

Using an ATM or a Web site to manage your bank account means that you are engaging in some form of virtual money. Using the Internet to pay bills, allowing a merchant to automatically deduct money from your bank account, or allowing your employer to pay directly into your bank account also means that you are engaging in some form of electronic payment. Fortunately, although there are one or two stories of folks who have gotten close, no one has broken into these networks and gotten away with it (at least, that we know about) in the history of their deployment. (Knock wood.) The vulnerability we all face if we use these systems is in how we as individuals manage a key piece of identifying information: our PIN or password. How well are you doing?

Score the level of security your PIN for your ATM/debit card offers.

____ Write down the number of digits in your PIN.

____ Multiply that number by 2 and write that on the line.

____ If you have your PIN written down somewhere accessible (note that your securely stored ID kit that you made in chapter 2 is not considered accessible), multiply the number of digits in your password by −2 and enter the result on the line, otherwise enter 0.

Very Important Note: If you have written down your PIN and it is stored within ten feet of your ATM card, this is no time for games. Stop reading this right now and go directly to the Taking Action section. Not only are you extremely vulnerable to fraud, you may find recovering

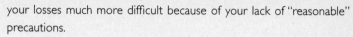

your losses much more difficult because of your lack of "reasonable" precautions.

___ If you let others swipe your ATM card or watch as you input your PIN, write a −3 on the line.

___ If you regularly use ATMs at places other than a branch of your bank, write a −5 on the line.

___ If you loan your debit/ATM card to anyone or share your PIN with anyone, write a −10 on the line.

___ If you know your daily cash withdrawal limit, write a 3 on the line.

___ If you review your bank statements as soon as they come in, write a 5 on the line.

___ If your PIN contains any of the following, enter the number of digits in your PIN on the line, otherwise enter 0.

- your name
- your address
- your date of birth
- your telephone number
- your Social Security number

___ If your PIN contains a word found in the dictionary, multiply the number of digits in your PIN by 2 and enter the result on the line, otherwise enter 0.

Now add up all the numbers. What's your score? If you ended up with a negative number, it's time to brush up on the liability sections of the EFTA, because you're a sitting duck for an unauthorized transfer. You would do well to read the first section of Taking Action, too. If you scored a 0 you can do better. If you were solidly in positive integers, you're at no more risk than the rest of us. As long as you keep your head, you should keep your money.

How Many Privacy Notices Have You Thrown Away?

According to one bank, they sent out 30 million privacy notices last year. Of the 30 million recipients, only 5 percent wrote or called back asking to opt out of information sharing. The bank's response?

They thought customers trusted them to market their names. The real reason? When confronted with a pamphlet written in microscopic type and using sentences that run on for pages, most of us shake our heads and throw the stupid things out.

While many privacy notices are written by (and for) lawyers, understanding them isn't really that important. They all basically do just one thing: they provide you with information on how to opt out. You don't need to read them. You simply need to decide if you care enough to take the time to call the 800 number they provide.

On a scale of 1 to 10, how much do you hate the following?

___ Getting junk mail
___ Feeling exposed
___ Getting phone calls from telemarketers
___ Being vulnerable to identity theft

If you rate yourself more than a 5 on any of the items, you should consider paying attention to privacy notices—or at least to the second section of Taking Action.

Should You Suspect that You're on a Debit-tracking Blacklist

This last quiz has to do with problems you may get into specifically by using checks. If you answer "Yes" to any of the questions, you absolutely need to investigate (see the third section in Taking Action). If you can say no to each of the following, pat yourself on the back for being a good financial manager.

- Have you ever had a store refuse your check as payment?
- Have you ever been turned down for a bank account?
- Have you ever had your checkbook stolen or lost a check?
- Have you bounced more than a few checks in the past seven years?

TAKING ACTION

Although the convenience of electronic payments can't be beat, they do raise issues of your need for protection and your loss of anonymity—at least to marketers. Based upon how you scored in the checkups, you may need to increase how you protect sensitive financial passwords and information, you may want to decrease how much financial information is shared between companies for marketing purposes, and you may need to contact a debit-tracking company to protect yourself from mistakes or to make sure that any information about you that is being shared with retailers and banks is accurate.

Protect Your Information Assets

If you didn't score so well on the password test, the good news is that small changes in your behavior can lead to dramatic improvements in the safety of your money. Banks understand that crooks want to steal your money. Bank networks were built to be safe, and they have proven pretty reliable over the years. You are the main point of vulnerability in compromising your accounts. And you have the power to change what you do.

If you want to increase your personal protection, consider taking the following steps:

- Memorize your PIN. Destroy any place that it is written down (with the exception of your securely locked Identity Kit—see chapter 2). Do not share your PIN with anyone. Not your family, not the manager of your bank.

- Follow the golden rule of passwords in setting up your PIN (see chapter 2). If you were a little less than careful, change your PIN to something better. *Now.* In Canada, having an obvious password like your birthdate or your first name is considered so stupid as to be legally negligent. Under Canadian law, victims of fraud who had an obvious password are fully liable for their losses—as they should be.

- Keep your ATM/debit card in a safe place. If that's your wallet, that's fine. Just understand that it isn't safe in the hands of your little sister or a coworker. If the worst ever happens, report the loss or theft of your ATM/debit cards to the bank right away. Be sure to document your communication with them. Note the call in a log, follow up with a letter. Because your liability is a function of when you report the problem, be especially careful to include when you noticed the card was missing, and when you reported the loss, in your letter (less than 48 hours later, right?).

- When you give your card to someone else to swipe (like at a retail store or restaurant), keep an eye on it. Watch for double swipes or anything out of the ordinary.

- Use ATMs that you're familiar with. Check the ones you know for anything that looks like a fake front. Chances are quite small that you'll ever fall victim to the fake ATM trick, but who knows? Stranger things have happened.

- Reduce the potential damage someone can do to you by lowering your daily cash withdrawal limit to what you absolutely need.

- Review bank statements as soon as they arrive. Remember that if you do discover something, the clock that determines your limits of liability started running when the statement was mailed.

- Keep your eyes open when you go for that cash at the ATM. Don't let someone shoulder-surf you.

How to Opt Out of Sharing Your Financial Data

Remember that part of the law that allowed major financial services companies to merge was a requirement that you be given some control over how your personal information was used for marketing purposes. If your response to the checkup on privacy notices suggests that you hate junk mail and telemarketing calls, or worry about exposure of private information and the danger of identity theft, it's worth it to you to take some small action to reduce them both. Here's how you do it:

First, gather a sample bill or statement from all the financial services companies that send you mail.

- Banks you have accounts with
- Credit card issuers you have cards from (not VISA or MASTERCARD, which are really just trade associations, but the actual bank that issues the card)
- Brokerage firms you've bought stock or mutual funds from
- Brokerage firms for any retirement plans you or your company has set up
- Insurance companies you've bought insurance from
- Loan companies—from student loans, to mortgages, to home-equity loans

Next, see if you have any privacy notices from them floating about. Perhaps you got one in the mail and just haven't thrown it out yet. If you find a notice, all you have to do is find the section with instructions on how to opt out, and you're off and running.

If you don't happen to have any of the privacy notices lying about, don't worry. You are allowed by law to opt out of information sharing whenever you want to. The only hitch is that you have to follow whatever process a company has set up for this. If they set up a toll-free number, you have to call it. By law, they don't have to pay attention to a letter.

The easiest thing to do is call the customer service number listed on your statement and ask what that company's procedure is for opting out of information sharing. Remember, the financial services law, the Gramm-Liley-Bleach Financial Services Modernization Act (GLB), covers opting out of sharing personally identifiable financial information with unaffiliated third parties. The two credit laws allow you to opt out of sharing information with the company's affiliates. When you're on the line with customer service, be sure to ask how to opt out of every kind of information sharing possible under *all* of the GLB, the FCRA, and FACTA.

Finally, even though financial institutions are required to send an annual notice, you are not required to opt out every year. Once you make an opt-out choice (or make no choice) your decision with be in effect for that account until you change it.

What to Do If You Suspect You're on a Debit Blacklist

If the last checkup indicated that you should investigate the debit tracking companies, your first job is to figure out who you need to talk to. If you lost your checkbook, or it was stolen, and you believe that no bad checks have yet been attempted, you can probably get by with contacting just Telecheck and ChexSystems after you call the bank. Until a bad check is actually passed, you don't have to do much more than alert the companies that a theft occurred and ask them to flag your account for possible fraud. Do be careful to consider checks you've written but haven't yet been cashed, and talk to those vendors up front. You certainly don't want to get reported for checks that bounce on an account you closed because of a theft.

If you have ever experienced a problem with a merchant or bank about using a check or opening an account, you should ask what company supplied the information that was used to make the decision. As we noted earlier, there are two main suppliers (Telecheck and ChexSystems) but also a variety of smaller information brokers. Your next step is to contact that company for their report on you.

Telecheck
1-800-366-2425

ChexSystems
1-800-428-9623 to order forms, then fax the completed form to 972-241-4772.
The order form can also be found online at www.chexhelp.com

What You Should Look For

Once you get the report, the biggest thing to check is that you aren't being flagged when you shouldn't be—either through a mistake or as a result of the theft of your checkbook. Each tracking company has its own policies for reporting fraud, but a good, basic way to begin is to file a police report and send a copy of it, along with a letter from the merchant confirming that fraud occurred, to the CRA. If you do have a file because of a legitimate problem, you want to make sure that the info it contains is correct and that all the positive info is also included—such as resolution of payment. Retailers may be slower to report resolution than the original problem.

Be forewarned: There have been stories of how difficult some of these agencies are to deal with. These companies are less publicly discussed than credit reporting agencies. They are much less prepared to offer good service to the public. But, like Equifax and TransUnion and Experian, they are reporting agencies subject to the Fair Credit Reporting Act. You *do* have rights. Be firm, knowledgeable, and persistent.

And at the end of the day, given the unpleasantness of dealing with stolen checks, please, please consider once again why you use them at all.

RESOURCES

When it comes to sorting out problems with the check tracking companies, you can turn to the consumer groups listed in previous chapters. If you become concerned about violations of information sharing by a financial supermarket, a number of consumer groups focusing on combating excessive junk mail may be able to offer assistance. Those groups are listed at the end of chapter 7.

If you have concerns about how your bank is handling your account, or you are not getting satisfactory results following a report of an unauthorized transfer, you will need to contact the government agency that regulates your particular type of financial institution.

There are a number of agencies that each serve a different type of bank. You may need to do a bit of calling before you end up in the right place.

- **Federal Deposit Insurance Corporation.** Regulates state-chartered banks that are not members of the Federal Reserve System. (www.fdic.gov)

- **Board of Governors of the Federal Reserve.** Regulates state-chartered banks that are members of the Federal Reserve system, bank holding companies, and branches of foreign banks. (www.federalreserve.gov)

- **Office of Thrift Supervision.** The OTS regulates federal savings banks and savings and loan associations. (www.ots.treas. gov)

- **Office of Comptroller of the Currency.** Regulates banks with "national" in the name or "N.A." after the name. (www.occ. treas.gov)

- **National Credit Union Administration.** Regulates federally chartered credit unions, which are nonprofit cooperative financial institutions owned and run by members. (www. ncua.gov)

- **Securities and Exchange Commission.** Oversees the nation's equity markets, which include stock exchanges, broker-dealers, associated persons of broker-dealers, and investment advisors. (www.sec.gov)

- **Federal Trade Commission.** The FTC investigates consumer protection and consumer fraud matters that are not specifically within the jurisdiction of another federal agency. (www. ftc.gov)

6. Uncle Sam Wants (to Know All About) You: Government Records

IN THIS CHAPTER:
What government keeps records on, how technology is changing that, what records you can see and how

We've covered credit bureaus, insurance companies, and banks. The next big, well-known, and obvious tracker of your personal information is Uncle Sam—the U.S. Government.

Government offers us services. It offers us education. It provides money for medical treatment when we can't otherwise afford it and covers bills when we're out of work. It protects us from fraud and crime and fire.

To do this, various government agencies catalogue us from the day we are born, collecting a wealth of information that we cannot restrict. A new initiative, eGovernment, will make information more accessible.

The good news is that easy access to this and other information assures transparency of government. The bad news is that information that is more widely available is more open to abuse. Unless we have a decent awareness of our rights *and* a willingness to exercise them, the benefits of greater government efficiency can lead to greater danger in our daily lives.

A NATIONAL ID CARD

When the Department of Homeland Security brought up the notion of a national ID card, realists stated the obvious: one already exists for a large portion of the U.S. population in the form of the driver's license. This database contains your picture, sometimes your fingerprint, a physical description, your residence, and details of the car you drive. What else could someone wanting to identify you need? What's more, it is law that you must carry the license with you whenever you drive a car—which means that most of us carry it most, if not all, of the time we aren't at home.

WHO USES GOVERNMENT RECORDS?

Absolutely everyone. Employers use them for background checks. Attorneys and private investigators use them to find people and dig up dirt on them. Insurance companies use them to set rates. Marketers use them to find names of people to market to. Car makers use them to find out who to inform about safety issues or recalls. Any court or law enforcement agency acting on behalf of the federal, state, or local government can use them to further an investigation.

And then, of course, there is you. We all use government records almost every day to demonstrate that we are who we say we are and that we have a right to certain services or privileges. For most of us, the most basic government record is our driver's license.

WHAT TYPES OF INFORMATION ARE COLLECTED BY GOVERNMENT?

Government collects a wide range of information about each of us. Most major life events are marked. How we use certain privileges that we have qualified for, like driving, are tracked. And how we make and use money is recorded.

The way information is treated depends loosely on a combination of the history of collecting it and the way it is meant to be used. There are three basic types: public, confidential, and secret information.

Public Information

Public information is, as its name implies, available to anyone who asks to see it. As part of a basic assumption about how our country works, information that catalogues the population is public. Everyone has a right to know how many citizens live in each district, in order to be able to verify that the representation accorded to us in Congress and the Electoral College is appropriate. In addition, information about social contracts such as marriages, divorces, and bankruptcies, are public knowledge. This allows each of us to be able to know the "official" status of the people around us and to make sure that there aren't abuses of these institutions.

As part of living in an open society we have little choice about when, where, and how this information is collected. There are virtually no restrictions on who can access it or what purpose they can use it for.

Confidential Information

Information that describes your individual relationship with the government is confidential.

A lot of this information is confidential because we have a societal tradition of treating medical and financial issues as private. This information includes what you pay in taxes or social welfare benefits you have accepted. Sometimes information collected by government may be a residue of a criminal arrest or prosecution—a database of DNA samples or fingerprints, for example. Because it serves no other purpose than to identify you when more common forms of ID aren't up to the job, DNA samples aren't all that useful in everyday situations. Society's need for the information is limited. Consequently, the sharing of it is limited, too.

Release of confidential information is restricted to the person the information describes and to those people who can justify a legitimate use for the information. This means that you are allowed access to your own file, but, without being able to demonstrate a valid reason, you can't look at what the government knows about your

IF ONE GOVERNMENT AGENCY HAS INFORMATION ABOUT ME,
HOW MANY OTHERS CAN SEE IT?

A report from the General Accounting Office (GAO) states that, in their investigation of the issue, "personal information was shared extensively with other federal agencies, other government entities (state, local, tribal, and foreign), and private individuals and organizations." They came to that conclusion after examining what happened to information collected for programs administered by four different government agencies: an application for federal student aid, a loan request for farmers, a worker's comp claim for a federal employee, and a passport application.

In each and every case, information collected on these forms was shared with law enforcement. In two cases, data was compared against IRS files. In three cases, FBI records were checked for suspected drug offenses. HUD, OMB, OSHA, the INS, Selective Service, the Social Security Administration, and even the U.S. Postal Service were sent information for review, depending on the type of form. Nongovernment agencies with access to the application information included attorneys, physicians, colleges, credit bureaus, labor unions, and banks.

In no case was the information sharing illegal or even extraordinary. It was just extensive.

neighbor. "Legitimate use" may mean a check by another government agency to verify eligibility for benefits, or it may mean sharing information with law enforcement to further an inquiry of some sort.

Secret Information

The final type of information collected by government is secret. This information is collected in the interest of national defense or to assist with criminal investigations. Because simply knowing that information is being collected may compromise its value—a drug dealer aware he is under suspicion may behave differently, for example—we don't necessarily know about this information. It may be difficult to find out that it exists. And it may be impossible to know exactly what it is. Although we will review two important laws that regulate government record keeping and disclosure, these safeguards may offer no help if an overweening interest of the state is accepted.

Why one type of information gets classified as one or the other is sometimes not as clear as we would hope it might be. As technology development forces our hand and government and consumers become savvier about information as a commodity, we can only hope for more thoughtful consistency in this area.

HOW IS GOVERNMENT RECORD KEEPING CHANGING?

Technology has had a terrific impact on government activity. The Internet, in particular, has created a hugely effective vehicle for disseminating information and facilitating routine government transactions electronically.

In 2000 the state of Florida passed a law that required all state government documents to be posted online by the year 2006. At a local level, many county clerks are putting online the two most commonly used document types, property records and court cases. Hamilton County, Illinois, as one example, offers an online interface to its database of tax liens, arrest warrants, bond postings, and a wealth of other court-related documents.

The result has been a transparency of government—and an exposure of its citizens that has been both rewarding and uncomfortable. Mothers Against Drunk Driving (MADD) likes online records because they make it easier for crime victims to track the progress of a case. Firefighters use floor plans available as part of property records to guide them when a fire alarm is raised. Consumers can look at past cases of lawyers they are thinking about hiring to determine how good they really are. Businesses can check on whether a potential partner is going to be tied up in embarrassing or expensive litigation. One woman, using the Hamilton County Web site, found out that a man she was dating was already married.

On the other hand, there are the cases of real estate agents who use the database to determine if sellers are going through a divorce and are more likely to be pressured into a lower price. Or the embarrassment caused for divorcing couples who find that their friends now know all about the intimate details of their marriage and financial situation. And, of course, the information is a treasure trove for creative identity thieves, and burglars can find as much use in publicly available floor plans as firefighters can!

Some privacy advocates believe that government should be in the business of making information available but that they should not be responsible for publishing it broadly. Making paper documents stored in a courthouse or county seat available on request provides truly motivated researchers with the information they are seeking. Putting the contents of those documents online, a few clicks away from millions of prying eyes, merely satisfies our prurient curiosity in one another.

Still other experts suggest that it isn't the technology that is the problem but the definition of what is public. The Privacy Rights Clearinghouse argues that providing access to files with certain sensitive information such as Social Security numbers blacked out protects individual citizens without damaging the fundamental transparency that fuels democracy. They also recommend posting online only indices of documents, not the full contents, or the rulings in cases, not the full case complete with gory, gossipy details.

As the risks and rewards of online access to government records are becoming clearer, legislatures are becoming more careful. After two years of trying to put all government records on the Internet, the state of Florida amended its original mandate to preclude posting military discharges, death certificates, and family court filings.

WHAT KIND OF RIGHTS OR PROTECTION DO I HAVE WHEN IT COMES TO GOVERNMENT RECORD KEEPING?

There are two laws that form the basis of protecting both our rights in information collection and our rights as citizens in a free democracy to oversee what our government is doing. They are the Freedom of Information Act and the Privacy Act.

As with so many other social contracts, the relationship of citizen to government was reevaluated during the 1960s, resulting in the passage of the Freedom of Information Act in 1966. Before the FOIA, a citizen needed to demonstrate his or her reason to want to see a government record. Following the FOIA, a citizen's access was established as a given. It was the government that now had to show why secrecy was justifiable.

Generally speaking, the Freedom of Information Act spelled out policies for how government should make you aware of information and procedures for how you could request access to it. First, federal agencies had to become more transparent. According to the FOIA, they are required to publish a description of their organizational structure, a general description of how they function and what they do, and an overview of their policies. They are also required to spell out exactly what information they collect.

Second, agencies are required to disclose records requested in writing by any person, group, or corporation. A later expansion of

---

How Black Lung Can Lead To Identity Theft

Sometimes carelessness, not the Internet, is the cause of unnecessary exposure from government record keeping.

Even in a world with awareness of identity theft, the Department of Labor catalogued benefits claims for black lung disease according to the claimant's Social Security number. By suing for benefits, a coal miner from Virginia found that his Social Security number had become a case number that was part of a tracking system available to other claimants and their employers.

Because the benefits claim involved legal action, the number was also made available to lawyers interested in the case and was introduced into a number of legal research databases. The miner has sued the Department of Labor for its mishandling of sensitive information.

THE INSIDE JOB

A problem created by government record keeping is that, while there may be a legitimate reason to collect information, collecting it also creates an opportunity for a nonlegitimate use. We've talked about criminals misusing publicly available information, but what about government employees abusing their access to information they help collect? IRS employees have been dismissed for "file browsing," pulling up tax returns for purposes other than doing their job in order to amuse or help out friends and family. One DEA agent made money on the side by selling top-secret information from criminal investigations to private detectives. Two FBI agents used their inside knowledge to smear company executives and manipulate stock prices.

the FOIA, the EFOIA, also allows online access to material. Of course, there are exceptions to what information must be made available. Broadly speaking, federal agencies have discretion to deny a Freedom of Information request if it would damage national security. Information that might interfere with a court case or the ability of the agency to do its job is exempt. Information that somehow relates to personnel data or policies for that agency is off limits. And information that is made unavailable by other laws can't be released by the FOIA.

Thankfully, in those cases where an individual's request for information is turned down, the FOIA also defined a system of appeal using the courts.

The second key piece of legislation is the Privacy Act of 1974. This act is the one we discussed in chapter 2 on Identity Theft that protects your Social Security number. More generally, it also restricts government record keeping. The Privacy Act gives you the right to see any file that the government has on you. It requires that government agencies get information about you directly from you, not from any other source, and gives you the right to challenge the accuracy of any information they keep. Most importantly, the Privacy Act specifically requires that information only be used for the purpose it was collected for. Remedies through the courts are also defined.

Just as with the FOIA, there are loopholes that weaken the Privacy Act. Information can be withheld if it involves law enforcement activities, national security, any litigation, civil service exams, or confidential government sources. And the Privacy Act only covers records that are a part of a system of records. In other words, other people must be subject to the same pattern of record keeping for the record you want to see to be covered by the Privacy Act protections. If the FBI is profiling you along with only a handful of others, that doesn't constitute a system of records and you have no rights. The American Civil Liberties Union (ACLU) notes that when it comes to actually trying to see government files, the Privacy Act exempts more information than the FOIA.

Other big differences between the FOIA and the Privacy Act are that anyone can use the FOIA, while the Privacy Act only protects United States citizens and permanent resident aliens. And the statute of limitations to file a lawsuit under the FOIA is six years, whereas the Privacy Act allows only two.

Despite some of the worrisome details, both pieces of legislation, and the principles they stand for, are to be applauded. The FOIA and the Privacy Act form the basis for keeping our government accountable for the information it collects on each of us. Try getting that in most of the other nations on this planet.

CHECKUP

There are countless records created at the local, state, and federal level. Some are freely available to anyone who bothers to ask for them. Some are only available to the record subject and anyone who can demonstrate a justifiable use for them. Others live in an "eyes only" world of secrecy. It's time now to see how much sense the whole system makes to you.

Guess the Government Policy

Below are listed some of the records that local, state, and federal government compiles on us. It is by no means exhaustive, but does show the variety of what is tracked. For each type of record, guess whether you think it is classified as public, confidential, or top-secret.

___ Birth certificate

___ Death certificate

___ Bankruptcy filing

___ Civil court record

___ Felony conviction

___ Tax return

___ Census survey answers

___ Car registration

___ Voter registration

___ Property record

___ Arrest record

___ Misdemeanor conviction

___ Sexual offense conviction

___ Pilot's license

___ Record of crime facts

___ Record of fingerprints and mug shots

___ Bank Suspicious Activity Report

___ New hires by business and government

___ National Instant Criminal Background Check System

___ Driving history

___ Plane registration

___ Marriage certificate

___ Tax liens

___ Family court record

___ Political contributions

___ Domestic violence conviction

___ Fishing license

___ Identification from driver's license

___ Driver's license suspension

___ Boat registration

___ Medicaid record

___ List of drug crime suspects

___ Record of computer hacking incident

___ Social Security earnings

___ Veteran's benefits

___ Medicaid record

___ Record of DNA sample

If you actually got through this rather dizzying list of information tidbits the government collects, congratulations. Read on to see how closely your notion of privacy and protection matches the current policies. For each record that you classified incorrectly, give yourself an "x."

When you're finished scoring, count the Xs. If you got 4 or less, make the results of this checkup public! If you marked 5 to 10 Xs, you'd probably better keep your results confidential. If you tally up more than 10 mistakes, definitely classify your performance top secret. In any case, read the first section in Taking Action to see what records you need to learn more about.

Public Records (Freely Available to Anyone Who Requests Them)

Birth certificate: A birth certificate is generally recorded in the county in which the birth occurred and oftentimes, at the state level, in a department of vital records. Birth certificates record the name of the child, the parent's full names, the date, time, and location of the birth. Some areas have made birth certificates confidential, so categorization of birth certificates under "public records" may not be accurate for everyone. On the other hand, there are cases where the state records department doesn't restrict access to birth data, regardless of the policy at the local level.

Marriage certificate: Marriage certificates are generally on file at the county level. They contain the name of the bride and groom, the county where the application was filed, and the date of the marriage. It is possible in some jurisdictions to request that this information be sealed from public access.

Death certificate: Similar to marriage certificates, these are generally housed at the county clerk's office, although a state office of vital records may track them as well. Certificate information available to the public includes name of decedent; date, and location of death, and the decedent's Social Security number.

Voter registration: Voter's registration is stored at the county clerk's or registrar of voters office. Registration includes your name, address, phone number, occupation, voting precinct, prior voting registration information, and party affiliation. It may or may not contain a history of when you actually voted. Some states restrict access to everything but your name and zip code in order to prevent harassment. Some states sell all of the information in voters' files to political parties or legitimate candidates for public office. Still others put all your information on the Web. If you're concerned about any of this, you can move to North Dakota, the one state that doesn't register voters at all!

Property record: Any real estate purchase is tracked by the county assessor's office to make sure that your tax bill is right. The actual record may be housed at the assessor's office, the tax collector's office, or the county recorder. Records include the location of the property, the owner's name and address, previous owners' names, the dates of sale, a description of the property, which may be detailed enough to include photographs and floor plans, and a value. Remember that if the bank is actually the owner of your property, your mortgage info is available as well. Property records are largely unrestricted just about everywhere.

Fishing license: In some states, getting a fishing license is like buying a pack of gum at the local convenience store. It generates no record at all. In other states, applications for a license containing your name, address, and the area and season you fish (or hunt) are tracked and made freely available to anyone who requests it.

Airplane registration: Both a listing of authorized planes and pilots are maintained by the Federal Aviation Administration and are publicly available. Aircraft data includes owner name, make and model of airplane and engine, the dealer who sold the plane, where the plane is based, and the registration number (called an "n-number") that is uniquely assigned to that plane. Airman data includes name, date of certification, and highest level of certification. Interestingly, information that would not be released about a car or driver is readily available about planes and pilots.

Arrest record: These records are kept by the arresting agency but may also be reported to state and federal databases. A record of arrest containing the name of the person arrested, the name of the victim, and the details of the incident are public. This information can later be sealed if the individual is found innocent. In cases where the safety of the public or an investigation might be jeopardized, information from arrest records may be closed to the public.

Any court record: Civil, criminal, and family court cases are all public documents. The only exception to this applies to juvenile records, which are considered confidential. Court records are kept by the court reviewing the case (county, state, or federal) and include the names of the parties, details of the issue at hand (the complaint, any response and motions), and the resolution. Court cases of public record also include any tax liens or bankruptcy filings you may have made.

Misdemeanor, felony, domestic violence, and sexual offense conviction records: Because a conviction is part of a court record, all convictions are by extension public records available to anyone who wants to read them. One class of crime has been elevated to an even more public status: sexual offenses. Not only are records of convictions of sexual offenses available to anyone who asks, but the names of offenders and their whereabouts are publicized. Megan's Law, named after a seven-year-old girl murdered by a convicted sex offender who had moved in across the street from her, is designed to warn communities about the presence of known offenders. Court records can be accessed at the courthouse and increasingly via Web sites. A growing number of companies offer criminal records checks. Megan's Law listings can be obtained through local law enforcement or your state's attorney general.

Political contributions: Federal rules for fundraising require that anyone who contributes more than two hundred dollars to a candidate or political party also supply their name, address, and employment info. This becomes a matter of public record, so that we can find out who might be in the pocket of any politician we elect.

Confidential Records

In the following cases, individuals are allowed to request their own file. Anyone else must demonstrate a legitimate use. Some employers, those of child care workers for example, are *required* to check applicants against these databases.

Driver's license: This information is kept by each state, although records are now being shared between states on a regular basis. License information includes identifying information (more restricted) and information about your driving history (routinely shared with individuals and companies, like insurers, who can come up with a justifiable use). Driving information includes things like accidents that you were in regardless of who was at fault, license suspensions or revocations, driving violations, license restorations, and point/insurance reduction course completion.

Suspension of a driver's license: This information is also tracked by a special database called the Problem Driver Pointer System of the National Driver's Registry. It is used by employers and state motor vehicle departments to find out if you have ever had a license suspended or revoked.

Car and noncommercial boat registration: This information, including the owner info, vehicle make and model, vehicle identification number and vehicle history, is stored at a state level. Generally, it is not available to the public but is shared with any requestor who can demonstrate justifiable use.

Tax returns: Returns are kept at your regional IRS department for federal returns. State returns are kept by the state government. Records contain your name, occupation, Social Security number, and the details of your income and expenses. Other people can request access to your returns for a court proceeding; other government agencies can use your returns to assist with the collection of child support payments. The Social Security Administration and the Department of Education can look at your tax records and request that a refund be withheld if money for student loans or old tax bills is owed to the government.

Social benefits programs: Depending on the program, you may have records at the state and federal level. Records contain your identifying info as well as details of your personal and medical history. Veterans' files also include a history of military service. To minimize fraud, government benefits agencies are required to publish a list of beneficiaries along with their Social Security numbers to tax authorities. These agencies may also run a check on you for unpaid taxes or child support obligations before finalizing your assistance.

Social Security earnings record: This information includes your name, date of birth, address (taken from your last tax return), and a history of your income as reported by your employers (or from Schedule SE of your tax return if you are self-employed). Some income, such as military or railroad service income, some government employment, and some foreign earnings, are not covered by Social Security and will not be shown. These records are housed at the Social Security Administration.

Federal Parent Locator Service (FPLS): The FPLS offers access to a network of databases maintained by the Social Security Administration, the IRS, the Department of Defense Office of Personnel Management, the FBI, the Veterans Administration, and the NDNH (National Directory of New Hires). This last database, established by the Personal Responsibility and Work Opportunity Reconciliation Act of 1996, requires a company to report all new hires to the state within twenty days. Each state sends that information, along with information about unemployment insurance claims, to the NDNH. In addition, the National Directory of New Hires has recently been expanded to track down defaulters on student loans. Although private citizens or their attorneys can request that a state agency use the FPLS to help collect delinquent child support payments, they are not provided information directly.

Census survey answers: The Census bureau goes to great lengths to protect the confidentiality of respondents. The same law that authorized the surveys, Title 13 of the US Code, also makes a clear requirement of confidentiality. That said, it is important to remember that even this rule can be bent when a national security interest is identified. During WWII, it was information from the census that allowed government agents to identify and locate the nearly 112,000 Japanese-Americans who were interned for the remainder of the conflict.

NICS (National Instant Criminal Background Check System): This database was established by the Brady Law to prevent firearm sales to convicted felons, fugitives from justice, and other disqualified buyers. Gun dealers submit info about potential purchasers. This info is checked against a federal database of people not allowed to buy guns. Although it is not supposed to be recorded, one privacy consultant notes that the purchaser identification information submitted by dealers is kept in audit logs for up to six months. The database of disqualified buyers contains the following info: name, gender, race, any other personal descriptive data, date of birth, state of residence, possibly a unique identifying number, and the criminal information that disqualifies ownership of firearm.

CODIS (Combined DNA Index System): CODIS is the FBI database of DNA material collected during an investigation of a crime (especially sex offenses) or a missing person case. This national database was established by Congress in 1994. By 1998 all fifty states had passed laws requiring local police departments to collect DNA samples to be submitted to the national system. As of March 2004, 1.7 million individuals were tied to samples in the database.

NCIC (National Crime Information Center): NCIC houses the FBI's collection of seventeen databases of all information relating to criminals and crime. Databases include wanted persons, sexual offenders, gang members, foreign fugitives, deported felons, missing persons, persons subject to protection orders—as well as stolen guns, boats, securities, and just about everything else. Law enforcement at all levels reports the details of a crime and all the participating parties (including the victim).

IAFIS (Integrated Automated Fingerprint Identification Systems): This is a set of FBI databases that includes the histories and mug shots of 45 million criminals, along with the largest collection of fingerprints in existence. Fingerprints are gathered primarily from arrests but also include images taken of federal employees, anyone serving in the military, and certain registered aliens and naturalized citizens. Individuals wanting to access their own record must supply a set of prints.

Top Secret

In addition to the information the FBI tracks as a result of criminal prosecutions, there are also a variety of databases maintained to track anyone who is simply suspicious. These databases are known to exist, but are not accessible to you and me. If you think you might be in one of them and want to see your record, you will have quite a fight on your hands.

In addition, there are undoubtedly databases that we know nothing about. We can only wonder about files maintained by the Secret Service, Customs, the INS, the CIA, the NSA, the Defense Intelligence Agency, or the intelligence units of the Army, Navy, Marines, and Air Force.

TSC (Terrorist Screening Center): This is a relatively new program administered by the FBI that consolidates terrorist watch lists from different government agencies into a single database. Information in the database is made available to federal screeners and law enforcement officials around the clock. Information on suspects is collected from the CIA, the Department for Homeland Security, the State Department, and the Justice Department.

NDPIX (National Drug Pointer Index) and NVPS (National Virtual Pointer System): This database is maintained by the Drug Enforcement Agency to identify all targets of drug investigations. Information on suspects is entered by law enforcement and used by law enforcement at the local, state, and national level to identify instances where the same suspect may be under investigation in different jurisdictions (in a wonderful example of bureaucratese, this is called "deconfliction" by the DEA). Recently, efforts to expand the system of sharing information on suspects and ongoing investigations to cover all crimes have gained significant ground. While law enforcement can access these records, they are not available to individuals.

FinCEN the (Financial Crimes Enforcement Network): FinCEN is a network of databases and financial records maintained by the Treasury Department. FinCEN collects information about suspicious financial activity from money service businesses across the country, which is shared with investigators from dozens of agencies, including the Bureau of Alcohol, Tobacco, and Firearms; the Drug Enforcement Administration; the Federal Bureau of Investigation; the U.S. Secret Service; the Internal Revenue Service; and the Customs Service. Agencies can investigate names, addresses, and Social Security numbers through FinCEN.

IAIP (Information Analysis & Infrastructure Protection): Formerly known as the National Infrastructure Protection Center database, this agency catalogues info on attempted and suspected hacking submitted by U.S. companies. The incident report requests information about the nature of the intrusion, the degree of damage, the response to the incident, and the suspected source or perpetrator. These records are not made available to the general public or anyone suspecting they are the subject of a report.

TAKING ACTION

If you're aware of what government records are kept and how they are treated, your only real action is to assess the records that are likely to be kept on you, and gain a better understanding of any specific policies or options in your city, county, or state that affect whether that information can fall into unknown hands. As part of that process, it's a good idea to get informed about how to use the two pieces of legislation that give you access to government records. If you were surprised by your score in the last checkup, you might also want to consider letting someone in power know about that.

Find Out About Government Policies Near You

As we noted above, there are variations in how different counties and different states restrict access to information. If you identified any records that you felt exposed you unnecessarily to identity theft, burglary, or even embarrassment, you should seek out the appropriate agency to inquire about their policies and, in particular, their plans for online access. In some cases, you may be offered the opportunity to restrict the record from public view.

The first step is to identify the records you care about. Go back to the list in the checkup section and put a star next to any record that applies to you. Highlight any record that contains information that you don't want made available to the guy down the street. Now you know what agency you need to contact. If you are a property owner, it is especially important to ask what information is kept about your real estate transactions. This information can be highly personal—ranging from intimate financial details to the location of your bedroom—and is generally subject to fewer restrictions than comparable data found in other government records. If you do nothing else, learn more about this.

Your government blue pages in the phone book should provide all of the contact info that you will need. County records can be found by going to your county clerk. State records can be found by contacting your department of motor vehicles, your state's attorney general, or office of vital records.

Procedures for determining if you are listed in any FBI databases can be found by visiting the FBI Web site. You must make a request to each individual program, and requirements on how to make the request will vary from program to program. The NICS (National Instant Criminal Background Check System) database, for example, requires a notarized signature; the NCIC (National Crime Information Center) will not accept written requests, but asks you to go to your local law enforcement office and present ID.

Know How to Become a Freedom Fighter

Some day you might find yourself in a situation where you want to make a request for information under the Freedom of Information Act. You are anticipating a detailed background check for a job; you become curious about monitoring of your political activity; you simply want to know more about what your government is doing. The ACLU routinely assists citizens wanting information on consumer product safety, environmental hazards, public health, and government spending. In each case the FOIA has assured your right to ask questions.

Under the FOIA, you also have a right to ask questions if you are a permanent resident alien, foreign national, corporation, or university. Even state and local officials or members of Congress have the right to use the FOIA to ask other branches of government what is going on.

Curiously enough, the reverse doesn't always apply. The FOIA was designed to monitor the activity of federal agencies. This is defined as agencies, offices, and departments of the executive branch of the federal government, regulatory agencies such as the FTC and Environmental Protection Agency, and corporations controlled by the federal government such as the Post Office, the Smithsonian, or Amtrak. Local and state agencies are not subject to FOIA provisions. Nor are the U.S. Congress, federal courts, or the executive office staff who advise the president.

How To Make a Request

There are several very good guides available for free that walk you through the process of making an FOIA request. The Electronic Privacy Information Center (EPIC) has made available on its Web site a U.S. Government publication on using the FOIA. Public Citizen's Litigation Group also offers assistance and publications on using the FOIA through their Freedom of Information Clearinghouse. And, of course, the ACLU virtually wrote the last word on the topic.

- *A Citizen's Guide to Using the Freedom of Information Act and the Privacy Act of 1974 to Request Government Records*, available online at www.epic.org/open_gov/citizens_guide_97.html
- Public Citizen's Litigation Group Freedom of Information Clearinghouse (www.citizen.org/litigation/index.cfm)
- *Using the Freedom of Information Act: A Step-by-Step Guide*, available from the ACLU or online at www.aclu.org/library/foia.html

Make Your Opinion Count

When you're all done with cleaning up your personal situation, you might want to consider the landscape of records that are kept on you as well as the nature of the information they contain (public, etc.). If you find that you guessed wrong about how records were treated in more than a handful of cases—in other words, your sensitivities were out of whack with the current practice—you may just decide that a letter to your legislator saying so is worth your time. After all, a government driven by the will of the people has to know what the will of the people is in order to be effective. Lobbying groups that seek to challenge government's use of information are listed in the next section. A letter or donation to them will also make your opinion known.

RESOURCES

Lobbying groups watching government's use of information include the ACLU, EPIC, the Electronic Frontier Foundation, The Center for Democracy and Technology, Public Citizen, and The Privacy Rights Clearinghouse. Contact info for these groups can be found below or at the end of previous chapters. The Federation of American Scientists also has a long-standing program to track government secrecy and record keeping.

- Electronic Frontier Foundation (http://www.eff.org)
- The Center for Democracy and Technology (www.cdt.org)
- Federation of American Scientists (www.fas.org)

7. Deciding What You Do and Do Not Want: Lists of All Kinds

IN THIS CHAPTER:
Why and how lists are made, how to evaluate whether a list is good or bad, what to do about bad lists

By this point, after reading about how credit reporting agencies, insurance companies, banks, and the government seem to be recording your every move, you're probably beginning to accept the idea that privacy is a thing of the past. Some organizations report on you; others access those reports to evaluate you. We've talked about how all this reporting isn't necessarily such a bad thing. It's tied to your ability to get the things that most of us need as adults in today's world.

But in talking about all this tracking and reporting, we've merely scratched the surface of how technology has allowed all kinds of organizations and businesses to note down things about you. It seems that everyone these days has a database—from the local dry cleaner to regional supermarket chains to national telecommunications companies.

Rather than wade through an endless catalogue of every list that's out there, a more reasonable approach is to take a step back and consider how listing can affect you—good and bad—and decide how much you care. Once you've done this, you can evaluate each new possibility as it comes up and weigh the risks and benefits that are appropriate for you.

It's time to develop your philosophy about lists.

WHO KEEPS LISTS?

Businesses wanting to know who their customers are—or might be—keep lists. A lot of times, you sign up for these lists even if you don't realize that's what you're doing. Anytime you subscribe to a magazine, donate to a charity, make a purchase online, or fill out a warranty card, you get on a list. Anytime you fill out a form to win a free trip to Hawaii, you get on a list. Anytime you call an 888, 877, 866, 800, or a 900 number, you get on a list.

There are also companies that exist to compile lists for other people. You generally get "drafted" onto these lists without your consent. Sometimes, as with credit reporting agencies, these companies coordinate reports from other companies that deal with you directly. Sometimes information comes from public records. Taking a job, earning a professional degree, or becoming licensed for something gets you drafted onto lists. Buying a house, having a baby, or going to jail also gets you drafted onto lists.

And while there are many companies whose sole business it is to compile, manage, and sell lists, there are many more companies out there whose primary business is something else—fixing cars, selling groceries, providing cable TV—but that nonetheless engage in the practice of selling lists of their customers. The industry term is "data mining," and it can be a big business.

WHAT ARE LISTS USED FOR?

Lists are used by all kinds of organizations to keep track of members, employees, customers, and prospective customers. Although there are probably as many uses for lists as there are lists themselves, list are used primarily for three major applications: The first is to market to you; the second is to keep tabs on you in case you need to be contacted (sometimes, whether you want to be or not); the third is to warn others against you.

The use of lists for marketing is a huge industry. Your name is collected in any number of ways and tied to some fact about you, such as that you just had a baby, or to some pattern in your purchase

LISTING VS. REPORTING VS. PROFILING

It's important to begin to distinguish between different kinds of tracking afforded by technology. The distinctions that we'll adopt in this book aren't always clear-cut, but it is important to have some means of separating one form of information collection from another to determine the potential impact a particular instance of tracking can have on you.

Listing occurs when companies or government or other organizations place your name, and perhaps some limited set of identifying characteristics or contact information about you in a central place. The information is generally updated only when there is a change in the information. There is no regular reporting of any transactions. The fact that you are on the list is information about you in itself. Lists can be sold, rented, or exchanged between organizations. You have the power to control whether or not you appear on some but not all lists.

Reporting occurs when companies supply information about your transaction history to a central company that in turn makes that history available—for a fee—to other companies considering doing business with you. Reporting often tracks sensitive information, and unauthorized access to it makes you vulnerable to identity theft. You generally don't control whether or not you are subject to reporting.

Profiling occur when information about you is examined and predictions about your behavior are made based upon the actions of other people *like* you. For an insurance company to rely on the fact that you've made three claims in two years is an example of their use of reporting. When they consider a score that ranks your likelihood to make a future claim based on the actions of other people who in some way are similar to you, this is an example of profiling. Most of the time you don't control whether or not you are being profiled.

Profiling has become something of a dirty word lately, so it's worth a little more explanation. The truth is that we all engage in profiling from time to time. Consider what happens when you meet someone for the first time at a party. Based on his or her answers to your questions, you draw upon your experience of similar people to fill in your image of the person you've just met.

There are times when profiling has the possibility to become sinister—when you are not fully informed that it is being done and how, or when you disagree with the connections a profiler is making between one piece of information and another. Profiling can be especially dangerous when no additional individual information is considered or when it is used for very important or enduring decisions. These times warrant your attention and are worth your voicing an opinion.

habits, such as that you purchased something from a catalogue. Sometimes lists are simply used to identify you as a relevant target for a marketing message or—if you're lucky—coupons. Other times, marketers look at your purchase behavior and use that knowledge to try to figure out what other products you'd consider buying. In other words, they try to figure out what other catalogues to send you.

List that can help track you down are used by high school classmates, law enforcement, lawyers, debt collectors, and, unfortunately, stalkers. They have also been used by parents seeking abducted children and single moms going after deadbeat dads. These lists are generally the product of large information brokers who earn money by compiling data. One of their biggest clients: the U.S. Government (specifically, the DOJ, FBI, INS, and IRS).

Finally, some lists mark you as a person that a company doesn't want to do business with. While some lists are specific and limited, others are broad and touch each of us. You may not be on the Terrorist Watch List, but it's a good bet that your phone and electricity service wasn't hooked up until after a list had been checked.

WHAT PROBLEMS CAN BEING ON LISTS CREATE FOR ME?

By far, the most common negative side effect of being on a list is that it might be used for direct marketing. Someone gets your name and starts sending you junk mail, calling you at dinner or flooding your inbox with spam. There are, however, a couple of other problems with listing that can give you headaches.

As was a concern with the reporting that we've explored so far, the information on a list may be incomplete or just plain wrong. One woman suffered the emotional trauma of losing her newborn infant. Unfortunately, the marketing list showing that she was a new mother wasn't updated to reflect her tragedy, and for years afterwards the woman received catalogues, coupons, and information geared to mothers of young children. Picking up her mail became daily torture, as she never knew if the pain of her baby's loss would be awakened by what she'd receive.

Wrong information can be especially problematic with negative lists. A law-abiding citizen kept getting turned down for potential jobs because his name had been mixed up with a felon in a database of criminals checked by most of the employers in his area. Or there may be extenuating circumstances that don't get noted, so you get singled out unfairly. One apartment renter withheld rent until a dispute with her landlord was resolved. When she finally moved out in frustration over the quality of her housing, she discovered that her landlord had reported her to a blacklist for the rental industry. She was unable to rent an apartment for the entire five years that her name remained on the list.

Another problem is uncertainty about how information will be used in the future. Although you can be quite happy with the privacy protection and the way that your information is being used when your name gets on a list, you have little control—or indeed knowledge—of what will happen down the line. One dot.com company promised everyone who registered with them that it would only use their names or e-mail addresses for the service that they were signing up for. It stated clearly that it wouldn't sell or rent their information. While the management of the company respected this promise during the time that they ran the business, the debtors seeking to recover what they were owed after the company went belly-up were less careful. The list was sold to whoever would pay for it, making the unfortunate registrants prey to a large number of spammers.

Finally and most importantly, the protection that a list owner offers you is typically subject to a very important condition. If the information is ever subpoenaed for any kind of legal proceeding, most list owners tell you up front that they will give up the goods. Even if they put up a fight, the courts may force them to disclose their data anyway. What you thought was private may become very public indeed.

In a case that has become somewhat infamous, the U.S. Drug Enforcement Agency subpoenaed discount card data on a few suspected drug dealers from a supermarket chain. The feds wanted to know if the suspects had purchased a lot of plastic baggies, presumably to package drugs for sale. Although supermarkets have been very careful not to share data on purchasing habits to target individuals for direct marketing, they had no protection from releasing the information to law enforcement.

Another famous example came up during the 1987 Supreme Court confirmation hearings for Robert Bork. In a heated battle over his nomination for the nation's top court, records of his videotape rentals were subpoenaed and used to indicate something about his sexual interests and personal integrity. Before that time, no one had considered the implications of tracking someone's movie preferences. One year after the Bork hearings, Congress passed legislation specifically protecting the use and storage of information about a consumer's video rentals. This legislation is remarkable for the specificity of its content (as well as its aura of addressing a problem where the horse had already been let out of the barn). We probably shouldn't rely on similar protections appearing as each new breach of information etiquette arises.

Now, it is unlikely that the vast majority of us will be subject to confirmation hearings for a seat on the Supreme Court. It is even unlikely—though less so than it once was—that you'll become the target of a drug or terrorism investigation. On the other hand, it is sad but true that for a lot of married folks it isn't quite as unlikely that you'll find yourself in a divorce court. Divorce is a legal and public proceeding, and because of that, trails of information that are otherwise protected can be subpoenaed and brought out in public. In one rather nasty case, the attorney for the husband wanted to make a point about the wife based upon the prescriptions she'd been taking for the past five years. He served Rite Aid with a subpoena for her pharmacy records—and got them.

Indeed, no one is off the hook when it comes to legal action. Because we are a society that likes to settle things through lawsuits, any kind of relationship has the potential to end up in court. Here's another example. The Recording Industry Association of America (RIAA), a trade group representing major music labels, wanted to make examples of college students known to be downloading copyrighted music files from the Internet without paying for them. Before the RIAA could sue the file sharers, it first had to sue their Internet provider, Verizon Wireless, to find out their names. Although Verizon didn't want to, a court forced them to hand over identifying information and Web-surfing habits on a handful of its customers.

Being tracked or being on a list may offer you a lot of rewards and opportunities. It may also make it possible for other people to draw incorrect or unfair conclusions about you. It may expose you in ways that you hadn't expected or desired. Or it may just get you more junk mail.

ARE SUPERMARKET CARDS AS BAD AS I HEAR?

Consumer loyalty programs represent a special kind of list opportunity, because they seem to be about one thing, but in truth are actually about something very different. These programs illustrate how difficult it can sometimes be to evaluate the tradeoff of risks and benefits offered by lists.

Many of the concerns about supermarket loyalty programs initially raised by privacy advocates have failed to pan out. Generally speaking, loyalty clubs offer rewards to keep you shopping at a particular store or buying a particular product. Managers of these programs don't want to anger you—that wouldn't keep you shopping the way they want you to—and, at least up until now, data collected by loyalty clubs hasn't been used too obnoxiously. Individual

---

SWAPPING SHOPPING IDENTITIES

If you do decide that you are indignant about the use of information gained from supermarket cards, you may enjoy knowing how a few outraged but creative souls are working to turn the system back on itself.

A Web site producer near Sacramento, California, will e-mail an image of the barcode from his Safeway club card to anyone who asks. By attaching his barcode to the back of their Safeway cards, the barcode's new recipients can enjoy savings and help build a profile that is, to say the least, confusing. At last count, somewhere around three hundred people were shopping as the same person.

On the other side of the country, a Web-site developer in Maryland has put up a site that posts downloadable images of barcodes submitted by site visitors. By affixing any one of these barcodes to their own cards, volunteers can essentially swap identities with one another.

---

shoppers have not been barraged with direct-mail offers as a result of signing up.

In fact, direct contact information hasn't seemed to be all that important to the grocery stores that use rewards programs. One chain in the Pacific Northwest has even gone so far as to say as much outright. In an appeal to those customers who feared privacy invasions and excessive direct marketing, it sent a letter that actually encouraged them to register under a false name.

If stores don't care about getting your name right and these programs aren't about marketing to you specifically, then what are they about? Profit and profiling.

Profit first: By presenting you with a deal that looks pretty good, loyalty programs keep you shopping at that store. The hidden catch is that the deal you're getting may not be quite as good as you think it is. Studies by consumer groups and media reporters suggest that loyalty club cards buy savings that are very much in line with savings offered as a matter of course by supermarkets without loyalty programs. Other studies suggest that loyalty cards actually cost you money. In one shopping comparison, a member of a consumer group opposing supermarket loyalty clubs went to four of his local grocery stores and purchased the same ten items at each one. When he was finished, he found that the total for the purchases varied dramatically. Taking the nonsale or nonclub price for each item, the cost of the ten grocery items was 49 percent higher at the stores with loyalty club programs. In other words, unless you get savings on absolutely every item you buy, the club cards may not offer you any savings at all in the long run.

And then there is profiling. Happily, exploiting knowledge of your individual behavior hasn't been that interesting to grocery stores. Instead, they are interested in grouping you with customers who shop like you. One group of particular interest to just about any business is those customers who spend the most money. A study conducted a few years ago suggested that 30 percent of grocery shoppers account for 75 percent of a store's profits. The trick has been to figure out who those 30 percent are and what they want to buy. Enter the loyalty program.

Although this is not stated as the purpose of the program, and certainly the name doesn't suggest this, "loyalty" programs are an attempt to track a large population of shoppers to understand how different people buy. Shoppers are grouped and evaluated according to their purchase habits. Once a store identifies its most profitable customers, it works to offer goods and services that appeal to those customers, to keep them from shopping with a competitor.

Some consumer advocates are concerned that by tailoring a shopping experience to meet the needs of 30 percent of shoppers, the majority will be underserved. Here's an example: A store determined that its most profitable customers bought a lot of baby goods and didn't buy a lot of candy—so they halved the amount of candy they carried and increased the number of baby food products. Single people with a sweet tooth were out of luck.

Some people are concerned that this kind of segmentation will lead to a world where rich people can buy the groceries of their choice while poor people are forced to dine according to someone else's tastes. Regardless of whether you think this is something to worry about, it's certainly worth it to recognize a larger lesson from the case of supermarket cards. These programs were designed with a hidden purpose. Sometimes information is collected from you for reasons that aren't fully explained to you. Laws offer you some protection against people who collect information to commit fraud against you, but even information collection for purposes that are legal and seem okay to one person might be too much for another.

WHAT ARE SOME EXAMPLES OF NEGATIVE LISTS THAT MIGHT AFFECT ME?

Negative lists have a tendency to grow from simple lists of wrong-doers into more extensive lists that track good guys, too. While this often happens as part of the need to distinguish the good from the bad, inevitably, collecting information about upright citizens becomes a business unto itself. Even if you have a 100 percent squeaky-clean background, you're probably still in some blacklister's database.

"Blacklist" is a somewhat emotional term, conjuring images of the McCarthy era. For our purposes, we will use the term "blacklist" in a more general sense to refer to any accounting of who is no longer eligible for a service or product because of a past indiscretion, most often nonpayment or a criminal act. You can also use it to refer to a list of companies and individuals who shouldn't be patronized because they don't perform as advertised. Some examples include online bettors listing casino Web sites that don't really pay out winnings, hoteliers listing nonpaying customers to warn other chains, and consumer groups listing chiropractors who have a history of complaints filed against them. The Nevada Gaming Board has its delightfully euphemistic list of "excluded persons" to help Las Vegas casinos keep out known scam artists and cheats.

Some of the most mainstream blacklists are used by landlords concerned about skipped rent or property damage. Landlords know all too well that while the vast majority of people who rent apartments are not criminals, the reverse is not true. People who commit crimes don't tend to settle down in houses where they can be easily found. The vast majority of criminals rent apartments.

To help landlords protect themselves from this potentially dangerous class of renters, a number of competing blacklists were created. These lists essentially contain information on anyone who has a criminal background, anyone who was a party in a court case involving a lease violation (evictions, late payments, or vandalism) whether they were in the right or not, or anyone involved in a lease violation that didn't end up in court but was reported by previous landlords. Landlords and property managers consult these lists to reduce their number of deadbeat tenants, or tenants who might damage a building or create problems with other tenants.

Fairly recently, tracking for the rental industry has gotten a lot more sophisticated. Just as the blacklist of bad-check writers has grown into an industry to sell bank account information on people with skimpy credit files, tenant screening has become an opportunity to score potential tenants on their desirability, regardless of any particular wrongdoing. These days, if you rent one of America's 32 million apartments, you are probably a part of this system.

When you apply to live in a large apartment complex, your application plus a listing of what other apartments you've applied to,

WHO'S TRACKING RENTERS

One of the biggest players is First American Registry, founded in 1978 to identify criminals to potential landlords. These days, First American says it has over 33 million court records in its system, and it now offers online access to an instant and accurate employment and salary–verification database that includes over 40 million employee records from more than one thousand of the country's largest employers, organizations, government agencies, and state governments.

and a score (based on your credit report and whether or not you have any court records) is used to make rent/no rent decisions, or decisions, about the amount of security deposit that will be required. Once you've gotten settled in, your positive—as well as negative—payment record is reported by your current landlord month after month, to be on file for review the next time you move.

Another far-reaching consumer blacklist is used by utilities. In the 1990s, telecom companies were having a terrible time with cell phone accounts. Deregulation gave consumers more companies to choose from and offered more opportunity to switch from one mobile phone service provider to another—sometimes without paying that final bill at the old company. Beginning in March 1998, nine large telecommunications companies created a nonprofit organization called the National Consumer Telecommunications Data Exchange (NCTDE) to maintain a database of "defaulted and/or fraudulent telecommunications accounts"—in other words, a blacklist of deadbeat phone customers.

With each application for new service, phone companies check the list to determine if they should refuse to open an account, or what amount of deposit to charge. Roughly 10 percent of all applications for new service come from folks who are rather gently labeled "high-risk accounts." Collections departments of utilities or other companies also use the list to find anyone who "skipped" out on a payment. As many as 33 percent of all skipped accounts owners are tracked down this way.

The NCTDE was such a hit with the telecom industry that a few years later information provided by water, electricity, and gas companies was added. The NCTDE officially became the NCTUE, the National Consumer Telecom and Utilities Exchange in March 2002. As more and more utilities are deregulated across the country, these companies are fighting the same battles as the telecoms with unpaid accounts. They want a way to know who should get water when they turn on the tap. Given that the combined exchange contains information on more than 10 million defaulted accounts representing $3 billion in unpaid fees, they have some reason to ask.

The actual database work for the utilities exchanges, by the way, was subcontracted to Equifax, the company that that knows all about your credit history. Given what we know about how two other blacklists—check-tracking and tenant-screening—have grown in function and usage over time, it is worth watching to see if the NCTUE grows into a full-scale profiling operation before too much longer.

CHECKUP

Understanding your reaction to lists will help you define how you want to respond when someone puts you on a list, or tries to. Testing for warning signs can alert you that you've been inducted onto a list that you definitely don't like. The following checkups help you do just that.

Three Lists to See If You Belong on Lists

Developing a philosophy of lists rests a lot upon your worldview, your situation, and the degree to which you believe you're vulnerable to information abuse. If it is important to you to be left alone, for example, that suggests one course of action. If you are more of a laid-back, live-and-let-live type, that suggests another. If you're a single parent counting every penny, you will make a different set of tradeoffs than an executive at the peak of his or her earning power. If you just feel in your bones that something bad is going to happen, you might want to take additional steps to seek protection.

The following checklists below are designed to assess the three areas that play a role in developing your philosophy of lists. Check the box for each statement below that describes you.

Section A

❏ I vote in every election, even the local ones.
❏ I do all I can to protect the environment.
❏ I have been known to boycott products or companies that trouble me in some way.
❏ I worry about the growing divide between rich and poor.

❑ In terms of annoyance, on a scale from 1 to 10, telemarketers are an 11.

❑ I throw away more mail than I read.

❑ I get angry when salespeople call me by my first name.

❑ I believe that privacy is a basic right.

Section B

❑ I use coupons all the time.

❑ I love getting a good deal. I shop around for everything.

❑ You could almost call flipping through catalogues a hobby of mine.

❑ I take advantage of perks whenever I can.

❑ When I want to buy something, I want to do it with minimum fuss.

❑ I have no problem creating a profile if it means that a store can personalize what it offers me.

❑ Selling my name is worth a 10 percent discount.

❑ I'm happy to get mail, even when it's addressed to "resident."

Section C

❑ I worry when people I haven't met know things about me.

❑ I worry that huge companies are really running the world.

❑ I believe that government needs to be watched closely to keep it in check.

❑ Due to my job or lifestyle, my name is in the public eye.

❑ I've done well in life and have a number of assets in my name.

❑ Some of my family members have serious financial, legal, or substance abuse problems.

❑ My job requires me to work with the public or with people outside the mainstream of society.

❑ I want to be prepared for a divorce or breakup of a business partnership.

Now count the checkmarks in each section. Which section contains the most? That will determine your predominant set of considerations when deciding if you want to play along, whenever you might get on another list. In case of a tie, you get to make the judgment call about which one best describes you.

If section A has the most checkmarks, then you're a **Conscientious List Objector.** You believe that individual actions affect society at large, and you've shown your willingness to step up to the plate and be counted on more than one occasion. For you, listing (as well as reporting and profiling) have implications that go beyond your personal situation. You should approach listing opportunities not only with a view to how you are affected, but also to how you're setting a precedent or supporting a system that affects others. You will want to be very aggressive about investigating and monitoring listing opportunities.

If section B got the most checks, then you're a **List Player.** You participate in the system in a different way. Your focus is on the individual impact of your behavior. You use coupons to save money and you want to continue doing so. You like storing your credit card number with the online shopping site so that you don't have to enter it each time. Either the convenience or the financial rewards of tracking are perfectly acceptable tradeoffs in your book. You will want to be fairly liberal about listing opportunities.

If you checked more boxes in section C than the other two, then you're a **List Screener.** You have a fairly high level of concern for your personal safety, or at least a set of rational reasons to think that you're more vulnerable to malicious acts than some of your neighbors. You will evaluate listing opportunities more carefully than the other two types. You won't be so concerned about the social impact of listing, or the gain it offers financially or in terms of convenience. You will evaluate listing opportunities for their potential exposure. If the exposure is too great, the benefit offered doesn't outweigh the risk to you.

To see how each philosophy is applied practically, read the first section in "Taking Action," below.

Should You Suspect You're on a Blacklist?

Determining if you're on a blacklist can be a little tricky. The biggest thing about blacklists is that you don't necessarily know if you're on them. If a hotel chain is trying to track down nonpaying guests, it doesn't necessarily want you to know that they're looking for you. They want to catch you the next time you check in. It is very rare that you will be told up front about your appearance on a list. All that you can do is watch out for certain signs, and when you see them start asking questions.

If any of the warning signs below apply to you, you should do a little investigating.

- Your application for something takes longer than you expect.
- Processing your application is taken over from a frontline person by the manager.
- You are turned down and you aren't given a satisfactory reason why.
- The vendor you're dealing with becomes rude.
- You've had a dispute with a vendor at some point.
- You have sued a vendor or service provider at any point in the past 10 years.
- You've been a victim of theft (especially of your identity, your wallet, your PDA, or your cell phone).

TAKING ACTION

Now that you've figured out how you feel and if you should be concerned about negative reporting, it's time to decide what to do. The first section defines action strategies for different list types. The second offers advice on the best way to investigate and resolve blacklisting situations.

Start Your Own Blacklist—and Whitelist

Lists are with us. Your job isn't to try to make them go away—that will never happen. What you *can* do without going crazy is understand your personal tolerances for being tracked and to approach each listing opportunity accordingly. In the first part of the Checkup, you assessed various elements that go into determining your list philosophy. In this section we'll explore how that philosophy affects what you do.

Even the most permissive person will have limits. Everyone

needs to become more conscious of listing and to categorize each opportunity as either something you will accept or something you won't. In other words, start your own good list (some call it a whitelist) and blacklist.

Every time that you are asked to fill out a form or give your name to anyone, or are asked if you want to be put on a list, evaluate it according to the appropriate criteria for you, whether you're a List Objector, Player, or Screener. If you approve, mentally note that lister on your whitelist. You don't need to do anything more. If you disapprove, put that culprit on your blacklist and take action.

Evaluating Risks and Benefits

Evaluating if someone belongs on your whitelist or blacklist is an individual process. You must look at each case and understand it according to your own set of priorities and needs. Here are some questions to get you thinking.

Conscientious List Objectors will want to know:

- Do I approve of the objectives of this listing?
- Do I think that this listing will create more harm than good?
- Do I believe that there is a hidden agenda for this information?
- Do I think there is strong potential for future misuse of this information?
- Do I believe that access to this information about me and others will benefit society as a whole?

List Players will want to know:

- Is the value offered for this information real? Or does it simply cover up a more expensive program?
- Is there a potential that the bargain on offer is actually a con of some kind?
- Is there a potential that what I sign up for with this list can get out of hand?
- Does signing up for this program require information about my bank accounts or other specific information that might endanger my bank accounts?

List Screeners will want to know:

- Do I believe that the organization handling this data is stable and secure?
- Who can access this information?
- Can I limit what is done with this information?
- Do I have any legal rights to confidentiality?
- Is this information subject to the FCRA/FACTA, HIPAA, or any of my state's privacy legislation?
- Is this information too personal? Can I make it less so?
- Can the information requester justify their need for the information they want?
- If this information were made public in a courtroom, would I be able to handle it?

What to Do with Your Own Blacklist

If you put a list maker on your blacklist, then you need to do something. Conscientious List Objectors might consider bringing a list owner's actions to the attention of the media, your government representative, or a consumer-advocate group. List Players will probably want to monitor their file on a regular basis by requesting a report. List Screeners should ask not to be put on a list; opt out of any program that uses that list, and write to list owners to minimize the use of information sharing to the extent they can.

If you don't have any control over the fact that information will be collected, no matter your list philosophy, you can choose to be as vague as possible (e.g., don't list bank account numbers in a public divorce decree) or you can choose to provide false or misleading data. Obviously the latter option doesn't apply to all cases, but it is an option to transpose the digits of your phone number when signing up for a video club membership.

What to Do If You Suspect You're on Someone Else's Blacklist

Basically, you don't need to worry about being blacklisted until something happens to suggest that you've got a problem. If you are turned down for any kind of service, you will want to inquire. If you think you know what the problem is and it's legitimate (in a youthful act of indiscretion, you really did skip out on that mobile phone bill), then you might want to find out about any listing to determine how long you will continue to have problems. Most industries retain information from anywhere from three to seven years. Some, however, may keep you there indefinitely.

If you suspect that you have a problem because a dispute with another vendor is unfairly damning you, you may want to see about either eliminating or explaining the record from that vendor. If you suddenly discover that you're a victim of someone else's indiscretion, you will definitely need to work to clear up the situation and report the problem to agencies that track ID theft issues.

No matter whether you feel it is justified or not, if you ever suspect that someone has used a blacklist to deny you service, you will want to tread carefully. There will be a lot of suspicion and defensiveness on both sides. You have two basic tasks: the first is to determine that some kind of list was actually a factor in the decision to deny you service. The second is to find the right company to deal with to seek the resolution you're looking for.

Was a List Really a Factor?

To determine if a blacklist is in play, you can try asking your vendor directly for an explanation for your denial. Certainly, given the potentially inflammatory nature of your question, it is a good idea to request a response in writing. In the case of utilities or telephone service, you can explicitly ask if the National Consumer Telecom and Utilities Exchange (NCTUE) was used. Landlords can be asked directly about their screening procedures. Employers also have legal obligations to tell you when they rely on third-party information to make a hiring decision.

If you don't get a response that satisfies you, you can try contacting your state government to determine what trade association governs the vendor you're having difficulty with. A casual call to the association may uncover useful information about application review procedures, including the use of industry lists. You should also see if your state's consumer affairs division can offer you any insight into information practices by that type of vendor.

Make Sure You Talk to the Source

Once you determine negative information was used against you, contact the reporting company that provided it and ask for a copy of your file as well as a copy of their information-collection and information-retention policies. If you discover that the company simply reports information from another agency, stop dealing with them. It's a waste of your time. They aren't reporting on you—they are reporting on someone else's report on you. This difference is key, because you need to go directly to the agency that compiles the report in order to have the weight of the Fair Credit Reporting Act and the Fair and Accurate Credit Transaction Act (remember chapter 3?) on your side. Once you can invoke the FCRA and FACTA, you have a much better chance of forcing an acceptable resolution to your problem—whether you want to have incorrect information eliminated, negative information amended, or simply understand how long negative information will be available to vendors you want to do business with.

If a blacklister doesn't respond, even after you've displayed your impressive command of the terms of the FCRA, you will need to contact a consumer-advocate group or attorney to help you out. You should also seriously consider writing a complaint letter to the FTC. This won't do a whole lot for you personally—except perhaps give you the opportunity to complain—but it will document your case. If enough complaints come in, the government will begin to notice.

RESOURCES

If you want more detailed information about different kinds of marketing programs, there are a number of consumer groups that seek to educate the public about what's going on around them. You can contact any of them for thought-provoking material. If you fear that you have a problem with any type of listing you can contact the FTC. Most of the consumer and privacy groups listed in the previous chapters will also be able to offer assistance.

Now that you've thought about how you feel about listing, you're ready to take on the most aggressive listers of all: direct marketers.

- Consumers Against Supermarket Privacy Invasion and Numbering (CASPIAN) (www.nocards.org)
- Direct Marketing Association (www.dmaconsumers.org).
- Council of Better Business Bureaus, Inc. (www.bbb.org)
- Federal Trade Commission (www.ftc.gov)
- A list of trade associations who may be able to offer insight on industry lists can be found at the Federal Citizen Information Center's Consumer Action Web site (www.consumeraction.gov/trade.htm)

8. KEEPING IRRITATION TO A MINIMUM: DIRECT MARKETING

IN THIS CHAPTER:
How direct marketing works, how to get the amount of direct marketing aimed at you just right

Now that you've mastered the basics of listing and you've developed your own personal philosophy of how you want to handle it, it's time to wrap your mind around the most prominent use of information in the good ol' U.S.A.: direct marketing.

Sometimes marketing provides you with information to make good decisions as a consumer. Sometimes it creates unwanted noise and makes you mad enough to scream. Upwards of 4.5 million tons of junk mail are delivered to you and your neighbors each year, and that's a lot of junk (and that's not counting the billions of pieces of electronic "spam" mail).

No matter if it makes you feel good or bad, junk ads ought to make you proud: direct marketing is a peculiarly American invention. Sure, it can sometimes seem like a battle when the barrage hits: on your telephone, in your mailbox, at your front door and, coming soon, over your TV. But with a little help from you—consider it your patriotic duty—marketers can find the right balance between information and noise. Cue the "Stars and Stripes" and keep reading.

HOW IS DIRECT MARKETING AN AMERICAN INVENTION?

A little more than one hundred years ago, a railroad clerk in Minnesota found a case of pocket watches. He knew how important watches were to those in his profession, and, using a list of railroad clerks in the Midwest, he sent out a letter making it known that he had watches for sale. Before very long Richard Sears had sold his watches and invented the mail-order catalogue.

Sears Roebuck, as his new business came to be called, sold a variety of items across the vast expanse of America. Because most of his customers in the developing territories were too remote to have access to suppliers, Sears' catalogue business actually made it possible to settle in the remote West. You might say he supported the pioneer spirit of our country. And in providing this valuable service, Sears laid down the tradition of what has become the direct marketing industry of today.

HOW LIKELY IS IT THAT I'LL BE MARKETED TO DIRECTLY?

By some estimates, direct marketing is a $1.5 trillion (that's a "t", folks) market. Major list vendors claim to sell information on 175 million people living in 110 million households. The marketers who rent that information use it to send *tons* of direct mail to our mailboxes each year. Over 10,000 different catalogues have been developed.

And if your head isn't spinning yet, think about this: at one point the telemarketing industry employed a whopping 2 million people to call you at dinnertime. The need to keep all those people busy, plus lowering long distance rates and improvements in automated dialing technology, has lead to a fivefold increase in telemarketing calls in the past decade.

In other words, unless you live in a one-room shack in the middle of nowhere—and possibly not even then—you're already being marketed to directly.

WHAT ABOUT SPAM?

Spam, the sending of unsolicited e-mail advertisements to huge numbers of people, is an exception to what we'll discuss in this chapter. When marketers send you mail, call you on the phone, or ring your doorbell, they bear the cost of contacting you. They pay postage or long-distance charges or transportation costs.

As a result, most marketers are genuinely interested in learning that you don't want to hear from them. It keeps them from spending money that they won't get back and helps them focus their spending on those folks they might actually sell something to.

The cost structure of spam is backwards from other direct marketing because the sender doesn't have to pay for the system that he's using. When you pay your ISP for a connection to the Internet, you are paying for the e-mail system that the spammers are freeloading on. The result has been a genuine abuse of both technology and the consumer. Spam is, quite frankly, the bastard child of a proudly capitalist tradition. The FTC estimates that as many as two-thirds of spam contain untruths or are attempts to defraud you. No matter how tempting, don't fall for the pitch in an unsolicited e-mail. Ever.

How Do Spammers Get My E-mail Address?

Spammers use any number of tactics to seal e-mail addresses from Web pages and servers.

One favorite tactic is called Web scraping or e-mail harvesting. Spammers create or use automated software called "robots" to visit lots of Web pages and extract everything that looks like an e-mail address. While scraping most often affects people who put up their own Web pages and include a "here's how to reach me" e-mail address on them, there are other times you may be vulnerable to this.

Have you ever posted anything to a bulletin board on a Web site, say for a classified ad or an auction bid? The way identified yourself is now fodder for spammers. Does any site you joined offer a way to search for other members? Spammers can automate search requests and then scrape the page listing that results.

Other nefarious tactics involve duping mail servers of legit Web sites to forward spam to the addresses they contain or to publish their contents for spammers to steal. More recent virus attacks have forced infected machines to reveal the contents of their e-mail address books.

Although it is becoming less common, another way spammers get your e-mail address is by buying it from the Web site you gave it to. Did a site you signed up with post a privacy policy? What did that policy say? Privacy statements often contain a lot of very confusing language but phrases like "valuable offers," "share your name with trusted partners," or "unless you opt out" are clues that you're not providing information to just one company.

IS DIRECT MARKETING EFFECTIVE?

Absolutely. If it wasn't, it wouldn't be the industry it is. Forty percent of Americans purchased something over the phone last year. More than half have bought something from someone who came to their door.

In truth, not that many of the people targeted for an individual direct marketing campaign generally respond. Consider direct mail. By some estimates, 44 percent of all unsolicited mail is never even opened. Of those people who do open the letter or read the postcard, typically about 1 or 2 percent buy something because of it. While this sounds pathetically low, think about it this way: direct mail costs somewhere between $500 and $700 per thousand pieces of mail. If you mail out flyers to one thousand people, and 1 to 2 percent or ten to twenty of those people buy your product for $70, then you've made somewhere between $700 and $1,400. You've at least made back and possibly even doubled the money you had to put out in mailing fees. What's more, you've also gained the addresses of several hundred people who like what you have to sell.

One direct marketing consultant who works on credit card offers estimates that getting someone to sign up is worth closer to

MEET A LIST COMPILER

Founded in 1969, Acxiom is a list vendor currently headquartered in Conway, Arkansas. They sell InfoBase, the most comprehensive collection of U.S. consumer, business, and telephone data available from one source. Annual sales for the company exceed $866 million.

According to Acxiom's corporate literature, the InfoBase contains files on 176 million individuals in over 111 million U.S. households nationwide. Given that the U.S. Census only revealed 105.5 million households in the U.S. in the year 2000, the fact that InfoBase tracks 111 million of them should be considered something of an achievement. Acxiom's self-reported numbers certainly suggest that the list compiler, motivated by profit and devoting its entire energy to collecting data on each and every one of us, is doing a pretty thorough job. The end result, according to Acxiom, is "one of the largest multisource databases in the world, containing current demographic and lifestyle information" on just about every U.S. household.

$700 per year to a credit card company, not $70. In our hypothetical campaign, it only takes one person out of a thousand to sign up before the credit card company starts banking money.

Now, add a bunch of zeroes to everything and you've got the economics of direct marketing. It's no wonder they do it.

HOW DO THE MARKETERS KEEP FINDING ME, EVEN AFTER I MOVE?

You tell them. You don't directly write to each marketer and give them an update, but chances are pretty good you told your post office where you were going. When you file a National Change of Address (NCOA) form with the post office, you agree to let the post office release your new permanent address to anyone who can prove that they know your old address.

This includes the companies you've never heard of, but who have been selling your old address for years. As you might imagine,

READING THE FINE PRINT ON THE POST OFFICE NATIONAL CHANGE OF ADDRESS FORM

"Filing this form is voluntary, but your mail cannot be forwarded without an order. If filed, your new permanent address will be provided to individuals and companies who request it. This will occur only when the requester is already in possession of your name and old mailing address."

The key here is "permanent." If you don't want your name updated with list vendors, simply indicate that your change of address is "temporary."

sending out information about your new address to thousands of direct marketers is a big task. That's why the post office only agreed to do it if the direct marketing industry would take care of it. About twenty companies, including familiar names like Axciom, Equifax, Experian, and Fair Isaac, have been granted inexpensive licenses to take updated USPS NCOA data every two weeks and resell it to countless list vendors and direct marketers across the country. The cost per thousand addresses ranges from $2 to $5. If you've moved in the last ten years, you know that this network of companies manages the information on the 41 million Americans who change addresses annually with great efficiency.

WHAT PROBLEMS CAN I HAVE BECAUSE OF DIRECT MARKETING?

The obvious issue is one of nuisance. However, there are a few other considerations.

First, there is the question of justifying the use of natural resources to create mail campaigns that are expected to be a waste approximately 98 percent of the time. Environmental groups estimate that producing junk mail kills 100 million trees a year, costs $320 million to dispose of, and fills 3 percent of America's landfill space.

The other big issue with direct marketing is fraud. Although e-mail spam is a growing source of fraud, the telephone is still one of the most effective vehicles for weaseling money out of unsuspecting souls. According to the FTC, Americans lose an estimated $40 billion a year to the 14,000-plus telefraudsters who call consumers each day. The National Consumers League commissioned a survey a few years ago that suggested that 92 percent of American adults had received a phone call that was an attempt at fraud.

Senior citizens are the most frequent victim of aggressive tele-crooks. Despite representing approximately 16 percent of the U.S. population, the National Fraud Information Center reports that 36 percent of fraud victims in the first half of 2003 were over sixty. On the other hand, it's a mistake to forget that almost two thirds of victims were in their twenties, thirties, forties, or fifties. It is probably not a good idea to think that you won't be a target just because you aren't eligible for the AARP.

The final major concern with direct marketing is the one created by making information about you available to such a broad number of people. Despite reasonable efforts, no company can guarantee that all of its employees or customers will handle your personal

---

THE TOP 10 TYPES OF TELEMARKETING FRAUD ACCORDING TO THE NATIONAL FRAUD INFORMATION CENTER (2003)

- Credit card offers (including credit repair and credit loss protection offers)
- Prizes/sweepstakes
- Work at home (including stuffing envelopes and processing medical claims)
- Magazine sales
- Advance fee loans
- Lottery schemes
- Buyers clubs
- Travel/vacations
- Telephone long distance service
- Business opportunities/franchises

data with the respect that it deserves. The result is that information about you can get into the hands of identity thieves or worse.

WHAT LEGAL PROTECTION DO I HAVE?

Here's the good news: you have tons of legal protection against direct marketers. Being just a little informed about it will take you a very long way.

We have already discussed the law that created provisions to allow you to opt-out of information sharing by the new, huge financial megacorporations. Other laws address telemarketing.

The Telephone Consumer Protection Act (TCPA), regulated by the FCC, set out the following protections:

- Companies were required to keep a list of everyone who asked not to be called again, called a "do-not-call list," and to honor that request.
- If a company doesn't honor that request, you can sue them.
- If you don't have a prior business relationship with a company or you haven't given your consent for them to call, it is illegal for a company to call you before 8 A.M. or after 9 P.M.
- Sending telemarketing faxes was declared illegal, because the marketer is effectively making you pay for the ad since you had to buy the paper and toner.
- It is illegal for a company to use a prerecorded message when it calls you.

A few years after the TCPA, Congress passed another law to address the growing issue of fraud. This later act reinforces the earlier bill, but, in addition, requires that all sales calls include prompt disclosure that the caller is actually trying to sell you something, what it is he's trying to sell, what company he represents, and the terms of the sale. In other words, telemarketers are not allowed to lie by leaving something out or by saying something untrue.

Finally, the federal government has established a national registry to list telephone numbers of anyone who doesn't want to receive telemarketing calls with the Do-Not-Call Implementation Act of 2003.

WHY DO I GET PRERECORDED PHONE CALLS?

Hey, wait a minute! Don't you get prerecorded calls all the time? Prerecorded messages are legal in certain cases: in the event of an emergency or when consumers already have a business relationship with the caller, or if the call is noncommercial (has George Bush or Bill Clinton phoned lately?) or doesn't contain an unsolicited ad. The last two exceptions are used by creators of most recorded messages to justify what they are doing. Consider the messages telling you that mortgage rates are dropping (and it just so happens that if you call these guys they can help you take advantage of it). The companies behind these messages have argued in court that they are providing a service to consumers, not selling to them.

The federal do-not-call list allows individuals to register their phone number in a database. This registry has been carefully constructed so that identifying information beyond the number itself isn't tracked. Once registered, telemarketers have up to three months to eliminate your number from their calling roster. Registration keeps you from getting calls for five years, and if a telemarketer does contact you when he shouldn't, you can file a complaint that could result in a big fine to the offending company. The most up-to-date information on the status of the registry and details on how to participate can be found at www.donotcall.gov or 1-888-382-1222.

IF I SIGN UP FOR A DO-NOT-CALL LIST, WILL I STOP GETTING TELEMARKETING CALLS?

No. By registering a number, you can reduce the number of calls that you're likely to receive, but you will not stop telemarketers altogether. Political groups, charities, and researchers are still free to give you a ring.

Companies that you call are also allowed, with certain limitations, to call you back. Even if you're in the Do-Not-Call registry, once you buy something from a company, they have a legal right to call you for the next eighteen months. If you simply call a company to inquire about a product or service, they're allowed to call you for the next three months.

CHECKUP

Before figuring out what to do about junk in your life, it's a good idea to understand just how much and what kind of junk you get. The following checkup helps you quantify and characterize your junk mail, but you can apply the same technique to any kind of junk that drives you crazy.

How Much of Your Mail Is Junk?

A lot? Not that much? Write down a quick guess at how many individual pieces you receive in a week. Now let's see how your sense of the amount of junk mail you receive matches up to reality.

This checkup requires a paper bag and a week. For the next week, simply take every piece of junk mail that comes to you and put it into a bag. At the end of the week, take a look at what you've got.

How many pieces are there in total? The Native Forest Network estimates that the average American receives 10.8 pieces of junk mail a week. Are you above or below average? Is the number higher or lower than you thought it would be? How much of your junk mail is truly "junk" and how much of it is interesting or useful?

Funny enough, most of the people who've tried this test are surprised to find out that they actually receive less junk mail than they think they do. The real lesson for them is that it isn't the *amount* of junk mail that's so annoying. It's the fact that it's *junk*.

If you're like these people, you can focus your efforts on something that's eminently realistic. Instead of trying to make all junk mail go away, you can simply aim to reduce the stuff that you have no interest in. If, on the other hand, you really want to stop all unsolicited mail, there will be a few tips in the Taking Action section for you, too.

If you want to try the selective reduction strategy, you have to do a little more work for your checkup. First, take your pile of junk mail and sort it by type. Sort out any stuff that you want to keep

SPECIAL ISSUES WITH CHARITIES

Americans have big hearts. We rally to causes like no other society on the planet, and we often express our sympathy or support with our dollars, to the tune of more than $240 billion annually. That's why direct marketing on behalf of charities can be so effective.

There is, however, a side to this kind of direct marketing that you should be aware of. Only the biggest charities invest in the infrastructure to conduct telephone solicitations. When you get a call to support your local fire department, it's unlikely they installed a bunch of phone lines and recruited a small army of phone dialers to make the calls. Instead, smaller charities, youth camps, and local fire and police departments contract out the fund raising. This would be fine, except that telephone fund raising for small charities has become big business for a handful of companies that specialize in this.

One such firm has over twenty telemarketing facilities across the U.S. and Canada. They call you on behalf of hundreds of "badge" groups, such as firefighters' associations and fraternal orders of police, asking for donations. According to published reports, on average, only about 20 percent of what they collect actually gets to the nonprofits they solicit for.

The rest goes to the telemarketer for "costs." It's such a good business that in the many years it's been around, the company has been profitable for all but one of them. If you're concerned about giving the most you can to a particular charity, the next time you get a call that pulls on your heart (and purse) strings, politely say no and write a letter with a check directly to the organization in question. That way, 100 percent of your donation goes to help those you want it to, instead of lining telemarketers pockets.

receiving—coupons from a store you frequent, perhaps, or a catalogue that you like to flip through. When you're left with the stuff that is a waste of your time, and consequently also a waste of the marketer's money, sort that into piles by type. Create a pile for junk mail addressed to "resident" or "occupant." Create another pile for mail addressed to the people who used to live in your house or apartment.

Create a pile for credit card offers, insurance quotes, and other finan-cial products. Create a pile for catalogues. Create a pile for telephone, cable TV, and Internet-access offers. Create any other piles that make sense for you, or just a final one for all the miscellaneous stuff.

Now take a look and determine what the two biggest piles are. Those piles indicate the two types of direct marketers you can tar-get to eliminate the majority of your junk mail. In some cases, like the credit card offer pile, this is as simple as calling a single 800 number. In others, it may require talking to a few vendors. But, in just about every case, a few simple actions will go a long way to cut-ting down on the piles that bug you most.

TAKING ACTION

You know by now that there is no way to eliminate being on a mar-keting list somewhere. What you can do, however, is help mar-keters target you more efficiently. Consider it your contribution to capitalism.

To do your part for society, there is a three-step process. The first is to clear the boards as best you can to eliminate the bulk of poorly targeted material. The second is to work with businesses and organ-izations you do want to engage with to achieve the right level of com-munication that works for you both. The third is to protect yourself against overly aggressive companies that just don't get the message.

Actions That Have Limited or No Effect

Since you are going to have to invest some of your precious time in this project, it is important to use that time as wisely as you can. The following actions will have little to no effect and will probably only serve to make you crazy, when the junk mail and unsolicited calls keep coming. Don't waste your time.

- **Don't hang up on telemarketers.** Yup, you read it right. Don't just hang up. First of all, the person on the other end is probably just some poor Joe like you who is trying to put food on the table. Unless you get the rich fat cat at the top of the organization, save your ire. Second, hanging up isn't considered all that impolite in telemarketing circles. Hanging up might simply mean that you had a bad day and didn't feel like talking. If they call again tomorrow things might be different. Similarly, if you recognize a telemarketing call and hang up before talking to anyone, the autodialer simply records the time that you answered and calls again at that same time on another day.

- **Don't say "no thanks."** As with hanging up, this means that you weren't in the right frame of mind—this time. Anything less than "put me on your do-not-call list" simply tempts the telemarketer to try again.

- **Don't get an unlisted phone number.** Presumably, having an unlisted phone number means that you don't want people to find you, including telemarketers, and a handful of states have made it illegal to solicit to unpublished numbers. However, the majority of states have not, and the fact is that having an unlisted number makes you *more* attractive to marketers. Their reasoning is that, because you are harder to find fewer companies have found you to sell to you. Therefore, you should be more receptive to the few offers that do get through.

  How do they find you? Simple technology. A computerized dialer calls number after number in sequence. Upon successfully initiating a ring, it identifies the number it called as a working one. Periodically, the list of numbers found by the autodialer is compared to a directory of published numbers. When your number, which is now listed as "working," isn't found in the published directory, you've been found. And your number has now been put on a list that can be sold to any marketer who wants to buy it.

- **Don't send junk mail back to the sender.** The equivalent of hanging up on telemarketers in the junk mail world is sending the mail back. There is only one time that it makes even a little bit of sense to do this, and not really even then. In the rare case that a piece of junk was sent via first-class mail or has "address change requested" printed on it, you can cross out the address, circle the first class postage, and write "refused: return to sender." Drop it in any mail box, and it will be returned to the sender. The problem is that, although the mail will be returned, it will probably only get returned to a sweatshop processing firm—often in another country. It will never get anywhere near the people who maintain the list of addresses, especially if the list was rented from another company and the mail was returned to the sender. If, as is much more likely, the junk mail was sent with a bulk mailing permit, the post office will generally try to redeliver anything you try to refuse. Bulk mail fees don't include return service, and the post office is required to provide the service that was purchased—i.e., getting it in your mailbox.

Clearing the Boards of Unwanted Telemarketers

Okay, now that you know what not to do, it's time to gear up for actions that you can and should take. The two important phrases in your vocabulary are "opt out" and "do-not-call list."

Antitelemarketing Action #1
Reducing telemarketing calls has gotten a lot easier since the creation of the national do-not-call registry. Signing up is incredibly easy and incredibly effective. It takes less than a minute, really, and the result is dramatic. Unlike registries maintained by the direct marketing trade association, which have spotty effectiveness, this registry simply lists numbers that ought not to be called and makes it easy to punish offenders. Registration is good for five years. Each time you change phone numbers you will need to register the new number. For information on how to register, you can go online to www.donotcall.gov, call 1-888-382-1222, or visit your state's Web site.

Antitelemarketing Action #2
If, for whatever reason, you don't want to sign up for the do-not-call registry, you have to deal with each caller individually. And this

is okay, because most companies are pretty responsive if they sense that you know your rights. How will they know? There's that simple, magic phrase.

When the phone rings answer it and politely say "Put my number on your do-not-call list." I know of some folks who soften the blow by adding "I never do business over the phone."

Anything else keeps the door open to future calls, but those magic words will signal to the salesperson that you know about the law. The company who is calling may take six weeks to drop you from their call list, but after that they can't legally telephone you for ten years. While you're at it, you can list more than one number at a time (e.g., if you have two lines in your house). And, if you have time, ask for the caller's name, company, and phone number or address to track violations. You can also ask if they call on behalf of more than one company. If so, you can ask not to be called for any of these companies as well.

If you're feeling feisty, you might even ask for a written copy of their "do-not-call policy" while you're at it. Telemarketers must have one by law. If the person on the telephone says that they can't or won't send it to you, you can sue for $500.

If you suspect that anything is up with the company, you should probably also ask for their registration number. In most, but not all, states, telemarketers of certain kinds (e.g., companies offering prizes, investments, and items below normal costs) are required to register with the state attorney general. You can report companies that can't or won't tell you their registration number. Who knows? By reporting them, you may be doing a good turn for somebody else who is actually considering buying from that company over the phone.

In most cases, however, it is pretty likely that you'll just pick up the phone, say the magic words, and be done. The salesperson will stop his or her pitch immediately, tell you how long it will take to process your name, and say good-bye. If a telemarketer that you've talked to does call you again (note that they are allowed to make one mistake and that it can take up to six weeks before your name is entered onto the do-not-call list), you have a right to sue them, ask your state attorney general to sue, or file a complaint with the FCC, which can assess fines.

Antitelemarketing Action #3

If you just don't want to deal with intrusive phone calls, you might consider buying one of the many devices that are available to help out. My favorite is called the Phone Butler. It plugs into your phone much like an answering machine, and when activated plays a recorded message that asks that you be placed on the caller's do-not-call list. For more on the Phone Butler and similar devices, see www.privacycorps.com.

I don't really recommend devices that try to fool computer auto-dialers into thinking your line is out of service. Every time you answer the phone, these devices play the funny series of beeps (the Special Information Tone, or SIT) that signal that the line has been disconnected. Computers will hang up at that point. Unfortunately, the tone will also play for friends and family when they call, too, and you might scare off people you actually want to talk to. The real problem with this gizmo and others like it, however, is that using technology to fight technology rarely works for long. There is the inevitable escalation. Indeed, there's a company that has recently announced a counterdevice to help direct marketers identify fake SIT recordings. Also, given how frequently telephone numbers go out of service and get reassigned to someone else, I'd doubt that even if you fool a telemarketer into thinking your number was a dud that they'd wait too long before trying it again. Picking up the phone and asking to be put on the do-not-call list costs you nothing and buys you years of peace and quiet.

Antitelemarketing Action #4

A final antitelemarketing action that you might consider if you get called by a lot of charitable fund-raisers is to opt out with companies that handle telephone solicitations for charities in your area. Information on these companies can be obtained from your Better Business Bureau. You may also want to opt out with Xentel DM, a large charitable telemarketers that makes calls nationwide. Up-to-date information on how to contact Xentel can be found on its Web site, www.xentel.com, or in the Fort Lauderdale, Florida, phone book.

Clearing the Boards of Unwanted Junk Mail

All junk is not created equal. Some is based on sophisticated customer profiling, some is based on carpet bombing your address, some is leftover from the previous resident. Credit card offers are a category unto themselves. For each type of junk mail that you've elected to target, find the summary below to learn how to reduce the bulk of it.

Credit Card Offers, Insurance Quotes, and Other Financial Products

You can eliminate a lot of insurance quotes and offers for financial products by exercising your rights and opting out with the companies, as we discussed in chapter 5. Other than that, probably the most important action you can take is to get on the opt-out list for preapproved credit card offers. This is easy, effective, and *very important* to help prevent identity theft.

One phone call to 1-888-5OPT-OUT (1-888-567-8688) will remove your name from prescreened credit or insurance offer mailing lists from Experian, TransUnion, and Equifax. When you call you will be given a choice to opt out for two years or permanently. If you elect to opt out permanently, you will be mailed a Notice of Election to Opt Out Permanently. Once the credit reporting companies receive your request, it will become effective within five days. As with other suppression lists, it will probably take several months before your request propagates to the databases of all the companies who have bought your name already, and you actually see a reduction in the amount of offers.

Mail Coming to "Resident" or "Occupant"

If you want to reduce the deluge of coupon paks or missing children ads, you will need to contact a handful of companies that make this their business. One company, Valpak, requests that you mail them a copy of their mailing label to make sure that they find you in their system. It's generally not a bad idea to do this with everyone. You increase the odds that your efforts will have an effect. The biggest

DO THE MISSING-CHILDREN ADS WORK?

Before you call the toll-free number for ADVO, you might want to consider one thing. The National Center for Missing and Exploited Children claims that one in six of the kids pictured on mailings from ADVO and a few similar companies are recovered because of them.

players are listed below. If you're really serious, a consumer group called JunkBusters lists more on their Web site (www.junkbusters. com).

ADVO-System, Inc. (the ShopWise and Missing-Children folks)
ADVO Consumer Assistance
P.O. Box 249
Windsor, CT 06095
1-888-241-6760

Valpak Direct Mktg Sys, Inc.
Attn: Opt-out
8605 Largo Lakes Drive
Largo, FL 33773
1-800-676-6878
(This is the company that requests that you send the Valpak envelope to them; suppression requests are honored for two years only)

Harte-Hanks, Inc. (they do the Penny Savers and Potpourri mailings)
Attn: List Maintenance
6701 Bay Meadow Drive, Suite D
Glenburne, MD 21060
1-800-456-9748

Mail for Former Residents or People You've Never Heard Of
Representatives of the post office say that the best thing to do is leave a note for your mail carrier explaining that such-and-such

person doesn't live at your house anymore. The carrier will input this information into the post office system and that should be that. Isn't it nice to have someone else doing all the work?

Some antijunk advocates have suggested filling out a change-of-address form for the nonresident and listing yourself as the agent authorized to do so. Although a "moved, left no forwarding address" may stop the mail, it also technically makes you liable for a $10,000 fine. Probably better just to chat to the guy who actually brings you the mail.

Catalogues

If you want to try to do away with all catalogues, you can try opting out with the main vendor of names to the catalogue publishers. Abacus Direct runs a cooperative database where thousands of publishers trade names. If you've ever bought from a catalogue, one of those names is undoubtedly yours.

> **Abacus**
> P.O. Box 1478
> Broomfield, CO 80038
> 1-800-518-4453
> optout@abacus-direct.com

Telephone, Cable TV, and Internet Access Offers

Companies that provide you with service know a lot about you. Telephone companies know what numbers you dial and what numbers are used by the people calling you. They have to—it's how they connect one caller to another. And by tracking how often you call a number and how long you stay on the line they know how much to bill you. In the process of performing the service you request of them, they have the ability to accumulate a lot of information. What a telecom company knows about you based on your use of a network that it offers you access to is called Customer Proprietary Network Information (CPNI).

Telecommunications companies that also offer Internet access, mobile phone service, and possibly even cable service, learn a lot about what you do using those networks, too.

CPNI has the potential to be pretty personal and sensitive. Happily, there are some restrictions on how the information can be used. Although CPNI can be used by its own company to sell you more of what you already have, it cannot be shared with third parties to market to you unless you give your approval. In some cases, telecom companies use an opt-in system. They will not share your information unless you tell them that you want them to. Others use the all-too-familiar opt-out plan. They assume it's okay to share your details until you tell them it isn't.

In order to reduce your telecom-related junk mail, you need to find a bill from every telephone, cable, and Internet access provider you have. Look up the customer service number and call them. Ask about their use of CPNI and what you can do to control it.

All Other Junk Mail (Part 1)

For a general decrease in all mail, you can put yourself on an opt-out list managed by the main trade association for the direct marketing industry. The Direct Marketing Association (DMA), established in 1917, is the oldest and largest trade association for direct marketers. In addition to lobbying on marketing-related legislation, the DMA also acts as a central repository for people to request removal from mailing, telephone, or e-mail lists. The DMA opt-out lists have their problems—which is one reason the federal government stepped in with its own do-not-call system—but for junk mail it's the best you've got.

To get on the DMA junk mail opt-out list, you can go to their Web site or write a letter with your request. The DMA charges a five-dollar fee for online registration but will honor written requests for free, so send a letter. Although the DMA warns that it will take longer to get your name processed, marketers only update their files four times a year anyway. There is no reason that the association representing the problem should make you pay to eliminate the problem. Besides, the DMA isn't doing this out of the goodness of its heart. They make money selling the opt-out list to marketers. Once registered, your opt-out request is good for five years. You should receive postcard confirmation that you've been added to the opt-out list a few weeks after your request is received.

There are a couple of problems with the DMA opt-out list to know about ahead of time. First, it is required that the roughly 3,600 DMA members honor this list, but it's totally voluntary for other marketers. Undoubtedly, junk mailers who are not part of the DMA will still send you material. Second, the way you list yourself in your request letter has to exactly match what the direct mail marketer has or he sends the mail anyway. For example, if you submit an opt-out request as James but a marketer lists you as Jim, your name isn't going to be eliminated from that mailing. You can, of course, increase your chances of success by including every variation of your name that you can think of in your request letter. While there are no limits on how many variations of your name you can include in one letter, you must write a separate letter for each family member you're protecting.

Even with all of these problems, however, it's worth noting that the DMA estimated at one point that submitting your name to its opt-out list would eliminate 75 percent of national mailings.

Direct Marketing Association
http://www.the-dma.org (remember that online opt-out requests incur a fee)
Mail Preference Service
ATTN: DEPT 12057543
P.O. Box 282
Carmel, NY 10512

All Other Junk Mail (Part 2)
In addition to the DMA master list, you can also opt out directly with the top list sellers. Fortunately, there are several organizations that are willing to help you out.

JunkBusters is probably the most prominent. Their Web site, www.junkbusters.com, contains an incredibly rich collection of information about direct marketing, as well as a fairly comprehensive listing of major list vendors that you might want to opt out with. JunkBusters also offers an automated letter creation service (you put in your information once and crank out whatever letters you wish) that is quite handy and free.

Alternatively, you can sign up with Private Citizen at www. private-citizen.com or Stop Junk at www.stopjunk.com. Private Citizen compiles a directory of members that is distributed to the largest junk mail vendors, as well as to over fifteen hundred tele-marketers. Stop Junk offers to send you preprinted, postage-paid postcards to sign and send out. You need to do less work in both cases, but you pay a little bit more for the privilege. You must pur-chase membership with Private Citizen to be included in the direc-tory, or pay a fee for the Stop Junk package.

All Other Junk Mail (Part 3)

Stop sending in warranty cards. Warranty cards are nothing more than a flagrant excuse to get profile information on you. In most cases, keeping the blank card with the terms and the receipt offers you all the protection you need.

Getting the Level of Communication Right

Once you've done your bit to clear away the stuff you don't want, you should take a break for three months. It will take this long to see just how much you accomplished. For fun, you might want to repeat the experiment of collecting all the junk mail you get for a week to see how much lower the volume is three months on. When you think the dust has settled, it's time to look at the stuff that's still coming.

Probably you are still receiving a lot of catalogues. Given that there are more than ten-thousand catalogues out there that can be mailed to you, it would be surprising if you didn't. With luck, your request to opt out of mailings has reduced the really junky cata-logues that you used to get, but if you've ever bought from a cata-logue, chances are quite good that you're still receiving it and related ones as well. The trick with catalogues is that they're expen-sive to make and expensive to mail. Companies don't mind sending them to you if you want them, but they really don't mind leaving you alone if you don't.

Given that you might not want to eliminate catalogues altogether, you will need to wage an ongoing campaign to keep companies informed about what is okay to send you and what isn't. It sounds daunting, but it's actually pretty simple. Every time a catalogue comes in, find the company's 800 number, usually on the inside front cover or the order form in the middle of the catalogue. With the label in hand, call the 800 number and do one of two things: either ask to be taken off their mailing list, or thank them for the catalogue but request that they not sell your name to other mailers. I've never known anyone who had a customer service rep say no to either of these requests. If you want to buy from a catalogue, contrary to popular wisdom, it's fine to do so—as long as you make clear at the time of purchase that you don't want your name sold to other companies. In order to get your money, the catalogue company should readily agree.

Once you've had a taste of how easy this is to do, you can try it next with magazines you subscribe to. Before long, defining your relationship with each company you do business with will become natural and the phrase "Please do not sell or rent my name" will fall off your lips like second nature.

Another proactive approach you can take to help marketers target material to you appropriately is offered by JunkBusters. JunkBusters has pioneered a service in which you create a "declaration" that indicates the types of information you are willing to receive. You simply need to visit its Web site and step through a simple Web-based form. Once you're finished, you can post the declaration at your own Web site or have JunkBusters deliver the information to the marketers it works with. This service is free for consumers, and represents a truly novel approach to controlling your personal information.

Protecting Yourself Against a Specific Marketer

Now that you've saved the trees that otherwise would have died to sell you stuff you didn't want, and established a meaningful two-way communication with companies that sell the stuff you do want, the time has come to take on the jerks in the marketing world. These are the companies that violate the do-not-call list or send you offensive material.

If it has been three months since you signed up for a government do-not-call registry and you receive a call from an organization that isn't a charity, a market-research company, or that you haven't done any business with in the past year and a half, it's quite possible that the company calling you is in violation of the law. You can submit a complaint to your state's attorney general, the FTC, or the FCC. All that you need to tell them is the name of the company or the phone number of the caller that you feel is in violation. Since recent regulations from the FCC require all telemarketers to transmit caller ID information, learning an offender's name and number should be relatively easy.

If you're receiving explicit mail that is a problem, you can take advantage of one of two U.S. Postal Service programs to stop it. In order to protect children from viewing sexually explicit material, Congress has passed legislation that allows you to file a form with the post office that puts you on a list of people who should not receive such mailings. The second program allows you to specify a specific mailer that you do not wish to receive offensive material from. While the program was designed to eliminate pandering advertisements, the form that you have to fill out only requires that you identify the mailer and that you ask not to receive anything more from them. Offensive is in the eye of the beholder as far as the post office is concerned, and you can list any company you want.

In order to be listed either as someone who doesn't want to receive sexually explicit mail or to execute a prohibitory order against a specific marketer, you need to fill out USPS Form 1500. This form is available online at http://www.usps.com or at your local post office. After completing the form, you can give it to any post office employee or send it directly to the main processing center. Once your request has been processed, you will be notified and told how to report any mailer who violates the order not to send material to you. Your name will remain on the list for five years, unless you request otherwise. At the end of five years, you will have to fill out the form again to keep the prohibition in force.

RESOURCES

It's a bit of work to slow down all the direct marketing aimed at you, but, with a little patience and a focus on the stuff that bugs you most, you can make quite a lot happen. As you progress, you may find new ideas or just plain moral support from any of the countless private organizations devoted to helping eliminate the problems of unwanted marketing. You can try any of your local recycling centers or local government recycling offices for more information. You can also visit the groups listed below for general information on reducing unwanted marketing. A few organizations specifically fighting spam have also been listed.

For information on do-not-call lists, you can visit the FCC or the Federal Do-Not-Call List registry. And finally, for information on fraud by telemarketers, you can find information and assistance at the National Consumer League's National Fraud Information Center or the FTC. For reports on specific national charities and general advice on telemarketing efforts by charities, the BBB Wise Giving Alliance can get you started. You will need to contact your local Better Business Bureau for local charities.

- JunkBuster (www.junkbusters.com)
- National Waste Prevention Coalition (www.metrokc.gov/nwpc)
- Private Citizen, Inc. (www.private-citizen.com)
- Stop Junk Mail Association (www.stopjunk.com)
- Coalition Against Unsolicited Commercial Email (CAUCE) (www.cauce.org)
- SpamCon (www.spamcon.org)
- Federal Communication Commission (www.fcc.gov)
- The Federal Do-Not-Call List registry (1-888-382-1222 or www.donotcall.gov)
- National Fraud Information Center (www.fraud.org)
- Better Business Bureau Wise Giving Alliance (www.give.org)

9. TRACKING AND HACKING: INTERNET INVASIONS

IN THIS CHAPTER:
What Internet issues are most important, actions and technology that help you safeguard your computer

The Internet has revolutionized our world in so many ways. For starters, the Internet has made finding information significantly easier. It has also made taking information from you easier, too.

Different programs that you inadvertently allow into your computer track where you surf or what you enter when you type your e-mail address, your passwords, or maybe even your credit card number. Hackers try to take over your computer. Despite the hype, however, most personal computing security issues are fairly easily dealt with. By the end of the chapter you'll know what you need to get this under control.

The real danger—and the one that's harder to affect—comes from the computers owned by governments and the companies we trust our information to. These systems are the key targets. Even though you can't install better security on these computers yourself, you can still play a big role in controlling attacks against them. You may think a virus on your computer is simply a nuisance. But when that virus causes your computer, and millions of others, to overload a Pentagon server with e-mails, you've become a part of the problem.

One of the most destructive viruses to date has been the Sobig virus released in August 2003, which caused almost $30 billion of damage—an order of magnitude more than ones released before it. Given that the virus was timed to expire on September 10, 2003, some have speculated that Sobig was, in part, an experiment to determine how far and how fast the virus could spread—in preparation for a similar attack with a more destructive payload in future.

It's up to you to protect your own computer to keep it from being recruited for this kind of cyberattack. Osama bin Laden—and other less-well-known terrorists and criminals—are thinking about it. So should you.

SHOULD I ASSUME THAT MY WEB SURFING IS TRACKED?

Yes, tracking what you do online, what sites you visit, and what you do when you get there is surprisingly common. Some tracking is done by individual sites trying to learn more about their visitors to make the sites better. Some tracking is done by online ad networks hoping to figure out more about you so they can show you ads for things that will interest you. Some tracking is done by software companies who use what you do to help find bugs and other problems with their products.

Things that are tracked typically include what browser software you use, what kind of computer you have, when you visit a site, how long you stay there, what you click on while you're there, and where you go next. Anything you enter in forms on Web pages, including something you want to search for in a search engine, can also be tracked. More intrusive tracking includes logging everything you type, and scanning what software you have on your computer. Although tracking sounds very intrusive and scary, most of the time it isn't.

HOW CAN MY SURFING BE TRACKED?

Tracking technology is always changing, but for now, the basic tools of the trade are cookies and spyware.

Cookies

Cookies are tiny one-line files written to your hard drive by the server of a Web site that you visit. They often include some kind of ID unique to you, so that the next time you visit the site the Web server can check your cookie and figure out that you've been there before. If you've never given any personally identifying information to a Web site, the ID can only help a company track what your *computer* does, no matter *who* is at the keyboard.

If you register with a site, you start to provide personally identifying information that can now be tied to the ID assigned you in your cookie. Besides helping a Web site developer understand more about who is using their site, tying your information to a cookie ID can be good for you, too. Cookies will often store preferences that you ask a Web site to remember for you: like your shipping address or a log-in ID. Many Web sites won't work properly without cookies, because they are used by the software that generates each page to keep track of what should appear on the next page—information that has very little to do with you or your personal information.

Most of the time cookies are created by the actual Web sites that you visit. They are limited in what they can know about you, and really aren't worth a lot of concern. There's even a bit of built-in security. Cookies can be read only by the same Web site that wrote them to your disk. A cookie written by one Web site—say, for example, your bank's Web site—can't be read by any other Web site—such as that of an online book seller.

The one time that you might want to consider cookies intrusive is when they are created by ad networks. Many Web sites that display ads don't actually sell or serve up the ads themselves. They contract this work out to agencies that specialize in finding advertisers and delivering ad content to individual sites. The largest of these networks, called DoubleClick, served over 669 billion ads on countless Web sites last year. Because a visit to any one of those sites also triggers a connection to DoubleClick's Web server, the cookie that DoubleClick writes to your hard drive can collect information about your broader surfing habits, not just what you do on one particular site.

In reality, DoubleClick is less interested in playing Big Brother than in showing an ad for something that you might want to buy. This means that there are two very real pragmatic limitations on their information gathering. First, they aren't going to pay to store information that they don't really have to. Second, they need a way to crunch their data *really* fast. No Web company in the world is going to hire DoubleClick to serve ads for them if their site slows to a crawl because DoubleClick is taking too long to process your profile info.

The result is that DoubleClick doesn't track the name of each particular site you visit in its cookie. It tracks the type of site you visit. Each time you visit a site or search using a term that falls into a category it tracks, a counter for that category in your cookie is incremented. To borrow an example directly from DoubleClick, if you visit fashion sites, florist sites, and bridal sites and search on the words "weddings" and "bridal registry," your DoubleClick cookie might look like the following:

Cookie ID	Sports	Autos	Wedding	Fashion	Business	Technology
123	0	0	19	10	0	0

The information in the cookie is used to determine that the time is right to show you ads about wedding stuff. The information is also used to predict a little bit about you. Since the vast majority of people who are interested in fashion and wedding stuff are women, DoubleClick will guess that you're a woman. Consequently, you might also see ads for products that appeal to women in general. DoubleClick specifically does not track categories that are too personal or inflammatory, like health, financial status, sexual orientation or behavior, race or ethnic origin, or opinions about politics or religion. They just want to sell video cameras and shoes.

Really pretty benign, don't you think? Okay, there is one catch. Individual Web sites that you've given your name to can access a surfing profile from DoubleClick. These companies may also share customer information with other companies that will see that you are a customer of both Web sites. Furthermore, DoubleClick bought Abacus, a large-catalogue direct marketing company, a few years back. That company, which knows your name, address, and purchase history (although mostly from catalogues), can compare notes with the Web sites and pretty soon what you do online can be tied to what you do in the real world.

But even this isn't the huge problem we might have feared. DoubleClick is actually fairly careful about its use of cookies and its sharing of information. It needs to be since some disgruntled Web surfers sued them, alleging that they were not so careful. Up to now, companies like DoubleClick and WebTrends have only found it useful to paint a general picture of your actions. They are limited by technology so that they can only gather information from Web sites that have entered into an agreement with them. And there are a number of ways that you can remove yourself from the whole process, which we'll explore in the Taking Action section.

Spyware

The other big tool for tracking is called, provocatively, spyware. Spyware comes in three flavors: monitoring programs, diagnostic programs, and adware. In each case, a program that reports on your activity is placed on your computer, frequently without your knowledge.

Monitoring programs are designed to track what keys you type, what files or applications you open, what clicks you make, and what is contained in everything you store on your computer. They are often used by employers to watch over employees, and by parents who want to know what their kids are up to. They are also the spying method of choice for people with less-than-honest intentions.

Common wisdom is that physical access to your computer is required to install monitoring programs, but hackers have found security holes in certain types of servers that allow them to sneak this kind of software onto your Internet-connected machine without being anywhere near it. Once installed, monitoring programs capture a steady stream of descriptive data that chronicles your actions at the computer. This data is sent back to a central server on a regular basis, using your own Internet connection.

Diagnostic programs are created by software manufacturers. They are designed primarily to aid developers in determining what went wrong in the event the software crashes on your computer, so that they can fix the problem in a future release. Details of how you use their product can be transmitted automatically

---

IP ADDRESSES

Whenever you type in a URL or click a link to request a Web page, the Web server needs to know how to deliver that page back to you—in other words, how to find your computer out of all the millions of other computers that are also out there on the Net. It can find your computer, because every computer connected to the Internet has a unique address called an *IP address* (short for Internet Protocol address).

Whenever you're online your computer transmits its IP address to every server it encounters. And every server keeps track of the IP address of every visitor in a log file.

Inevitably, unless you use special software to hide your IP address, it is possible to trace a visit to a Web page back to an individual person. When you connect to the Internet, your Internet Service Provider (ISP) assigns your computer an IP address. Since your ISP knows who you are (you pay the bill) when you connect, and it knows what IP address it assigned to you, it's not too difficult to make the connection from an entry in a Web log of an IP address back to the person to whom it belongs. This is how the Recording Industry Association of America (RIAA) tracked down all those people who it claims were sharing music files illegally, in order to sue them. It simply noted the IP address of computers that were requesting music files, and then subpoenaed the records of ISPs to determine the name of the person to whom the IP address was assigned.

over the Internet. While it is also possible to misuse this data, most software companies don't *appear* to have stepped over this line. Each time you install a new program, it is quite possible that you are adding this kind of diagnostic software as well. The fact that you are is probably disclosed in some fine print in the license agreement.

Adware is a supercharged version of the cookie tracking we talked about earlier. It monitors your Web surfing and download activities to choose which pop-up ads it should—and will—show you. Some programs have been designed to transmit information about you back to profiling companies. One, for example, addresses the question of who signs up for certain services, what motivates them to sign up, and how long they stay a customer of the service once they do sign up. The software collects the information it deems relevant to these questions and sells that data to anyone who wants to buy it. Clearly, this type of monitoring is the most aggressive and intrusive. Adware is commonly included in free programs that you download. File-sharing programs that are so popular for downloading music rely on adware as their source of income. There really is no such thing as a free lunch after all, is there?

IS ONLINE SHOPPING SAFE?

Given all of the ways that we've talked about tracking, how can it be safe to input your credit card into a Web site and shop online?

First, consider that most tracking occurs by and for advertisers. It is created by companies and carried out only with the collaboration of a series of other companies. Annoying? Possibly. But criminal? No. Although theoretically the tracking tools that you undoubtedly have on your computer would allow unauthorized capture of your credit card number as you type it in to a Web site form, it just doesn't make sense for advertisers to disrupt the system for a relatively small amount of money.

Second, remember that your financial liability from misuse of your credit or debit card number is small to none. With credit cards, if someone steals your number but not your card, you have no liability at all. Since online shopping never involves your physical card, you have no financial exposure if someone steals your credit card number and uses it.

Third, the truly dangerous thing about online shopping has absolutely nothing to with your own computer. There has never been a case where someone's credit card number was stolen while an order was being placed. When you input sensitive information into a Web page, chances are very good that the seller has programmed its site to offer you protection by encrypting any data that you're sending it—a Web page that will encrypt information as it travels the Internet is identified by an icon of a key or lock in the bottom corner of your browser window.

More importantly, you are protected by sheer randomness. Of all the trillions of bits being shot back and forth over the Internet at any one time, what are the odds that someone is going to tag the ones coming from you? Most thieves will concentrate their efforts on bigger fish.

In this case, the "big fish" is the company you're doing business with. The Internet Security Alliance, which teaches businesses how to protect sensitive information, suggests that a company's computers, chock full of your credit card info and the info of all their other customers, are the ones that you really have to worry about. The bad guys who want to commit fraud are much less interested in tracking you individually than they are in breaking into a shopping site's database that stores your number along with about a million other people's. Before you give your credit card number to a Web site, you might want to know more about how they are making sure that your information won't be stolen and sold to criminal rings.

If it's a big player like Pottery Barn or the Gap, chances are good that the info you provide online is just as safe as the info stored in their databases when you buy over the phone or at their store. If the company is a smaller, Internet-only operation, you might want to do a little checking. Call customer service. Look for a Better Business Bureau or TRUSTe seal.

Once you recognize where the danger of online shopping lies, you can see that the question to answer is not "is online shopping safe" but rather "is online shopping with this Web site safe?"

In most cases, the answer is yes.

CAN WHAT I WRITE IN AN E-MAIL BE TRACKED?

Absolutely. And you can probably bet that it is. Although there is a law that makes it illegal to read or share the contents of an e-mail, there are a couple of important loopholes.

Employers monitoring employees aren't covered (technically, they own the computer, the network, and the software, so they have a right to access the things they own). If the person you send the e-mail to consents to share it, they don't need your permission. Or, as we've learned before, if law enforcement gets curious, they can take a peek with a court order.

Furthermore, anytime you send an e-mail from point A to point B, it goes through any number of Internet companies on its way. Each company has its own set of privacy policies and its own interpretation of its obligations and rights. You can't even be sure that the companies are all governed by U.S. law. Finally, the biggest and most important exception is that e-mail is considered private only when it is in transit. Once the text resides on a computer somewhere for more than 180 days, it enjoys much less protection.

All of these exceptions mean that, if someone really wants to, he or she can most likely read your e-mail. Practical obscurity, the fact that there are too many e-mails from too many people to make yours worth caring about, will probably protect you in all but the most unusual circumstances. But the safest bet is not to count on it.

HOW MUCH DO I HAVE TO WORRY ABOUT HACKING?

To understand hacking, you first have to understand the reason the Internet was created. In the throes of the Cold War, American policy makers worried about how to maintain communication between cities in the event of a nuclear strike. Some kind of network was needed, but any kind of centralized command center for this network would be too vulnerable to attack. The answer, thought up by the RAND Corporation, a government think tank, was built upon two important principles.

The first was that the network would be a decentralized collection of computers. They would all be joined together, but no one computer would be more important or more functional than any other. Because there was no gatekeeper or mastermind setting up a system of control, each node in the network simply needed to be able to understand the communication protocol in order to pass messages along.

The second was that any information sent over this network would be broken into pieces, with each piece being sent to the recipient's destination via a random, individual route. The pieces would be reassembled once they'd all arrived at the other end.

The result of RAND's design is that it's very easy for other computers to hook into the system. The first network linked four computers. In three years the number had grown to thirty-seven. Today, the Internet connects over 42,500,000 servers talking to countless individual computers in just about every country.

While this anarchic style of architecture has allowed for the rapid growth of the Internet, it has also institutionalized certain problems. Because the system was designed to handle a fairly simple exchange of basic information—not the sophisticated transactions for business that require verification and encryption—there are lots of holes. The result is that for every attempt to make the Internet secure, there is another creative way to break the system. It simply wasn't designed to be what it has become.

Because the underlying technology of the Internet makes it difficult to prevent hacking, a sensible way to deal with it is to look beyond technology fixes. You must understand what motivates the hackers.

In this light, it's easy to see that your individual vulnerability is limited. Hackers typically want to disrupt companies, either because of a grudge against them or to get media attention. It is not as common for a hacker to attack your computer at home and mess with your personal data. There is no glory. Don't get me wrong: it isn't unheard of. It's just not all that likely.

If someone wanted to get into your computer at home, he would most likely use a Trojan horse. A Trojan horse is a piece of code that is disguised as another program, video clip, or game that you can be persuaded to download and install in your system. Once installed, the Trojan horse may do any number of things, including giving the hacker access to all your files and e-mails, or the ability to mess with your operating system to create messages that pop up on the screen.

More often than not, however, Trojan horses are used to enable more widespread attacks. One of the most common reasons to hijack an individual's computer is to recruit it for a "distributed denial of service" attack. By duping a huge number of computers to visit a Web site at the same time, a hacker can overwhelm the Web site's servers and prevent legitimate users from getting on. One of the most famous denial-of-service attacks was launched a few years ago. First Yahoo! was hit. Then, a few days later, eBay, CNN.com, Amazon.com, E*TRADE, and other major sites were taken down. The overwhelming traffic to these sites caused them to go offline for hours, resulting in an estimated $1.7 billion in lost business and other damages.

More recently, individual PCs have been hijacked by another Trojan horse to serve as middlemen for porn Web sites. Instead of connecting directly to the originator, anyone clicking on a spam advertisement for porn would connect to some random individual's computer that had been hijacked. That individual's computer would then be forced to connect to the porn site, get the content and pass it along to the requester. In this way, the purveyors of the adult content were able to remain anonymous to the end user—and any law enforcement.

The program that forced unwitting PC users to become porn providers didn't cause huge economic losses, and in many cases went unnoticed by the PC owners themselves. But it does illustrate the basic point: hacking into your computer at home is probably about stealing your bandwidth. It is not likely to result in loss of your personal and critical data. Anyone who wants to do that is going to hack into corporate computers—and into your accounts at major Web sites.

WHAT IS ACCOUNT HACKING?

Many seasoned Internet users take advantage of a number of online services. They may have sold something on eBay. They may use PayPal to pay for auction items. They may have an account with Amazon. They may use a password-management service like Microsoft's Passport. These services and Web sites are a favorite for a new kind of fraud: account hacking.

Account hacking involves tricking either you or the company you have the account with into giving up the information that is needed to pretend to be you online. In some cases, hackers rely on human gullibility, in others they rely on a weakness in software. In all cases, account hacking is the newest form of identity theft. It's just like a thief stealing your credit card number, except, in this case, it's your ability to use an online account that is stolen.

Where people are the weak link, the problem may be simply that they make the information that protects important services (like passwords and password hints) too easy to guess. The Web site eBay offers a classic example of how this might happen. When setting up an account, eBay asks you to create a question about something personal that only you can answer. Typical questions are things like a pet's name or the city of your birth. If you ever forget your password, you can go to your question screen and by answering the question correctly, start the process of creating a new password.

The problem is that the question screen is freely available to anyone to visit, and some eBay users, who obviously don't know this, also publish personal pages where they reveal all kinds of details about themselves, including the answer to their password question. A motivated account hacker can read a user's personal page, surf over to the question page and, with little difficulty, set the wheels in motion to change the password and to begin to sell fake items as the unwitting victim. In fairness to eBay, the company does send an e-mail to a user to verify his or her identity before granting access to the Password Change page. But not all sites are so careful about protecting users from their own stupid mistakes.

Another favorite trick of account hackers, called *phishing*, is to create a program that mimics the log-on screen for well-known sites, like PayPal. This screen is mailed to unsuspecting users along with a story about how the Web site is introducing a new feature or how the security department needs you to check your account. By typing your sensitive information into the faked screen, you send critical data both to the hacker and to the legitimate site. You never know that someone has now collected your password, or worse, your credit card number.

And then there are problems created by the software itself. Microsoft Passport is a system to store information on user names, passwords, and payment info, so that it can be shared automatically with sites you register with and shop at. This avoids the hassle of remembering passwords you don't use often or of retyping the same information over and over. Unfortunately, problems that make the system easy to compromise keep appearing. In the latest example, an engineer found that by typing in a URL with a Passport user name added on the end, he could request a password reset from the Passport servers. In other words, knowing only the user name for an account, he could effectively take it over.

If you choose obscure passwords and password hints, if you're careful about where you store them, if you ask questions about suspicious looking e-mail, chances are good that you'll stay out of trouble (see Taking Action on page 209 for more info). Now, if only it were so easy to protect the computers at the other end.

ARE CYBERTERRORISTS REAL?

The scariest kind of hacking occurs when corporations get broken into and your data gets stolen, or when the government systems meant to keep us safe are compromised.

Media has given us an image of hackers as juveniles with body piercing and green hair. Some security experts suggest that the kids get the headlines because they want them. They try to get caught. In truth, now that computers are more than a generation old, there is another class of grown-up hackers that we don't know much about. We don't know much about them because they don't want us to. These hackers are ex-CIA or KGB or Israeli intelligence agents. Or organized criminals.

In 2001, a huge hacking operation run by the Russian Mafia was uncovered. Systematically targeting over forty U.S. companies, hackers from Russian and Ukrainian groups had stolen the credit records of more than a million people. Following the theft, the victim companies were telephoned, told of the intrusion, and "invited" to pay for the consulting services of the group for protection. The director of an internet security center at Carnegie Mellon, CERT, reported almost 83,000 computer break-ins in 2002 (up from 9,859 in 1999).

While the targets of many hackers are large corporations, hacking attacks directed against government have acquired new urgency in the past few years. Information on the status of law enforcement investigations and data on individual citizens is all exposed. In the mid nineties, a group of hackers known as Phonemasters successfully invaded the FBI computers. In addition to playing pranks, they also notified drug dealers when they were being targeted by an FBI investigation.

The Department of Defense has long been an attractive target for hackers. A few years ago, it ran an exercise called "Eligible Receiver" in which employees of the NSA using commercially available software were asked to break into Pentagon computers. The results that we know about are less than encouraging. The team was able to take control of the Pacific command center, picking up power grids and the 911 system in nine cities along the way.

Even worse than messing with government computers, worries today include viruses that try to cripple our infrastructure. Phone systems, emergency coordination systems, power grids, water supply, law enforcement, and health systems—not to mention defense

WHAT IS THE GOVERNMENT DOING TO PROTECT AGAINST CYBERTERRORISM?

Even before 9/11, the U.S. Government was thinking about cyberterrorism. In 2000 a law that created an overall framework for managing information security went into effect.

As a result of that effort things have gotten somewhat better, but according to the GAO there is still work to do. By mid-2003, all of the twenty-four agencies they reviewed had poor security programs in place and poor control of who could access their systems. Almost a third of the agencies reviewed still hadn't gotten around to assessing all of the risks they faced. Twenty out of twenty-four agencies would be unlikely to continue functioning in the event of a significant cyberattack on their systems.

The good news is that the Department of Homeland Security is working on it. We can only hope that our bureaucracies can shore up their systems before the bad guys come knocking.

---

systems—increasingly are part of vast computer networks that can be brought down.

Given the high-stakes nature of these intrusions, we have a very legitimate reason to be quite alarmed indeed. Most security experts don't speak of *whether or not* we'll have a major terrorist cyberattack, but *when*. Raids in 2002, which turned up computers that suggest that al Qaeda has been training recruits to hack into these types of networks, indicate that the worries aren't entirely without basis.

CHECKUP

Now it's time to scan your systems. If you've been paying attention, you know that this means a lot more than looking at your hard drive. Online security is part technology and part common sense.

This checkup will give you a feeling for how you're doing on the both fronts.

Basic Understanding

Before launching a single program, we need to set the rules of the road. You need to be able to answer the following questions (or know where to find the answer quickly). In case you're getting nervous, these questions aren't about understanding technology. If the Internet is a car, these questions aren't about how the engine works. They are the equivalent of knowing which pedal is the brake and which is the accelerator.

If you can't answer any one of the following questions, you're like an irresponsible thirteen-year-old who is convinced that he can drive a car—until he runs into the tree. If you can't answer the following questions, get the manual, buy a computer book, or call up a trusted computer guru friend. You are in over your head.

- What operating system is running on your computer?
- What e-mail program do you use?
- What browser and version number are you using to surf the Web?
- Do you store passwords in your browser or other software program?
- What type of Internet connection do you have?
- Do you have your own personal firewall?
- Do you have antivirus software installed on your machine?
- Have you updated your virus definitions in the past week?
- Do you keep backups of sensitive data?

How Clean Is Your Machine?

Now that you've passed the basic test to drive on the Internet superhighway, it's time to check your defenses. The first task is to understand how much tracking you are subject to, if you have any viruses, and if you have known security holes waiting for someone to come through. For that, you want to assess your operating system, your antivirus software, how many cookies you've got going, and if you have unwanted spyware.

Patches and Updates

It's always a battle to determine when upgrading is worth the money, the hassle, and the potential for introducing more problems than you fix on your machine. But here's another consideration: software with known security vulnerabilities needs to be fixed. One way to fix them is to keep your operating system and browser on the latest version.

If you are too concerned that a new release just isn't stable enough, or for any other countless and valid reasons you don't want to upgrade at the moment, you need to stay on top of whether or not there are security patches available for your system. Not installing a patch is the number-one reason that computers get broken into. Check now: Is your operating system and browser software fully up-to-date? Are there any patches to solve security problems that you haven't installed?

If you don't know the answers to these questions off the top of your head, here are a few places to check for info:

Microsoft's site for Windows and Internet Explorer issues
www.microsoft.com/security/

Netscape's site for Netscape browser issues:
wp.netscape.com/security/notes/index.html

Apple's site for Macintosh issues:
http://info.apple.com/usen/security/index.html

Cookies

Do you know where to find your cookie file? If so, take a look at it. The codes probably won't make sense, but you can see who has been tracking you. If nothing looks too surprising or disconcerting, you're done. If not, you might want to take a few simple steps to reduce the cookie tracking that goes on. We'll talk about a few different ways to do this in the first topic of the Taking Action section. If you don't know how to find your cookie file, don't worry. Follow the suggestions in the Taking Action section.

Spyware

Next, download and install a program to scan your system for spyware. In several recent studies of broadband users and users of file-sharing programs, more than 90 percent of computers were found to have spyware installed on them. Remember that spyware is generally nothing more than aggressive ad tracking, so this isn't too much to get worried about. But it's worth a check every now and then. Both PC and Mac users will find a good source of free spyware-tracking programs at CNET's www.download.com.

Viruses

Finally, look at your antivirus software—which I'm *sure* you have. If you haven't done it in the past week, now is the time to launch your antivirus program. What was the last date the virus definitions were updated? Given that 250 to 450 new viruses are released each month, you aren't doing yourself a favor by waiting.

If your virus definitions are more than a month old, visit the Web site for the maker of your antivirus software to see if you can download more-recent information. If you can't do this for some reason, it's time to upgrade your software. Go to an online or real-world store and buy a new copy. Read www.consumerreports.org, or talk to a salesperson for recommendations.

Once you've gotten fully updated antivirus software running on your machine, start the program and double-check its settings. Make sure that your entire computer is being checked for viruses (one virus manipulated protective software so that the software wouldn't check where the virus was hiding), and that all file types get scanned when you open or download them. Now, run the thing and see how you do.

No matter how many viruses you uncover, by updating your software you've already passed this test!

Are You an Easy Target for Terrorists or Organized Crime?

We read a lot about viruses. They can be damaging to our own computers and take a lot of time to sort out. They can also bring the infrastructure supporting the Internet to its knees. Because becoming infected with malicious code that forces your computer to spam in-boxes or participate in a denial-of-service attack has an impact that goes far beyond your own hard drive, it's time to think about your vulnerability on this front as a danger to the country you live in.

Seriously. It is unlikely but not impossible that your unprotected computer could help terrorists do a lot of damage. The following questions are designed to help you understand how easy you make it for a terrorist or criminal to recruit your computer for their devious ends.

- Do you open e-mails from senders you don't recognize?
- Do you click on links in e-mails and instant messages from unknown senders when they appear interesting?
- Do you leave your computer connected to the Internet with your browser open when you are not using it?
- Do you forget to update and run your antivirus software at least once a week? Or do you not have it at all?
- If you connect to the Internet with a broadband connection, do you still need to get a firewall?

If you answered "yes" to any of these questions, you are in danger and you are potentially putting the rest of us in danger, too.

TAKING ACTION

Now that you've covered the basics by doing the checkup, you are ready to take steps to increase your protection online. A lot of protection can come from simple actions that reduce profiling, assure the safety of online accounts, and vet where you shop and register. Technology can also help keep your computer from harming other computers, but, as with all else online, what you do plays a bigger role than you might think.

Use the Information Technology You Were Born with (a.k.a. Your Brain)

The smartest software program in the world isn't going to protect you if you want to behave stupidly. So don't! Here are some basic commonsense things you can do to decrease the possibility of unwanted intrusions or becoming a victim of fraud.

If You Want to Reduce Profiling

- Think twice about what personal information you make available to Web sites—from giving them your e-mail for a free newsletter, to your credit card number for a purchase. You are often the source of your own data. Consider it this way, if you don't register with any Web sites, they can't track you. They may track your computer, but they have no idea who you are.

  Given how much is available on the Web these days, it's really unlikely that you won't find some special thing that you just have to sign up for. In those cases, elect to offer as little information as you feel is necessary, and, if the information isn't critical to the transaction, you can always choose to be a little bit less than complete or accurate, if you know what I mean.

- Next, change the cookie setting on your browser. Newer browsers offer very-easy-to-use tools to manage cookies. You should be able to find a privacy menu in your browser software that allows you to determine which Web sites you will allow cookies from and which you won't, or to delete cookies. GetNet-Wise, a partnership between computer companies and public interest groups, offers an online tutorial customized for your particular browser at http://privacy.getnetwise.org/browsing/tools/.

If you're having trouble figuring out the settings for your particular browser and a trusted computer guru friend can't help, you can create a cookie to opt out of tracking by the larger ad networks. This won't affect any of your other cookies, but it will set a flag for the two largest networks that you don't wish to be profiled anymore. Details on how to set an "opt-out" cookie can be found at http://www.privacychoices.org/ and http://www.networkadvertising.org/.

If You Want to Be More Secure from Account Hacking

- Use hard-to-guess passwords for important accounts. We talked about this in chapter 2 and it isn't any less true now. Don't use your name, your pet's name, or any of the numbers in your Social Security number. When programs allow you, use a mix of symbols and letters. Mix upper and lower case.

- For those accounts that are silly or don't contain essential information, feel free to use your name (or your pet's name) as your password. Really. Just don't use the same password you use for your important accounts. If you think the password guards something relatively trivial, the folks storing the passwords probably think so, too. They are much less likely to have put protection in place against serious hackers, and your password is more vulnerable. This is not the place to store the same password you use to protect valuable data. Chances are really, really good that Bank of America has more protection for its servers than the music fan club you just joined.

- As a rule of thumb, do *not* store your passwords in your browser. Get a paper notebook that sits beside the computer if need be (provided the location is secure—don't do this at work, for example). Given the problems that exist with password-storage services such as Microsoft's Passport, why would you volunteer to be a guinea pig for the fix? If you're not the type to sign up for the first human trials of an experimental vaccine, don't use Passport.

- And for goodness sake, don't fall for e-mails with fake information requests or share information about yourself online that gives someone a hint to your password (or, as we saw with eBay, your password hint question).

If You're Thinking of Registering or Shopping with a Particular Web Site

- Look for the company's contact info (generally found via an "about us" link at the bottom of the page). Make sure that you can get ahold of the company in more than one way. If you experience any kind of problems, it can be very frustrating to track someone down with nothing more than an e-mail address.

- Read their privacy policy. The privacy policy is a statement from the company that details what information about you is collected and how it is used. Most sites have a link at the bottom of their page to the privacy policy. If you have to hunt around too much for one, that's a bad sign, now isn't it?

- Check for any certification. Certification agencies like TRUSTe and the Better Business Bureau will vouch for the fact that a company is as advertised. If you have any problems with the site that is certified, you can complain to the certification agency, which will generally be quite active in helping you out. That's what they do, after all.

When Anti-This-or-That Software Makes Sense

Before you spend a dime on additional software to get rid of viruses or hackers, it's really important to understand that software is only as smart as the guy who programmed it. If that guy figured out absolutely every possible combination of events and read the future with perfect precision *and* wrote code that contained absolutely *no* errors, the software will be a magic bullet that can offer you absolute protection. Since that magic confluence of circumstance has never occurred, nor is likely ever to occur, you would do well to remember that software can't do your thinking for you. There is no magic bullet that will eliminate spam or keep you safe. You will always need to exercise judgment and restraint.

If you bear that in mind, there are many different kinds of programs that can help you in the battle for secure computing. Get-NetWise (www.getnetwise.org) has compiled a comprehensive but easy-to-read tutorial on all the basic issues. CNET (www.cnet.com), Anchordesk (www.zdnet.com), and *PC World* (www.pcworld.com) are terrific places to get started learning about (and even downloading) both free and paid programs.

How to Be a Good Cybercitizen

When it comes to corporate responsibility or government defense against cyberterrorism, there isn't a whole lot that you can change as one person. However, you can do your part to keep your computer from being recruited to be a part of the problem. You can protect other computers by protecting your own.

The Cyber Security Alliance, a partnership between government and technology companies devoted to educating computer users across the country, makes the following suggestions:

1. Use protection software ("antivirus software") and keep it up-to-date.
2. Don't open e-mail from unknown sources.
3. Use hard-to-guess passwords.
4. Protect your computer from Internet intruders—use "firewalls."
5. Don't share access to your computers with strangers. Learn about file-sharing risks.
6. Disconnect from the Internet when not in use.

7. Back up your computer data.
8. Regularly download security protection update "patches."
9. Check your security on a regular basis. When you change your clocks for Daylight Savings Time, reevaluate your computer security.
10. Make sure your family members and/or your employees know what to do if your computer becomes infected. (Just because you're smart enough to read this book, you can't expect everyone else who sits at the family computer to figure this out through osmosis.)

Let me add my own two cents. Don't open any attachment files that you get via e-mail unless you are absolutely sure that you know the source *and* you're expecting to get something. This is especially true of files that end in .vbs or .exe. Those extensions as much as tell you that someone is planning to execute a script that affects your machine.

And a final word about software called personal firewalls that offers you protection from Internet-based intrusions. The key to using a firewall is to make sure that it is set up properly. Studies show that more than half of the people who have taken the time to buy a firewall haven't set it up so that it actually offers them protection. For information on how firewalls work and advice on setting them up, start with CERT Coordination Center's Home Network Security Tips (http://www.cert.org/tech_tips/home_networks.html).

RESOURCES

The technology industry changes very quickly, but keeping in touch with what is happening at a high level is an absolute must if you use a computer. Some very good mainstream sources are listed below.

For insight into national security issues relating to viruses and the like, the CyberSecurity Alliance or the White House CyberSpace Initiative are both good places to start.

- GetNetWise (www.getnetwise.org)
- CNET (www.cnet.com)
- Zdnet Anchordesk (www.anchordesk.com)
- *PC World* (www.pcworld.com)
- Cyber Security Alliance (www.staysafeonline.info)
- The National Strategy to Secure Cyperspace (http://www. whitehouse.gov/pcipb/)

10. Watching Out for Monitors in the Sky and in Your Pocket: Mobile Tracking

IN THIS CHAPTER:
How mobile tracking works, how it is expanding, how you can affect and keep on top of what is developing

Gosh. It's starting to sound downright Orwellian. Someone is tracking every dime we spend, every e-mail we send, and everything we do in between. Is there anywhere we can go to escape the tracking?

Not really. More and more, thanks again to new technologies, there is no place left to hide. There is an eye in the sky, and in your car, and—very soon—even in your pocket. We're now being monitored just about everywhere.

This chapter is about mobile tracking—technologies that can track your every movement, whether you're driving across the country or simply shaving in your bathroom. We'll discuss two key aspects of mobile tracking: tracking the location of things (and people), and monitoring how things are used, no matter where they are.

As with just about every other kind of tracking we've discussed, mobile tracking is being developed with the best of intentions and with our convenience and safety in mind. The benefits are real, but, as with most things, they come at a cost, with the potential for misuse and abuse. As always, it's up to you to decide if the blanket of security afforded by these systems is comforting or suffocating.

In other words, despite the fact that some of what we'll talk about in this chapter is still under development or sounds a little bit out there, the same principle from previous applies: the more you know about who is doing the tracking and why, the better you can protect yourself from the downsides and take advantage of the upsides.

HOW IS MOBILE TRACKING USED?

Probably two of the most important changes in the modern world have been the ability to make things very small (and still functional) and the ability to put stuff up into outer space. The combination of the two has led to the ability to implant small transmitters into objects and then follow their signals with a network of satellites up in the sky.

This type of tracking has proven very popular for keeping an eye on "mobile assets." Taxi fleet operators, messenger companies, and rental car companies all find value in knowing where their cars are at all times. There are a host of antitheft tracking devices you can buy to keep your car from being one of the million-plus vehicles that get stolen each year. Emergency rescue networks looking for downed planes and missing boats have used tracking devices for years.

Rather than tracking vehicles, some companies are more worried about keeping an eye on what is inside them. As deliveries go from truck to warehouse to destination, the FBI estimates about $12 billion of goods goes missing. Little radio chips implanted in packages can be followed to monitor how, when, and where trucking companies move shipments about. Little radio chips may soon end up inside consumer goods, like razors, to help alert retailers when shelf stocks are low or when a suspected shoplifting is underway.

It shouldn't be surprising to learn that there is also a lot of interest in tracking people. Navy ships have supplied sailors and visitors with smart cards that can be tracked. Calling muster happens much faster now. Criminals with GPS ankle bracelets can be released from prison but still watched closely. Various kinds of tracking devices are also available to pet owners and parents of smaller children. Although parents generally opt for a bracelet of some sort, at least one company sells concerned guardians a microchip that gets implanted under the skin. Yikes!

In some cases, the tracking isn't used to follow where you go but to alert someone when you get there. Traffic congestion caused by a lot of cars in the same place at the same time can be reduced through the timing of traffic lights or freeway on-ramp lights. Little chips in passbooks or ATM cards can tell banks who is entering a branch—if you have a high balance, you will get better service the moment you cross the threshold.

Sometimes tracking is for convenience: a reader that identifies when you drive through a toll booth lets you pay fares automatically. Sometimes it's for protection: a 911 system for mobile phones will be able to pinpoint your location if you can't speak. Sometimes it's for national security: following a suspect truck as it travels across the country can help prepare for a potentially nasty event.

HOW DOES MOBILE TRACKING WORK?

Understanding all the details of the technology isn't terribly important, but it is worth understanding the basic advances that have allowed the mobile revolution to understand its weaknesses. Most tracking systems rely either on satellites or radio towers.

Satellites have been in the sky since Sputnik launched in 1957. Although they've long been used for a host of military and scientific purposes, not to mention weather forecasting, the biggest impact on each of us has probably been the Global Positioning System—GPS for short. Twenty-four satellites (plus three backups) make GPS work. The orbit of each satellite has been carefully calibrated with the orbits of all the other satellites so that, at any given point in time, at least four of the GPS satellites can be "seen" by a receiver on Earth.

Essentially, each of the four satellites sends out a signal describing its position relative to you. By combining the signals (using a process called triangulation) and by comparing your position to

HIDING CELL PHONE TOWERS

Creating a network of towers that relay signals to one another has proven to be an interesting challenge. Not only are there technical issues of where to place antennae for the best coverage, there are communities of people who are less than certain they want yet another ugly utility tower in their front yard. The need to work with the people living near planned antennae sites has spawned a wonderfully inventive new industry: tower camouflage.

Some camouflage is pretty simple: a fat flagpole is really a tower. Others are more wild: radio antennae have been disguised as palm trees, church steeples, rock formations, and in one notable case, an entire lighthouse. For a fun, quick peek at how creatively towers can be made to blend into the scenery, check out a few of the best practitioners in the field: Stealth Network Technologies (www.stealthsite.com) and the Camouflage division of the Larson Company (www.utilitycamo.com).

maps loaded into your device, your GPS receiver can figure out exactly where it is. Depending on the equipment used, GPS can pinpoint your exact location anywhere in the world to within six feet (the military version, which delivers smart bombs to precise locations and to determine the location of people and equipment on the battlefield, can get a bit more precise).

As spiffy as this sounds, there are technical glitches with GPS. The Earth's atmosphere, mountains, and large man-made objects such as skyscrapers can interfere with satellite transmissions. Also, the military occasionally degrades or disrupts the GPS signals for reasons of national security.

As an alternative to satellites, some tracking systems rely on land-based networks of radio towers. These antennae, about 130,000 throughout the country, assure us of cell phone coverage in a lot of places. Cell phone antennae are used much like GPS, except that, instead of triangulating a position using satellites, the position of a handheld device is calculated by comparing position information relayed by antennae. Shortcomings with this system are that, even with 130,000 antennae deployed, there are still big parts of the country without coverage.

Regardless of which system is used to determine your location, the next step is to communicate that information back to someone else. With some systems, another satellite is used. Your location (expressed as latitude and longitude coordinates), along with some unique code that identifies who you are, is uploaded to a satellite using a small dish. With other systems, your coordinates are transmitted using the land-based mobile networks—essentially making a cell phone call back to a central computer telling it of your whereabouts. The receiver of the information now knows exactly where you are—in real time, with pretty decent accuracy.

WHAT ABOUT TRACKING MOBILE PHONES?

The notion of using a cell phone to track location was introduced as part of the deployment of an enhanced emergency system called E-911. The goal for E-911 is to pinpoint the location of anyone calling the emergency number, which, not surprisingly, is helpful to rescuers trying to find someone who is lost or unable to speak. The ability to identify a caller's location from a land-based telephone has been in place for years—911 operators automatically get the exact street address of calls made from land lines without anyone having to say a word.

Today, however, the National Emergency Number Association reports that almost one-third of emergency calls come from mobile phones, and the government felt it was time to extend location identification to mobile users.

Although E-911 is currently available only in a few counties, the FCC has targeted December 2005 for a full network across the country. This may or may not happen. E-911 has presented a tremendous challenge to the entire wireless industry. It is proving to be a fundamentally different and far more difficult task to locate mobile phones than it is to locate stationary phones. The biggest problem seems to be developing a system that works in a variety of different environments.

Most wireless operators can already locate the nearest cell phone antenna being used during a call. But, as you can probably guess, there are more antennae serving the hoards of people using cell phones in crowded cities, and fewer antennae in rural areas where bandwidth isn't as much in demand. The result is that AT&T can pinpoint someone to the block they're on in urban areas, but only to a several mile radius elsewhere.

A few major carriers are trying a variation of antenna triangulation to build their bit of the wireless E-911 system—and struggling. If the antennae used to calculate a phone's position aren't plentiful enough, the precision of the predicted location isn't good enough. Other carriers are using GPS technology, but they've got problems, too. The GPS does well in rural areas but isn't as effective in cities, where the satellite signal is often lost in buildings or underground parking garages. Despite the current hiccups, it's a safe bet that some new technology or some efficient combination of technologies will allow the carriers to meet the FCC goals eventually. It's just not yet clear when or what those technologies will be.

WHY WOULD I WANT ANY MOBILE TRACKING?

By far the best things to come out of mobile tracking are the systems that offer help when you really need it. Some new cars are equipped with systems that detect when the car has been in an accident (by detecting the deployment of airbags) and will call 911 for help automatically, communicating your exact location via GPS to emergency personnel—even if you're unable to talk.

The E-911 system was proposed, in part, because of devastating phone calls to 911 where victims were unable to communicate their location. One nineteen-year-old woman managed to dial 911 from her cell phone after she'd been abducted from a shopping mall. Because she couldn't speak, operators were forced to listen helplessly for hours as she was driven around, assaulted, and eventually murdered by her abductor. Another woman was able to call 911 as her car plunged into a Miami canal. Unable to offer her precise location in the water, she drowned before emergency workers could locate her.

Sometimes you might want tracking very much indeed.

IS SOMEONE WATCHING HOW—NOT JUST WHERE—I DRIVE?

You bet. First, let's take a look at how this is done using the same technologies that determine where you are.

Consider this story. Acme Car Rental in New Haven, Connecticut, used a GPS system in each of its cars that reported back to the agency the location of each car in real time. When you know where someone is and what time they got there, it isn't too difficult to do the math and figure out how long it took the car to go from point A to point B—in other words, how fast the car was going.

So Acme programmed the system to record whenever the vehicle was speeding. According to the rental contract offered by Acme, "Vehicles driven in excess of posted speed limits will be charged a $150 fee per occurrence." Although the language appeared in bold type at the top of the contract, the wording was vague enough that

---

TRAFFIC CAMS

Most of these cameras take a picture of your license plate. Depending on local law, there may be restrictions against photographing drivers. In some cases it is illegal to photograph car passengers.

In cases where a citation may be issued—rail-crossing or toll-booth violations, speeding, or red light–running—pictures are examined by a police officer. In certain jurisdictions, where red-light running is classified similar to a parking ticket instead of as a moving violation, the vehicle owner is held responsible for the red-light violation, regardless of who was driving.

consumers got caught by surprise. One, in particular, was quite dismayed to find his bank account debited an extra $450 after he returned an Acme rental. The renter, James Turner, filed a small-claims case as well as a complaint with the state's consumer-protection division.

After investigation, the consumer-protection agency ordered the car rental company to stop its practice without better disclosure, explicit customer consent, and fees in line with the damage to the vehicle (more like 37 cents than $150). Despite this case, GPS systems still exist in cars, and the monitoring system used by Acme is still used by larger rental companies like Budget and Thrifty, although to provide directions or assist drivers who have unwittingly locked themselves out of their car.

At this point, the 2.4 million subscribers who pay a monthly fee to GPS tracking companies like OnStar haven't really experienced problems with monitoring, but there is at least one story of a man whose OnStar system fingered him as the culprit in a hit-and-run accident. Commercial companies are pretty careful with driver data, and reporting the hit-and-run case was entirely reasonable. However, the incident does underscore the fact that more active monitoring is possible and that the potential for abuse exists.

WHAT IF I DON'T DRIVE A RENTAL CAR OR PAY FOR A TRACKING SERVICE?

In the past ten years, mobile tracking has become a big thing for drivers of all cars. The U.S. government has been investing in something it has dubbed the "Intelligent Transportation System," or ITS for short. This program was mandated by Congress in 1991 to coordinate the development and deployment of new, smart, road systems in the United States. Intelligent Transportation is a broad program designed to address everything from managing freeway or city traffic to routing emergency vehicles to collecting fares automatically at toll booths and bus stops to presenting highway alerts on LED signs.

An increasingly common example of intelligent transportation can be found at toll booths across the country. By placing an identifying device called a "transponder" in their car, drivers simply need to whiz by sensors in toll booths or at the roadside, and computers automatically deduct the toll payment from their bank account. Processing involves validation of identification information and vehicle classification, creation of a transaction record, and— and this is what gets some folks thinking—double-checking data such as any overdue parking tickets, to see if you should be stopped for a quick chat with the law.

Because under the ITS program fare collection is part of the same organization working on freeway management, it shouldn't be too surprising that the two initiatives are getting tied together. As an example of a system that we will all be seeing very soon, San Francisco installed a hundred and fifty roadside sensors to collect information from drivers who had signed up for FastTrak, its automatic toll-payment system. The sensors are able to report the speed and location of the 200,000 FastTrak transponder-equipped cars over five hundred miles of freeway. All of this information is transmitted back to a central command center where real people look at it and make decisions based on it about how many emergency vehicles to dispatch to an accident, or if they should change ramp metering.

The information from central command is also made available over the Internet and by phone to each and every one of us. A few years ago, the FCC set aside the telephone number 511 for traffic-alert information. By calling 511, motorists in any area with smart highways can learn of up-to-the minute projections on estimated travel times between locations. They can also find out about crashes on their proposed route and other delays.

While you can probably imagine how this information can be quite useful to reduce your morning commute, consider how handy it is for anyone who drives for a living. As one courier working in Florida notes, he loves using the service to plan which way is best to crisscross his territory in any given hour.

Systems similar to FastTrak (or E-ZPass, or IPass in other parts of the country) are also being set up for riders of public

---

511 COMING TO A NEIGHBORHOOD NEAR YOU

As of spring 2004, twenty-one states had all or part of their territory covered with a 511 system. As more freeways come online, it's worth checking with the Department of Transportation Web site to see if you're covered (http://www.fhwa.dot.gov/trafficinfo/511.htm).

---

transportation. Fare collection for public transit fares and even parking fees generally rely on cards. These cards range from a cardboard or plastic "swipe" card with limited data storage capability to a "smart" card containing a lot more room and processing power. Payment processing can be initiated by direct contact like a swipe, or sometimes by proximity. As with toll-collection systems, a transaction record is created and stored in a central location. And, as with other systems, users are checked for violation enforcement.

By now you may be breathing a sigh of relief. You don't drive a rental car, you don't have a GPS and you don't have a FastTrack-type transponder. This issue doesn't affect you, right? Well, even if your car isn't equipped with this stuff, you might be surprised to learn that your driving is still being monitored.

HOW IS MY DRIVING MONITORED EVEN IF I DON'T HAVE A GPS OR A TRANSPONDER INSTALLED?

In a shift that has dismayed many weekend tinkerers to no end, computers were introduced into car engines in the early 1980s. These computers were originally little more than sensors that monitored engine temperature, air density, and accelerator force to calculate the right combination of fuel and air for the best gas mileage.

Since the introduction of fuel injection, the number of computers in cars has risen dramatically. Shifting gears in automatics transmissions, firing spark plugs, antilock braking, airbag deployment, and

What Your Airbag Knows about You

Data tracked by airbags varies from car to car, but probably includes the following:

- Vehicle speed (five seconds before impact)
- Engine speed (five seconds before impact)
- Brake status (five seconds before impact)
- Throttle position (five seconds before impact)
- State of driver's seat belt switch (on or off position)

even seat memory require simple computers, also called Electronic Control Units (ECUs).

With one notable exception, most of the information that your car currently collects gets discarded. There is simply no place to put it. That one exception is the airbag. In something similar to the black box recorder we've come to rely on for information on airplane crashes, many cars now contain reasonably sophisticated computers that record a wealth of data related to accidents or near accidents (defined opaquely as something severe enough to "wake up" the sensing devices). These are called Event Data Recorders or sometimes Crash Data Recorders.

In the past few years, a private company has introduced a software package that translates all of the data collected by airbag computers into something readable—and analyzable. Information from certain GM, Ford, and Isuzu cars can now be downloaded following an event to get a clear picture of the car's performance in the seconds before a crash. Other makes of car will be similarly supported soon.

Although designed to be used to find ways to increase the safety of moving vehicles, crash data is already being used by law enforcement and insurance companies to combat fraud. The National Highway Traffic Safety Administration is considering storing the data from airbag crash data in a central database.

The implications are significant: if you are speeding a little at the time of a crash, your insurance company could refuse to pay your claim. It's not hard to imagine that information like this will also be of great interest to employers, your parents (if you're a teenager), and anyone wanting to sue over an accident. Your car warranty could even be voided when your dealer discovers you've been driving too fast or otherwise "abusing" your car.

As with crash data, other information currently collected by your car will almost certainly become less disposable. Car industry gurus suggest that 90 percent of the changes to cars in the coming years will involve increasing the power of the ECUs. The result is a growing desire to want to be able to download new software into our cars' computers. Since it's a pain to find you and tell you to come into the dealer whenever an update is ready, part of the future vision includes being able to zap the information into your car remotely, using something like the Internet.

Once installed, the technology can work both ways. In addition to receiving updates from a dealer, you can also send them updates about your car. Even though you won't have a hard disk under your hood, the dealer can have one in his office. Add a GPS that pinpoints your location to the growing ability to send information from your car back to someone else, and suddenly things like how hard you hit the accelerator to make it through an intersection while the light was yellow can be logged. It is entirely possible that everything you do in your car, not just where you go, will be pieced together before too much longer.

WHAT THINGS BESIDES CARS ARE BEING TRACKED?

When computers were put in cars, no one envisioned their use to tattle on fast drivers. It's that aspect of information collection that has folks up in arms over the latest tracking gizmos: radio frequency identification (RFID) tags, often called simply "radio tags," that can be embedded in all kinds of consumer goods. Move over smart cars. Now we have smart razors.

Actually, RFID has been the basis of a fair bit of the mobile tracking we've already discussed. It is a basic technology in which a thing transmits information to something else, which then identifies the thing and processes the information it sends.

The recent change has been a simplification of the transmitter that has allowed RFID chips to become both small and very cheap. Today's tiny tags are about the size of a speck of pepper and do nothing more than emit a unique ID that can be picked up by sensors located nearby. Unlike bar codes, which, when scanned, can identify a product type, RFID chips can identify each and every unique bag of potato chips.

Although their use will undoubtedly become more pervasive in the next decade, right now RFID tags are used mainly to help stores keep track of their inventory. A few stores have pioneered smart shelves that read RFID tags to be able to alert a clerk when a shelf needs restocking. A few others have put smart checkout into place. Stroll by a reader with a cart full of tagged products and the scanning can happen all at once, instead of the item-by-item method required for traditional bar codes.

But a real limitation with RFID chips is that, in order to make them cheap enough to be put into something that you're only going to pay $2.95 for, they really can't do a whole lot. There is absolutely no way that the signal emitted from an RFID tag in your razor will be strong enough to talk to satellites in the sky or to the mobile phone networks to share the secrets of your shaving habits with the manufacturer. It can't go more than a few feet. This means that once you take your RFID-tagged razor home, unless you've gone to the trouble of installing sensors in your medicine chest, the manufacturer has no idea what you're up to. Some appliance makers do envision a smart refrigerator that can read its contents and order replacements from the grocer for you, but those developments are still a bit away.

Outside the home, it is true that you have less control about the presence or absence of sensors. Remember the smart passbook example? In this case, the tiny computer speck implanted in a passbook *is* read as you walk by the sensor the bank has put in its own door. Similarly, one clothing retailer experimented with the technology and thought that it could identify you as a previous purchaser when you passed by sensors embedded throughout their stores. Privacy advocates are concerned that chips implanted in shoes can be used to record who crosses a sensor in the entrance to a sporting event or political rally.

In all of these cases, the ability to figure out anything interesting about you requires a traditional database. The unique ID is meaningless, until it can be tied to your profile info collected elsewhere by the bank or retailer or cops. The jury is still out on how valuable this type of profiling will be to the companies who will have to pay for the infrastructure. When it comes to tracking inventory—a problem where common, everyday mistakes cost manufacturers and retailers up to $60 billion a year—the benefits make sense. Many stores have suggested that trailing the 200 billion plus individual products sold annually is simply too much data for them to use in a meaningful way.

We'll have to wait a little bit more to see how RFID impacts our daily life. The takeaway for the moment is that this isn't a tracking device, it's a profiling device. Depending on how much you care about profiling, you can decide how much you care about RFID.

SHOULD I BE WORRIED ABOUT ALL THIS MONITORING?

In case you're wondering if there is something to worry about here, it's worth considering a few mitigating factors.

With the exception of systems being set up to monitor commercial vehicles as they crisscross the country, most ITS mobile tracking systems have been designed to monitor a fairly local area. In cases where the scope is more local, the systems involve pretty simple receiving and transmitting devices. An array of sensors on roads that include things like radar, acoustic devices, infrared scanners, magnetic loops embedded in the freeway, and video cameras talk to a device that is located in your car. The device in your car transmits to each of the various road sensors it passes. In other words, the tracking isn't comprehensive in the way that it is with a satellite that peers down on the entire Earth. It's restricted to wherever sensors have been set up. Chances are extremely good that urban environments will find it cost-effective to create smart roads; more rural communities may not.

It's also encouraging to note that, unlike a lot of consumer-profiling systems that were created in more naïve times, the intelligent transportation network is being developed in a world where privacy considerations are already a concern. System architects are aware that consumers will not willingly sign up for a system that tracks their every move. Because automatic toll collection saves money for states, they want it to work. The tracking systems have been designed to assure that routine activity would not be monitored for other reasons.

The FastTrak system in San Francisco, for example, records exactly who you are and when you cross a bridge. It needs to in order to justify the fact that it just charged you a few bucks for taking the Golden Gate. The system that manages traffic flow, on the other hand, doesn't ever need to know who you are—simply that a car is somewhere. As each FastTrak car passes a sensor, the sensor reads the FastTrak ID, scrambles it using an encryption algorithm, and notes the scrambled ID in a log. This generic ID makes no reference to a car owner's ID or information. The next time you drive over or past a sensor, computers recognize your scrambled ID and calculate how long it took you to get from point A to point B. In this way, travel times can be determined and points of congestion identified, but no record that you yourself provided the data is ever made. What's more, all the data is purged at the end of each day. Since no 511 employee will ever have access to the FastTrak data (only the encrypted numbers), owners of speeding cars can't be tagged for tickets because of 511 data when they finally do slow down.

To show that they really mean business, the managers of the California 511 system suggest that there is a simple way not to participate in this new tracking: when you're not going through a toll booth, simply put a Mylar bag over the FastTrak sensor. They have even mailed bags out to all current FastTrak customers to make their priorities clear.

So, what about the privacy considerations of the E-911 system? Here, too, privacy concerns were addressed up front. Access to information about your cell phone's location is limited by law. The

Wireless Communications and Public Safety Act of 1999, the law that created the E-911 system, states that you must specifically agree to have your location information made available to commercial vendors. In other words, you have to actively sign up with companies wanting to sell you access to driving directions, restaurant recommendations, or other services that give you information based on where you happen to be.

Other monitoring, like in your car or using RFID, is more about profiling than watching where you go. In some cases, as with airbags, there is little that you can do about it, but the use of that information is relatively rare. As more information gets exchanged between your car and your mechanic, we will probably see increased efforts to address potential abuse. In the case of RFID, the architects of the new radio tags have been very clear to address possible problems up front. Each RFID chip can be "killed" upon request. If we do get to a point where your refrigerator does watch your calories for you and you don't trust the grocer to turn off the RFID chip, it isn't unlikely that a household device that zaps RFID chips will be invented. Think of it as the shredder for the twenty-first century.

Knowing about these safeguards, you may determine that the balance between convenience and intrusion has been struck fairly well when it comes to the systems we've been considering. By and large, I'd agree with you. The big warning, however, is that having an acceptable state of affairs today doesn't guarantee that we'll have it tomorrow. The use of data collected from mobile tracking is still new enough that big mistakes haven't happened yet. And it's not hard to imagine how the data collection can be expanded in ways that do cross a line. As we will see in the next chapter, restrictions on the use of tracking by law enforcement are a little less comforting.

CHECKUP

Tracking can be a lifesaver, literally. In cases where it begins to feel intrusive, it's still pretty easy to beat. The following checkups are designed to make you aware of the amount of tracking in your world and to determine what tracking is useful and what isn't.

Get to Know Your Mobile Phone

If you use a cell phone, get to know what it can and cannot do when it comes to E-911. You can try reading the user's manual, or going to the company's Web sites, but, for the real dirt, find a dealer near you. For best service, find a copy of your mobile phone bill. Who do you actually buy service from? Look for an 800 number on the bill and call it to find the closest authorized dealer.

Once you've found the right place and established a rapport with the sales guy there, you'll want to learn if your phone, and your mobile service provider, uses GPS location or some other technology to be E-911 compliant. You'll want to find out how you disable the system on your phone, if desired. You'll want to hear about all the services that mobile tracking makes available to you and why you shouldn't turn it off. You'll want to learn about the state of E-911 deployment in your area.

After you've had a good chat with the sales guy about E-911 capabilities and other location-dependent marketing programs available with your phone, you can determine if you want to disable tracking from your phone, buy a different phone, or possibly even switch to a different provider.

Do You Participate In a FastTrak or E-ZPass System?

You've already considered the implications of providing your personal ID and bank information if you've signed up for this. The extra consideration is the state of 511 deployment in your area. The quickest and easiest way to find out is simply to pick up the phone and dial 511. What happens?

If you find that 511 traffic monitoring is in place in your area, you would do well to go to 511 Web sites to find out what is happening and what safeguards of your data exist. The guys in California were pretty careful. Are the officials in your area equally as conscientious?

If you don't have confidence that you personally aren't going to be pulled over for a speeding ticket when law enforcement is short on their quota, you might want to reconsider participating in fare-collection programs. Or get a Mylar bag.

What Can Your Car Say about You?

Since 1999, every car coming off the assembly line is equipped with at least two airbags. To varying degrees, these airbags can tell mechanics, cops, and claims adjusters about any accident that you've just had. The key is to know what they can learn. First, visit the Web site for one of the largest dealers in software to decode airbag data, Vetronix (http://www.vetronix.com/diagnostics/cdr/vehicle/_list.html). Check to see if software has been developed for your car. If so, be forewarned that aggressive driving may not go unrecorded.

If software doesn't appear to have been developed for your car, it's still worth talking to a dealer. If your car is under warranty, have a chat with the mechanics at the dealership the next time you go in for service. Ask them about the use of computers in your car and the mechanics' ability to extract data from them in everyday and postaccident circumstances.

If your car isn't under warranty, your local mechanic may or may not be on top of this issue. He has little incentive to understand how the car succeeds or fails in emergency situations, since he's unlikely to be contributing to the design of new models in the near future. For that reason, it's a better use of time to visit a dealership that sells newer versions of the car you drive. Find an eager salesman and start pumping him for information. Remember, you don't have a lot of control over the information at this point, so your goal is to understand your exposure.

Does Your Local Police Use Traffic Light Cams?

In a way, it doesn't matter. You have no God-given right to drive a car. This is a privilege you earn by showing certain proficiency, both of operating the vehicle and of understanding rules designed to keep everyone as safe as possible. Since running red lights, speeding, and using the carpool lane when it's just you and the dog are all things you shouldn't do, you shouldn't do them, whether there is a camera there or not. If you're curious, www.photocop.com/locations is one of a few Web sites that track what locations currently engage in some kind of photo surveillance.

TAKING ACTION

Now that you've assessed how much you want to be a part of mobile tracking, you can adopt any number of simple- to more-complicated ways to elude the systems. You should also continue to be on the lookout for changes in how these new systems are being used.

Opting Out of Tracking

There are a handful of remarkably simple strategies that can help you avoid a lot of mobile tracking. This includes things like:

- Leaving the cell phone (or other signaling device) at home
- Turning it off
- Blocking signals from the tracking device—this is the Mylar bag tactic. Some reports suggest that sitting on devices interferes with them, too
- Disabling the feature on your phone or, if it comes to it, asking that the RFID chip be killed at checkout

If you're really concerned about the potential for misuse of data from your airbag, you may be able to get the government's permission to have an on-off switch installed in your car. Be warned, however. This is not a simple or quick process, and the fact that you do it gets recorded in still another database (also at the National Highway Traffic Safety Administration). For more information on on-off switches, and referrals to dealers and repair shops who can do the work, visit the NHTSA's Web sites on airbags at http://www.nhtsa.gov/airbags/.

And as systems become more fully developed and widespread, don't forget to keep an eye out for more formal opt-out methods.

The Department of Transportation (www.its.dot.gov), the FCC (www.fcc.gov/911/enhanced/), and the Consumers Union (www.consumersunion.org) are all good resources to help you stay informed.

Monitor the Monitoring

The key long-term action that is needed when it comes to mobile tracking is maintaining an awareness of what is going on around you. At the moment, there doesn't appear to be much abuse of information. The systems have been designed with a sensitivity toward limiting abuse, and much of the technology is not used widely enough for problems to have surfaced.

However, this calm state shouldn't be taken for granted. As mobile tracking systems become more mainstream, we can certainly expect mission creep, a gradual expansion of their methods and uses. As more information about the effectiveness of mobile tracking becomes available, you may decide that the benefits of a particular system actually don't outweigh the risks—or simply that there is a much better solution at hand.

Consider the case of red light cams. The Insurance Institute for Highway Safety reports that motorists who run red lights cause about 5 percent of all car accidents. Because of stats like this, it would seem reasonable to presume that red light cameras constitute a reasonable instance of monitoring to increase safety. Some studies suggest that red light cams work: the Insurance Institute found that red light cams in Oxnard, California reduced red light violations by 42 percent. Others find the opposite: the City of San Diego Enforcement System Review for 2002 showed that *accidents* increased at intersections with red light cams. Indeed, that study and others by the San Francisco Department of Parking and Traffic and the Virginia Department of Transportation suggest that simply increasing the time a traffic light is yellow by one second is far more effective at reducing collisions. It would appear that tracking, in the case, is not necessary to keep drivers safe.

In order to assure that tracking is justifiable and that the good intentions of system creators continue to guide its use, you should evaluate programs you participate in on a regular basis. Once a year, make a point of doing the checkup in the previous section.

RESOURCES

As you seek to stay informed about the development of mobile tracking systems, the following consumer groups and government agencies can offer assistance.

The best way to stay on top of what is happening with the government's Intelligent Transportation initiatives is to visit the Department of Transportation Web sites. To follow E-911 issues, the FCC has a Web page that links to quarterly reports from each of the wireless networks on their progress implementing E-911 services.

For information on red light cameras and a listing of state and local laws that regulate them, you can contact the Insurance Institute for Highway Safety. Updates on consumer issues associated with RFID are tracked by the Consumers Union or the group that also fights supermarket cards, CASPIAN. The Consumers Union is also active in lobbying for responsible use of airbag data in cars. They will have information about that, as will the National Highway Transportation Safety Administration.

- Department of Transportation (www.its.dot.gov)
- A state-by-state summary is available at www.its.dot.gov/staterpt/state.htm.
- FCC Enhanced 911 update (www.fcc.gov/911/enhanced/)
- Insurance Institute for Highway Safety (www.hwysafety.org/safety_facts/state_laws/auto_enforce.htm)
- CASPIAN (www.stoprfid.com)
- Consumers Union (www.consumersunion.org)
- National Highway Transportation Safety Administration (www.nhtsa.gov)

11. Deciding When Everyday Observation Turns Sinister: Surveillance

IN THIS CHAPTER:
What surveillance is possible, how it's changing, what you need to do as a result

So far, we've discussed lots of ways information about us is tracked. We've talked about understanding how that information can be used to get us more of what we want, and how limiting it can help us stop getting what we don't want. We've even joked a little about how participating in one of the biggest uses of information, direct marketing, was our duty as Americans.

Generally speaking, the use of information offers reasonable benefits for the risk it creates. And we've approached managing information about us as something to evaluate with a measured view.

This chapter will explore a different use of information that has the potential for far more sinister purposes than anything we've discussed before. This chapter is about a type of information that can be abused with devastating consequences and about how we have an absolute duty to ourselves and our country to pay attention to what is going on. This chapter is about surveillance.

Surveillance is the gathering of information about you by watching you closely. Surveillance used to be the province of peeping toms, cops, and stalkers. Increasingly, it is becoming the hobby of the overly curious as well. The ability to engage in surveillance has grown dramatically in the last five years with miniaturization of cameras, computer networking, and predictive modeling. Since the genie is out of the bottle, we need to understand that the world is always watching and behave appropriately.

WHY IS INFORMATION COLLECTED BY SURVEILLANCE MORE IMPORTANT THAN OTHER INFORMATION?

If a marketer makes a mistake in your profile and sends you a coupon you're unlikely to use, that's unfortunate. If the FBI misinterprets the reading material you've been checking out of the public library and hauls you in for questioning, that's a problem.

Since the increased emphasis on homeland security, the government—and the many different cops it employs in the FBI, the CIA, the NSA, the INS, the IRS, and the DEA—has become much more active. They are engaged in important and sometimes dangerous work, and we should applaud their efforts to keep us safe. However, we should also be cautious. Lately, stories of problems have been surfacing.

In a series of incidents eerily reminiscent of the Hoover era, there have been reports that the FBI is monitoring who attends political rallies and infiltrating the groups that plan them. The government has also begun taking a greater interest in what people are reading, writing, and photographing. Authorized by the USA PATRIOT Act, the FBI has been visiting libraries to ask after the reading habits of their patrons. Read the wrong material and you may hear a knock on your door.

Consider what happened to a freelance writer in Atlanta who was seen in a coffee shop reading an article called "Weapons of Mass Stupidity." A concerned—and apparently confused—citizen reported him to the FBI. As it turns out, the writer was reading up on media networks not bomb making, but the fact that someone reported him was enough to trigger an investigation.

The same FBI branch later arrested an amateur photographer for filming storage tanks. The photographer liked the interplay of light and shadow on the highly geometric shapes. The FBI didn't like his subject matter. Luckily, the photographer, who was also a highly respected attorney, was able to explain his way out of the situation.

About the same time, the Secret Service investigated a supposed threat to the president published in the *LA Times*. Michael Ramirez, a political cartoonist for almost two decades, spoofed a famous cartoon to show the president with a gun at his head. The Secret Service apparently didn't find the cartoon funny since they came a-knocking shortly after it ran.

While the government can and should do its best to keep us (and the president) safe, these stories suggest it can take things to an almost comical extreme. Indeed, we might just laugh them off, if they didn't hint at a much darker story that is still unfolding. During World War II, Japanese Americans were interned in camps in California for no other reason than that they were born in the country that attacked Pearl Harbor. In the years following the September 11 attack, more than one thousand Arabs living in this country have been detained for questioning—some for many months and without any communication with the outside world. The parallels to the suspicion, lack of knowledge, and fear engendered against Japanese Americans following Pearl Harbor are worth noting.

Of course, government agents don't have a monopoly on surveillance. And abuse of government power is not the only potentially dire consequence. There have been notorious cases of stalkers hunting and, unfortunately, murdering their unlucky victims. An old story, but one that clearly demonstrates the dangers of information access, was the murder of Rebecca Shaffer. Shaffer was an actress appearing on a popular TV sitcom when she attracted the notice of John Bardo. Bardo hired a detective who went to the local Department of Motor Vehicles, and simply requested Shaffer's records. Based on that information, Bardo found out where Shaffer lived. He went to her house and rang her doorbell. When Shaffer answered, Bardo shot her at point-blank range and killed her.

Another terrible story is that of Amy Boyer. Liam Youens, a high school classmate of Amy's, became obsessed with her. He kept a journal describing his interest in her, and expended considerable effort to follow her everywhere he could. Following graduation,

Amy got a job at a local dentist's office. Youens uncovered the address of her employer by requesting her file from one of the information brokers that compile identifying information on all of us. He waited for Amy outside her workplace one day and killed her as she left to go home.

The use of information gathered by watching you is more important than other information for two reasons. First, surveillance is generally undertaken for only the most serious reasons. You are a target for a crime or are suspected of committing one yourself. Second, the collection of the information is often done in secret (if you knew you were being watched, you would probably behave differently). Because they don't tell you what they're doing, it is more difficult to keep an eye on those keeping an eye on you. This means that information-collection procedures are not subject to review. And if you believe something is out of whack, you have far less recourse to fix things.

HOW LIKELY IS IT THAT I WILL BECOME A VICTIM OF STALKING?

According to the Department of Justice, one out of twelve American women is stalked at some point in her life. One out of forty-five men is stalked. Almost one out of seven college women is victimized by this before she graduates.

College stalking typically lasts about sixty days and includes psychological harassment and sexual pressure. It generally doesn't result in physical violence. Stalking of adult women is far more dangerous, lasting almost two years on average and ending in violence a third of the time. In the vast majority of cases—80 percent by some estimates—the stalker is a former spouse or intimate partner. Clearly, if you are a woman in an abusive relationship, or a young woman away from home for the first time, there is a reasonable probability that you will be stalked.

A relatively new phenomenon is stalking that occurs online. A victim is sent unwanted and possibly threatening e-mails or other electronic communications like instant messages or message board postings. A victim may also be "followed" as she enters chat rooms or goes to sites that allow community members to interact with one another.

As with real-world stalking, the online version generally affects women and generally is carried out by someone the victim knew previously. Statistics from Working to Halt Online Abuse (WHOA), an education advocacy group, suggest that unlike in the real world, where only 13 percent of women are the perpetrators, fully 33 percent of cyberstalkers are women. In about a third of all reported cases, online harassment turns into actual physical stalking. The full scope and nature of online harassment is only just becoming clear, but the reported numbers are still lower than real-world incidents. Estimates of the number of victims range from several thousand to 100,000 people a year.

WHAT IS VIDEO VOYEURISM?

A few years ago, the Washington State Supreme Court ruled that two men who had been caught taking pictures up women's skirts could go free. One voyeur photographed women's underwear in a shopping mall, the other at a food festival. In both cases, the judges ruled that because "casual surveillance frequently occurs in public," the women being photographed had no right of privacy to be protected.

Unfortunately, the two cases in Washington are just two of many such stories. There are instances of pornographers secretly videotaping over a thousand college athletes in locker rooms and selling the footage on the Internet, landlords who wired the apartments they rent with hidden cameras, and a man who is suing a major hotel chain because he allegedly found a camera hidden in a bathroom fixture. A search online brings up more than one hundred thousand Web-cam sites looking down on showers and up from toilets. Assuming that each Web-cam photographs about a hundred people— more than *ten million* people have been caught unaware and on tape.

As stunning as it is to imagine, videotaping people in places where they might reasonably expect some privacy, like a bathroom, is 100 percent legal in a lot of states. Ditto at the federal level. Although federal law made it illegal in the late sixties to record you while you're talking on a public phone, it is still okay today to photograph your underwear as you do it. Furthermore, it's okay to publish that photograph on the Internet for millions of viewers.

The lack of legal protection has to do, in part, with the complexity of what to prosecute, but it also has to do with the fact that a lot of miniature cameras are hard to see. Most of us are unaware of them and consequently aren't so outraged by the problem. In the past year, one type of camera that is more obvious has caught the attention of lawmakers. Of the 160 million cell phones in use by American consumers, approximately 6 million of them come equipped with cameras. These phones, popularized by television ads that show a cell phone owner sending embarrassing photos of a restaurant patron to her friend, have led to a general ban on *all* cell phones in the public bathrooms, locker rooms, and showers of a few jurisdictions. Similarly, some gyms have asked members to leave any cell phones at home. Unfortunately, these general bans penalize anyone simply wanting to carry a phone for legitimate purposes, and they don't address the much more pernicious use of cameras that have been hidden from view.

While it's unsettling to think about peeping at the gym or at the mall, it's also worth taking a second to realize that you're much more likely to get caught in an exposed moment where you work. According to one dealer of surveillance equipment, more than half its sales go to employers wanting to secretly monitor what their workers are doing. And that's completely legal, too.

HOW HAS GOVERNMENT SURVEILLANCE CHANGED SINCE THE WAR ON TERRORISM?

It is easy enough to know that government has been enacting some big changes to combat terrorism more effectively. It is less easy to understand exactly what it is doing. Even some of our elected representatives seem less than certain. News reports have suggested that the Uniting and Strengthening America by Providing Appropriate

THE FOURTH AMENDMENT

"The right of the people to be secure in their persons, houses, papers, and effects against unreasonable searches and seizures, shall not be violated, and no Warrants shall issue, but upon probable cause, supported by Oath or affirmations, and particularly describing the place to be searched, and the persons or things to be seized."

Although its cousin, the first amendment, is probably better known, the good old Fourth Amendment is getting a lot of attention from civil liberties groups lately. Designed to prevent unreasonable search and seizure, the Fourth Amendment is being used to challenge new legislation such as the PATRIOT Act and its follow-ons. Of particular concern with the PATRIOT Act is that the "probable cause" limitations have been made too loose, that the sneak-and-peek searches, particularly of homes, is "unreasonable," and that the roving nature of wiretaps allows for searches that do not involve places that have been "described," and therefore can be abused.

Tools Required to Intercept and Obstruct Terrorism (USA PATRIOT) Act was barely read by congressman eager to pass it in the days following the attacks on the Pentagon and World Trade Center.

One very big change to our society has been the creation of the Department of Homeland Security. This aggressive reorganization of government collapsed twenty-two agencies employing tens of thousands of workers into one department. The last time such a large shakeup occurred was the creation of the CIA at the beginning of the Cold War in 1947. The Department of Homeland Security is responsible for maintaining the security of the nation's borders, implementing large-scale emergency preparedness and response plans, conducting research into potential new types of threats, and collecting and analyzing intelligence information to identify and stop future attacks.

Government agencies that now fall under the management of the Department of Homeland Security include Customs, the Coast Guard, the Secret Service, and parts of the INS. New agencies to coordinate efforts of local, state, and federal governments and to interact with private sector companies (like high-tech firms) have been created. Another new agency, and one that is getting a lot of attention, is the Transportation Security Administration (TSA). Among other things, it is responsible for air-travel safety.

A second big change in society has been the passage of legislation to make it easier to find and prosecute terrorists. Clearly, the most notable law has been the USA PATRIOT Act, which broadened surveillance powers of law enforcement. Among other things, the act makes tapping your computer legally similar to tapping your phone, makes suspicion of terrorist activity a justifiable cause to order a wiretap on a person, allows mobile wiretaps to follow a person into different jurisdictions, and allows for searches to be conducted in secret without advance warning to the home or car owner. These so-called "sneak-and-peek" searches are particularly noteworthy, because part of what is authorized is entering your home and installing software on your computer that logs your every keystroke.

Another provision of the PATRIOT Act extends the type of material that can be requested for an investigation of a potential terrorist. Law enforcement has begun collecting all kinds of business records. In a December 2002 survey, 45 percent of companies admitted that they'd already supplied customer information to government officials. The diving instruction association, PADI, a major home-improvement store, and at least one major grocery chain have all turned over their customer transaction databases to the FBI. JetBlue, American Airlines, and Northwest have also admitted sharing customer data with the government or its contractors.

By far, the change with the biggest potential to really affect the way we live our lives has been the increasing attempts to collect, organize, and mine data from databases of information on average people. Shaken by the failure of intelligence that might have prevented the 9/11 attacks, the Pentagon and other spy agencies have switched gears. In addition to investigating people they have reason to expect are guilty, money and energy is being devoted to figuring out who is likely to be guilty at some point.

In other words, we are all being investigated without probable cause. The Pentagon, in particular, is pushing this approach with a number of projects managed by its Office of Total Information. In a move reminiscent of science fiction stories, the Office of Total Information is tasking computers with intelligently combing through vast amounts of everyday data to identify behavior indicative of criminal or terrorist activity. How do these computers decide who to point the finger at? The short answer is we don't know. And that's scary.

WHAT DO I NEED TO KNOW ABOUT WIRETAPPING?

As with other things in the modern world, telephone technology is getting more and more sophisticated. Today, digital telephony and the advent of other kinds of digital communication, like e-mail, have presented a real challenge to anyone trying to find and catch bad guys.

Basically, with old-style phones, the only hard part was finding a way to listen in to a conversation. Picking up a signal as it traveled across a wire was easy to do, as long as you could put a device on the wire and tap into it. These days, digital technology means that even though it's still easy enough to pick up the signal, the signal itself has been turned into a babble of scrambled packets, each containing only a small piece of the puzzle that—when reassembled properly—make up your conversation. Without a way to reassemble the pieces, a would-be eavesdropper has useless data. The result is that digital phones—mobile, cordless, you name it—have gotten a whole lot more secure—unless you're the target of an official government investigation.

And that's because the government passed a law that required telephone and Internet service providers to make decoding digital signals and reconstructing them into recognizable data possible for cops. This law, the Communications Assistance to Law Enforcement Act (CALEA), has been subject to court challenges for years, but the net result is that digital phones are just as transparent to law enforcement as the older, analogue ones. Indeed, digital phones are actually *easier* to get information from.

The reason they are easier has to do with the traditional way of defining wiretapping. There are two kinds of phone eavesdropping: one looks at the telephone numbers of everyone you talk to, the other involves actually listening to what you say. The ability to monitor just the numbers requires very little judicial oversight—when asked, a judge has no option but to grant law enforcement the right to look at the phone numbers of a target's incoming and outgoing calls. When asked to grant a wiretap that allows law enforcement to listen to the content of a conversation, however, a judge is required to examine the facts of the request. In this case, the tap may or may not be granted based upon its potential to violate a target's fourth amendment rights.

So, let's apply this logic to digital telephony. In today's world with Touch-Tone menus, the first type of eavesdropping can legally pick up any account numbers or passwords that you punch in. Law enforcement can learn about your banking transactions, your voicemail access codes, your credit card numbers, even your Social Security number, with the same ease that they can learn what the phone company already tracks—who you call and who calls you. Digital technology offers greater exposure at a lower threshold.

In the case of Internet communication, the FBI developed a software program called CARNIVORE (now called DCS1000), which allows them to do the equivalent of wiretapping for e-mail accounts. CARNIVORE resides on servers at Internet service providers and captures data coming from any Internet address that they've gotten a warrant for. The unfortunate news is that the program doesn't seem to be as specific as its designers had hoped, and an FBI tap on one user's account sometimes brings in random communications from nontargets as well. The furor over this wholesale collection of e-mails has led the Bureau to delete information it's collected on more than one occasion, for fear of tainting a prosecution through using information they weren't allowed to collect.

HOW DO YOU TRACK SOMEONE DOWN?

In order to watch you through a keyhole, someone first has to know where to find you. Government investigators who want to find someone don't simply rely on their own data gathering. As befits a free market economy, they pay private firms called Individual Reference Service Agencies for their data as well.

These agencies create massive databases cataloguing everyone they can find. The information is collected from public records, such as the telephone book, real estate records, and court documents. It may also be culled from news reports, professional directories, even high school yearbooks. Financial information isn't collected, although each of the big credit reporting agencies also offers its own reference service, so it isn't too hard to figure out how one might lead to the other.

Information collected by reference service agencies is used for two basic reasons: to locate someone or to verify they are who they say they are. Identity verification is used to combat fraud and allow consumers to check up on professionals they seek to hire. They have been used by both the Republican and Democratic National Committees to check up on potential donors.

When reference-service lists are used to track people down, the reason may be that someone wants to collect on a bad debt, unite separated families, locate heirs to estates or pension fund beneficiaries, locate organ or bone marrow donors (donor databases often get out-of-date), or enforce child support orders.

And, of course, reference-service databases are used to find suspected criminals. Federal courts, and state and local law enforcement are longtime subscribers to these companies. Thirty-five federal agencies, such as the INS, DEA, and the IRS also subscribe. Indeed, it is the reference-service databases that form the backbone of many of the "total" information programs being proposed.

WHAT ABOUT PROGRAMS THAT ENCOURAGE CITIZENS TO WATCH EACH OTHER?

As if spying itself or buying information from companies who spy wasn't enough, the government is also encouraging each of us to spy on one another. What's interesting is how eager we are to do it.

Neighborhood Watch is a long-standing program designed to

help prevent crime. Originally created in 1972 to promote cohesive-ness and afford greater protection for urban neighborhoods, Neighborhood Watch has recently gotten more funding and atten-tion. The program has expanded the training it offers to include identification of activities that suggest terrorism. The Air Force has created EagleEyes, a souped-up version of the Neighborhood Watch program for its members.

Local police are also joining together to create their own watch programs. Law enforcement organizations in the East and Mid-west have created a communal database with reports from citizen participants in the Community Anti-Terrorism Training Initiative. Better known as CAT EYES, the program was designed by former military officers. In this program, a structured hierarchy of watch-ing occurs. Individual blocks are monitored by captains charged with personally visiting each house. Captains report any suspi-cious activity to neighborhood coordinators, who take the infor-mation to their local police or sheriff. The police enter the data into a database, which is shared by the jurisdictions participating in the program.

Certain professional organizations have also launched pro-grams. The American Trucking Association launched a program in 1998 to encourage truckers to report on a variety of driving prob-lems—stranded motorists, drunk drivers, accidents, broken signs. Recently they have begun educating their members on what to look for that might indicate terrorist activity.

Perhaps the most far-reaching use of domestic surveillance is found in the system created to hunt down child kidnappers. In re-sponse to the kidnapping and murder of a nine-year-old Texas girl named Amber Hagerman, radio broadcasters in the Dallas/Fort Worth area banded together in 1997 to issue alerts whenever a child was kidnapped. The idea of harnessing the power of the me-dia to support manhunts evolved into the AMBER (America's Miss-ing: Broadcast Emergency Response) alert system, a name that not coincidentally is also that of the young victim.

Essentially, upon confirmation that an abduction has occurred, law enforcement contacts television and radio stations, which broadcast available information using their Emergency Alert Systems. Law enforcement also contacts local department of transportation officials to place alerts on LED highway signs wherever they exist. The resulting awareness of the crime—often with a vehicle description— has lead to the successful recovery of 122 children as of January 2004. Growing enthusiasm for the AMBER program is evident in a federal law providing funding to expand the existing programs into a nationwide network.

While reassuring that we are all adopting a higher level of vigilance, it is also worth asking about safeguards built into the system. Remember the fellow reading the article on "Weapons of Mass Stupidity"? Then there is the story of a group of Arab Americans reported for doodling "suspicious" pictures on a paper tablecloth at a restaurant. An FBI inquiry showed that there was nothing to worry about—except perhaps why the inquiry had happened in the first place. Random observations from untrained and potentially biased observers can turn otherwise innocent bystanders into casualties in the war on crime and terrorism.

WHAT ARE THE CHANCES THAT I WILL BECOME A TARGET FOR GOVERNMENT SURVEILLANCE?

Chances are certainly higher that you will be subject to government surveillance than you used to be. But as long as you aren't an immigrant from a targeted country, or otherwise fit the profile of a drug dealer, the chances you will find yourself the target of specific, aggressive eavesdropping are relatively slim.

The use of wiretaps grew significantly the year after the World Trade Center and Pentagon attacks. The number of content wiretaps currently averages about 1,300 a year, about a thousand of them for drug cases. The number of surveillance requests under the Foreign Intelligence Surveillance Act, a law used to find foreign spies (and now terrorists) on American soil, broke 1,700 in 2003, up approximately 500 from the year before. This means that roughly 3,000 wiretaps were authorized in 2003. While, philosophically, you may believe that 3,000 wiretaps is 3,000 too many, the practical

THE UNFRIENDLY SKIES

For those unlucky passengers who have been fingered, the process of flying has become a torture. Passengers report extensive and time-consuming screening, rude treatment, and unclear answers to justifiable questions. Many miss their flights; others have become known to business colleagues as the person *not* to travel with.

The confusion in the system is evident. One "high-risk" flier is a woman whose name is similar to the true suspect's, an Australian *man*; another is at least twenty years older than his suspected namesake. Still another man, whose name actually does match a detainee at Guantanamo Bay, missed his flight while waiting for a clearance. When all was sorted out, the airline gave him an apology and a meal voucher and booked him on a flight for the next day. The following day, however, he got to the airport only to find the entire lengthy process of suspicious questioning starting anew all over again.

While the airport experiences are bad, what's worse for these harassed travelers is that, when they take steps to remove their names from the no-fly list, many enter into a maze of referrals that leads nowhere. Some have turned to their congressman—which may explain, in part, why Congress is paying more attention to development of CAPPS II.

reality is that, in a country of more than 280 million, the chances that you'll be the target of one are pretty small indeed.

What is more likely for those of us who aren't suspects in a drug or terror case is that a general higher level of watching will make it harder for us to escape notice for smaller problems. You may not be planning to blow up anything, but the same zeal in sharing and comparing information means that the parking ticket you got on vacation two states away is going to follow you back home. There is going to be a lot less "getting lost" in the system than there used to be.

Indeed, much of the more intensive scrutiny adopted to find terrorists may be actively expanded to find other kinds of criminals. Take the case of CAPPS. The process of listing people who were suspected of intending to disrupt air travel (i.e., hijackers) has been in place since 1990. In 1998, this system was updated to include the Computer Assisted Passenger Pre-screening System (CAPPS), software programs that identify individuals not "tied to the community" and assign them a risk code. Some codes indicate that more questioning is in order; others preclude any air travel at all. Now, as a more advanced version of CAPPS with antiterrorism fully in mind is being developed, passenger information is being tied to more nontravel information, like family structure, income, and credit histories, for more exhaustive profiling. Even before it's finished, the desire to expand the use of the database to catch suspects for violent crimes has come up. It is not out of the realm of possibility that before much longer the travel-profiling database will discover your unpaid ticket and detain you at the airport until you cough up the fine.

Because of CAPPS, it is decidedly more likely that you will be scrutinized more carefully when you travel by air. According to testimony by the Deputy Secretary of Homeland Security, roughly 14 to 15 percent, or 1 out of 7, of all air travelers are currently identified as dangerous. Improved systems will still flag 1 out of 25 passengers. Good sense suggests that there are not as many as 13 million terrorists and drug dealers living in the United States. This also suggests that you have a pretty decent chance of being a pretty decent person who nonetheless finds your bags getting searched every time you fly.

What is absolutely certain about the changes in goverment surveillance is that we will all be forced to live in a society that views one another with suspicion first and open arms second. Without question, each and every one of us will be watched more in the coming years.

CHECKUP

In order to understand the true impact of living in a world full of one kind of surveillance or another, you need to consider the use of video cameras, determine if you're more or less likely to be singled out for more aggressive surveillance, and check in on how your neighbors feel about the subject—since they can be a source of significant information on you.

Say "Cheese"!

The first test is to check how many cameras watch you in a given day. Starting now, take the next twenty-four hours to look for any cameras you can find. Look on the ceilings at the bank and at work. Ask store clerks about monitoring of changing rooms. Look up at traffic lights or on street lights.

While you're counting the cameras you can find, consider this: in New York City, the average New Yorker is filmed seventy-five times a day. British citizens, with more than 2.5 million cameras lining their streets, are even more exposed. Are you finding more or less than that?

Once you've finished your twenty-four hours of watching, take that number and quadruple it. Why? Because it is virtually certain you didn't see all of the cameras that photographed you. The real learning is this: did you behave any differently during your day of checking? If so, you might want to consider changing your behavior on a regular basis, because, whether you're checking or not, the cameras are still rolling. Commonsense behaviors for a world caught on film can be found in the first section of this chapter's Taking Action.

How High Is Your Surveillance Profile?

Now that you've considered the passive surveillance none of us can escape, the next set of tests can help you determine if you have any special circumstances that suggest that you might be a likely candidate for something more.

Check any of the following that apply:
- ❑ You manage or have had to fire a disgruntled employee at your job.
- ❑ You have been in an abusive relationship.
- ❑ You have had a relationship with someone who has a history of abusive behavior toward others.
- ❑ You have recently ended a relationship of any kind.
- ❑ You are a woman in your first year of college.
- ❑ You are a woman in any year of college in a new relationship.

❑ You are active in online message boards or chat rooms.
❑ You are active in an online dating service.

If you checked any of the boxes above, the sad truth is that, statistically speaking, you are more likely to suffer a stalking incident in your life than someone who didn't check any. Stalking can be a very serious problem. If you checked the last two boxes, in particular, you may be at greater risk for cyberstalking.

Resources to help you learn more about what you can do are listed in the second section of this chapter's Taking Action.

Now consider the following statements.
❑ You have a highly visible professional position.
❑ You work in a company that develops technology of some sort.
❑ You deal with sensitive information in your job.
❑ You travel overseas on business relatively frequently.
❑ You are a vocal critic of government policy or support groups who are.
❑ You have attended a political rally in the past year.
❑ You are active in other controversial religious or social activities.
❑ You are involved in any kind of extensive or expensive legal proceeding.
❑ You fit a profile of a likely terrorism suspect.
❑ You have acquaintances who use or sell drugs.

If you checked any of these boxes, you are more likely than the average person to be a target for electronic eavesdropping. If you checked any of the first three boxes, in particular, you are more likely a target for industrial espionage. Checking any of the remaining boxes suggests that you may become a target of some kind of surveillance by a private investigator or law enforcement. You, too, should pay attention to the section on advice for anyone with a high-surveillance profile.

Do You Know Your Neighbors As Well As They Know You?

Finally, as part of being in a society where watching one another is becoming a national pastime, it is worth becoming aware of any

Neighborhood Watch programs in effect near you. The easiest way to do this is to contact your local sheriff. The phone book should have a listing, or you can visit the official National Neighborhood Watch Web site (http://www.usaonwatch.org/). Be sure to ask not only about Neighborhood Watch but any other citizen programs as well. Because most citizen programs involve some kind of partnership with law enforcement, the law should know what your neighbors are up to.

TAKING ACTION

Now that you know you're being watched—or possibly even followed—it's time to consider what to do about it. All of us need to adapt our basic behavior; high-risk individuals might want to take action to limit their exposure. Finally, as with mobile tracking, government surveillance is changing enough at the moment that it's worth a little extra attention to make sure that nothing gets too out of balance.

Common Sense for Living In a World That Is Always "On"

First and foremost, you need to understand that you are filmed without your consent absolutely every day. Except in the privacy of your own home—with the shutters or curtains drawn—you simply cannot behave as if no one were watching. It's probably true that most of the time this won't be a big issue, but for those times when you are letting loose a little, it is common sense to be cautious about where you do it.

You probably want to do what you can to avoid disrobing in public places. Experts who work with voyeurism victims especially warn against using tanning beds, a hugely popular hiding place for cameras. Hotel rooms, dorm rooms, and medical and dental offices are also well-known target locations. Other advice includes scanning unfamiliar locations for anything positioned to "look" down or up at you: gym bags in locker rooms, packages on floors, for example. And think twice about wearing light clothing in public.

Peeping creeps have taken to using infrared filters to photograph through it. Finally, because of the prevalence of security cameras in the workplace, a frank talk with your boss may also protect you from an even more frank picture.

If you're really concerned about unseen video cameras, you can use technology to fight technology. There are a range of countersurveillance devices that signal an alert when a camera or listening device is nearby. Buying an antibug or anticam widget may be a bit of overkill for the average person, but if you're not average, it is an option available to you. Two places to learn more about countersurveillance are www.spyzone.com and www.thespystore.com.

Second, determine for yourself where you want to draw the boundary line on surveillance. There is legitimate debate about the extent to which cameras should be used to watch our routine activities in the name of protection from crime and acts of terror. But taking a naked or near-naked picture of someone without their consent is surely unacceptable to the majority of us. If your state doesn't already have one, you may want to add your voice to a request for laws with teeth against this.

The Electronic Privacy Information Center (EPIC) has launched a video surveillance awareness project (http://www.epic.org). The ACLU (http://www.aclu.org) will be more than happy to help you get letters, e-mails, and faxes to the right people.

Don't Expose Yourself More Than You Need To

If you checked more than three of the boxes for the statements in the Surveillance Profile checkup, your situation suggests that you need to take steps to protect yourself from stalking or aggressive electronic surveillance. Generally speaking, there are three steps to take. The first is to secure the technology you use. The second is to limit or restrict information about you as much as possible. The third is to make sure you know where to turn to when you need to.

Securing the Technology You Use

First, look at your home. If you use a cordless phone, make sure that it is digital. Cordless phones that operate at higher frequencies (2.4 GHz or higher) or use multiple channels are more difficult to listen in on. Next, consider any other wireless devices that you might have in the house. Baby monitors, intercoms, and walkie-talkie signals can be intercepted just as phone signals can. Finally, think about how you've protected your house. If you have installed video cameras for home security, be aware that wireless cameras can broadcast images to receivers up to three hundred yards away. Some home security systems may actually offer you less security, if unwanted eyes are tapping into the broadcasts.

Second, think about phone technology that you use outside your house. Is your cell phone analog or digital? Do you have the tracking features mandated for the E-911 system turned on, or off? You might want to reconsider your subscription to any location-based services. If you are unsure of anything about your cell phone, a quick trip to your dealer is in order. Furthermore, if you tend to make or receive phone calls from airplanes, be advised that air-to-ground calls from airplanes are incredibly easy to monitor.

Third, if you use a laptop you should password-protect it and encrypt sensitive files. This is especially true if you travel. Hotel rooms are notoriously insecure, and your computer and personal papers are particularly easy to gain access to in this case. Be careful of where your laptop is while you're away at dinner.

Once you've completed a basic check, step back and reconsider your situation. While these pointers can raise your awareness of how what you thought was a private moment can be broadcast or shared without your consent, by no means do they offer full or adequate protection for truly high-risk individuals. If you fear for your safety, or genuinely believe that you may be the target of any sort of espionage, it is important to consult professional advice.

Restricting Information about Yourself

If you are living in any kind of fear, it goes without saying that you want to get an unlisted and unpublished phone number. You want to use a P.O. box instead of your home address for your driver's license, magazine subscriptions, and just about everything else. You want to talk to your employer about the absolute sensitivity of giving information to random callers or visitors, and you want to stay out of online chat rooms. You probably also want to stop using your full name whenever you can. The absence of a middle name or initial will make finding you in huge databases at least a little more difficult.

Additionally, you should probably seek to remove yourself from the major Individual Reference Service directories or reverse lookup directories. Many, which simply track public information, will not let you. Two agencies that do allow opt-outs are shown below.

Opt-Out
US SEARCH.com Inc.
5401 Beethoven Street
Los Angeles, CA 90066

LexisNexis Name Removal
PO Box 933
Dayton, OH 45401
FAX 1-800-732-7672
Online form at www.lexis-
nexis.com/terms/privacy/data/print_template.asp

Know Where to Turn

If you have reason to fear you will become the victim of a serious stalking case, you will want to take additional steps to make yourself more difficult to track down. This type of anonymity will likely require significant lifestyle changes. The National Center for Victims of Crime (www.ncvc.org) and the National Domestic Violence Hotline

(www.ndvh.org) are two excellent resources for information and services to help you.

If the government wants to bug you, let's face it, it will be able to
do so. Since there really isn't any way that you can protect yourself,
your best bet, if you believe there is potential for a problem, is to
prepare for how to deal with eavesdropping once you are aware of
it. It is a good idea to get chummy with organizations and people
who might help you if and when you need it. Groups like the ACLU
or the Electronic Freedom Foundation are a good place to start.
Your legislators are another.

Staying Informed

The final component of dealing with surveillance is to stay aware of
it. While many of the new measures are genuinely designed to keep
us all safer, there is a need for effective oversight of what is going
on. Remember the old saying: Absolute power corrupts absolutely.
With this very much in mind, our forefathers built this nation upon
the notion of checks and balances.

Happily, that system appears to be working. Many potential
abuses of information that the Pentagon and other government
agencies have proposed have been subject to significant questioning by Congress. You would do well to pay attention yourself. The
Center for Democracy and Technology offers a particularly useful
and user-friendly summary of pending and recent federal legislation, if you want to stay on top of government security programs.

RESOURCES

The following resources will help you learn more about surveillance issues and provide assistance should you ever find yourself in
a situation where you are being stalked or spied upon. If you need
to contact your legislators, Congress.org offers a quick lookup.

- National Center for Victims of Crime (www.ncvc.org)
- National Domestic Violence Hotline (www.ndvh.org)
- Working to Halt Online Abuse (WHO@) (www.haltabuse.org)

- EPIC's program on surveillance: www.observingsurveillance. org
- Find your local, state, and federal representatives at www. congress.org
- Electronic Frontier Foundation (http://www.eff.org)
- The Center for Democracy and Technology (www.cdt.org)

12. PROTECTING YOUR KIDS

IN THIS CHAPTER:
Danger to your kids from online predators, tracking by schools and marketers, how you can affect and monitor it all

Perhaps the most important checkup you can perform concerns your children. We all recognize their need for extra protection. The Internet holds special peril for them. Underfunded schools are "selling out" to marketers, and while educators have always maintained records, powerful and cheap desktop computers mean that the infamous "permanent" record is, in some cases, becoming the infamous "public" one.

The collection of information on children and the regulation of its use are the least clear-cut and most confusing of all the information issues we've been discussing. Your voice as a parent can make a big difference for your kids. It's time to get to that PTA meeting.

WHAT KINDS OF THINGS DO I HAVE TO LOOK OUT FOR?

When it comes to our kids—of any age, really—you want to look out for information misuse that leads to danger from predators and exploitation by schools and marketers.

The Internet has provided a powerful vehicle for criminals to target kids. While the actual number of kids abducted and murdered by strangers is quite low—about 1 out of every million—the number propositioned for sex online each year is outrageously high, almost 1 out of 5, according to one study. Not all dangers to your kids come from the Internet, of course, but the potential that your child will be approached online is strong enough to warrant your attention.

School records present another kind of danger to your kids. I know it sounds like the beginning of a joke, but school administrators can really set up your child for a lifetime of problems with a negative assessment in a school record. The problem isn't so much what the record says as much as it is that more and more people can get to it. Even pristine school records are a resource with tremendous information that often isn't as protected as common sense would suggest it should be. The University of Wisconsin at Stout, for example, proudly displays the name, e-mail address, street address, and often phone number of all its students and faculty on its Web sites. This searchable directory is available to anyone with a computer and an Internet connection.

Finally, realize that marketers want your kids. They tend to go after them a little more aggressively than you might think wise. Marketers know that kids directly or indirectly influence the way you spend money. These junior consumers indirectly influence as much as $500 billion in parental spending. If that wasn't enough to get someone's attention, some figures estimate that children nineteen and under spend another $200 billion of their own money each year.

Not surprisingly, kids' marketing profiles are highly sought after by companies seeking to establish lifelong brand attachment (notably soft drink makers and fast-food restaurants). And when they aren't targeting your kids by name, they're buying them textbooks and school stadiums in exchange for persistent, inescapable advertising.

Especially as more and more school boards struggle to close budget gaps, schools are becoming ground zero for a range of marketing deals. School buses have become moving billboards. Computer labs deploy screen savers with fast-food ads. Candy companies offer free samples to use in "scientific" experiments.

And, in one of the more controversial turns of all, current

events are provided by ChannelOne. Launched in 1990, ChannetOne produces a twelve-minute news broadcast that is beamed by satellite into approximately twelve thousand schools each morning. Those schools account for over 8 million students or about fifty times the teen viewership of MTV. However, according to one advocacy group, a substantial portion of the ChannelOne broadcast consists of ads and promotions that not only encourage kids to spend money with a sponsor but also entice them to enter contests or play online games—which suck up identifying information for the sponsor.

Think it's tough to be the parent? Just imagine being the kid.

WHERE DO MARKETERS FIND OUT ABOUT YOUR KIDS?

Marketers develop their lists from a number of sources. They may purchase the list from a vendor who takes the time to scour public birth and school records. They may collect the information themselves by sponsoring a contest. Or they may buy the name from your child's school.

Since we know that public records start at the moment we are born, it shouldn't be too surprising to learn that someone is reading them from the moment they are created. In addition to public birth records, list vendors have devised a number of tactics to gain information directly from expectant parents. How many of the following sound familiar?

- Want to be notified of upcoming sales on maternity clothing at our store?
- Sign up for the pregnancy calendar and get e-mails that describe your baby's development that day!
- Your first child's portrait is free!
- Use this coupon to save on diapers (but we will only honor it if you fill in the following info . . .)

Experian offers a New Parents Database that gets names from about fifty sources, including large retail stores, Internet sites, photography studios, and packaged-goods manufacturers. These sources, in turn, get their information anytime you fall for one of the gimmicks listed above. While knowing what month little Joey was born seems innocuous enough, add that to a full profile on mom and dad and Experian starts to know quite a bit about how you're going to raise your child and when you can be convinced to buy the stuff you need to do it. All told, public and private sources supply Experian with approximately 60,000 new target families a week.

Once your child has grown past two or three years, marketers no longer consider you a new parent. At this point, kids have graduated to their own files, and marketers are keen to know more about *them*. American Student List and Student Marketing Group are two companies that specialize in direct marketing to kids. ASL claims lists of 9 million names of kids between fourteen and eighteen years of age; 20 million from two to thirteen. Younger kids are found primarily through direct response sources—meaning warranty cards that you fill out. Older kids are tracked using public records, magazine subscriptions, and questionnaires that they volunteer to fill out.

In addition to buying names from list compilers, large companies targeting the "youth" market often use contests or giveaways to gather names on their own. In one school year, Houston schools sanctioned over one hundred different contests sponsored by companies wanting to market to children, like Duracell, Eastman Kodak, and McDonald's. Wal-Mart signed kids up for computer lessons. Papermate asked for a written movie review using one of their pens. In some cases, the information collected for the contest was used to market to kids later. And since 75 percent of kids think it's just fine to share personal information with a Web site in exchange for freebies, why not? The promotion, the branding, and the information collection are a compelling win for advertisers.

Not surprisingly, another big source of information on your kids comes from their schools. The ACLU has almost made a habit of suing schools over selling information about their students. Several years ago, they filed a class action suit against the Indian Creek School District in Ohio, which had allegedly volunteered lists of students and their private addresses to Advanced Financial Savings Bank for marketing purposes. More recently, they warned the University and Community College System of Nevada that a partnership with the credit card company, MBNA, was in direct violation of a law protecting student rights. In exchange for providing personal information about students that facilitated the marketing of credit cards to them, the College System received a portion of the profits on what the kids charged.

In some cases, schools are actively seeking alternate funding to bridge evergrowing budget gaps, but in far too many cases, they

---

THE ULTIMATE MARKETER: THE U.S. GOVERNMENT

One piece of legislation that protects access to student information also, ironically, requires its disclosure.

Public high schools are required to turn over students' names, addresses and telephone numbers to the military so that glossy images of Air Force, Navy, Army, and Marine careers can be sent out each year to the young men and women taking advantage of a state-sponsored education.

The list of names developed by the military is also useful to the Selective Service for tracking down eighteen-year-old males who have neglected to register for the draft (as they are required to do by law).

may be unwitting assistants to the marketers' ploys. In one notorious practice, a company made it its business to mail out surveys asking for financial and personal information from students. Over 100 million surveys were sent to guidance counselors at three quarters of the high schools in the country each year. The public mission of the survey was to collect Junior's profile data to share it with colleges who might want to offer him a scholarship. The not-so-public mission was less noble: The company also allegedly sold the student data to commercial marketers—like American Student List.

Because the FTC has recently cracked down on the financial aid survey companies, this particular misuse of information is less likely to occur in the future, but the moral of the story is still important. School employees, generally unaware of the practices of the marketing companies, were unwittingly encouraging kids to expose themselves. Think of the schools that accepted free computers or software without fully understanding that the "gifts" came prewired to track the students who used them. Although a lot of these problems have come under tighter control, thanks to greater awareness and new legislation, the need to ask questions of school administrators is still very much present.

HOW DANGEROUS IS THE INTERNET, REALLY?

In March 2003, twenty-five-year-old Saul Dos Reiss pleaded guilty to manslaughter and three counts of second-degree sexual assault. His victim was a thirteen-year-old girl he had picked up in an Internet chat room.

Although this is the kind of story that makes parents crazy with worry, it is also one, thankfully, that is relatively uncommon. Of the roughly 82,000 cases of child sexual assault that will get reported this year, approximately 90 percent of them will have nothing to do with any Internet activity. Instead, they will be carried out by a family member or close friend the parent allowed into the home. The truth is that simply keeping your kid away from the Internet won't keep him or her safe from assault.

But does this mean that the Internet stories you hear are all hype and you can stop worrying about predators like Dos Reiss? Not entirely. Although it takes a special combination of personalities and circumstances to result in a tragedy like the one that happened in that case, the Internet does increase the chances of the combination occurring in a few ways.

First, it offers a tremendously efficient avenue for child predators to reach out to more kids. By some estimates, there are 45 million kids online. One child advocacy group suggests that more than three quarters of our kids will be approached online by predators by the time they are fourteen.

Second, the Internet has rewritten the rules of social relationships. Kids taught from a young age not to accept candy from strangers will generally not follow someone they don't know down the street. They will, however, happily chat with a complete stranger online. That's part of the appeal of online chatting.

And finally, being removed from real-world verification of someone's circumstances has made it easier for predators to get close enough to a child to make an assault possible. Because each of us is essentially anonymous in a chat room, we have the option of revealing or not revealing things about us. A child molester can begin chatting with your child by posing as a peer. Only after the relationship between a predator and a child develops—sometimes over a period of years—does he gradually reveal more of his true situation. By the time the admissions are made, the child considers the molester his or her friend and is more likely to accept him without question. This process of developing a relationship from a casual encounter into one with sexual overtones, also known as "grooming," would have been much less likely if a grown man had to approach the child in a schoolyard.

Here, then, is the real danger of the Internet. The chances that your kid will be approached in some way are quite high. And kids are more likely to respond to an initial approach because the rules that warn them of danger (i.e., stranger danger) and the tools they use to evaluate a situation (i.e., the ability to gauge physical appearance like age) are missing. The trick is for kids to realize that something is awry at some point before a face-to-face meeting.

Thankfully, for the vast majority of kids, this realization will happen. Indeed, in a recent survey by the Crimes Against Children Research Center, none of the cases they reviewed actually led to physical contact. Most child activists stress that a little parental involvement goes a very long way in reducing the really scary physical danger of unwanted sexual approaches online.

For some kids, lonely and isolated from their parents, the predator may succeed in his seduction. Young girls might believe they have fallen in love; young boys might have become curious about a homosexual partner. If you're concerned your children may be like these others, there is a list of red flags to look for in the Checkup section.

WHY ARE SCHOOL RECORDS SCARY?

Aside from grades, records maintained by school systems range from the results of psychological and aptitude tests to career planning profiles to disciplinary notes to drug tests. Your child's participation in well-meaning studies about school violence or drug use offers information about his or her politics and personality. Many of these records are subjective in nature and potentially damning. But, believe it or not, that's not what's really scary about them.

It used to be that all the permission slips and doctors' notes were maintained by the teacher or nurse who collected them. Now that 95 percent of U.S. public schools are connected to the Internet, all those little bits of paper that incrementally detail both you and your child have been dumped into online record-management systems, along with teachers' evaluations, standardized test results, class grades, and any other comment added by a counselor, coach, or administrator. Once available online, the whole bit is shared over the Net with state departments, other schools, and even law enforcement. What's scary is that school records have become so public.

Sometimes the implications of making information public haven't been fully thought out. A few years ago, Yale put up a Web site that let applicants determine if they'd been admitted for that academic year or not. While this may have seemed efficient, the

---

SCHOOL SECURITY

As schools struggle with keeping kids physically safe at school, they are experimenting with many of the same technologies and programs as law enforcement. Public schools in Biloxi, Mississippi, are now wired with almost five hundred Web cams that monitor classrooms and hallways twenty-four hours a day. A school in Phoenix, Arizona, only has plans for two cameras, but they will be hooked up to face-recognition software in hope of finding missing kids and stopping known child molesters before they enter school property. In both cases, safeguards on who can view the video footage are in place. However, the schools' activities create obvious opportunities for questions by concerned parents.

Web site didn't use passwords or randomized login codes to protect access to the acceptance information. This meant that anyone with an Internet connection and some basic knowledge about a student could find out whether he or she got in or not. When an admissions officer at Princeton was fingered for perusing the Yale Web site, applicants, who feared their acceptance at one college would hinge upon their status at the other were, to say the least, dismayed.

Other times, new information management systems make sharing information unintentional. About the same time the Yale Web site was releasing student data, a Texas university database was hacked, compromising 55,000 students and faculty.

The weakness or naiveté exhibited by Yale and the University of Texas in protecting data is a natural outgrowth of how schools have behaved for years. Their mission as educators is based on a philosophy of free and open exchange of ideas and information—it's their knee-jerk response. They have also been custodians of a tremendous amount of information. But because so much of the record keeping was decentralized, there were few problems for any given student. Now that all the information is being gathered into centralized databases and shared via public and private Web sites, schools will need to reconsider their information policies more carefully. As a parent, it's good to ask questions of your child's school about these issues.

WHAT LAWS PROTECT KIDS' INFORMATION?

There are three laws that form the backbone of kid-information protection. One governs online information collection and the other two restrict what information goes into a school record and how that record is handled.

The Children's Online Privacy Protection Act (COPPA) seeks to protect the online collection of information about kids. Studies in the mid nineties suggested that, even though a lot of Web sites were collecting information on kids to target them for marketing campaigns, very few of these Web sites publicly acknowledged what they were doing. Concerned over the inability to effectively monitor information collection on minors, Congress passed a law that laid down basic rules.

Since April 2000, commercial Web sites have been required to obtain parental consent before collecting personal information from children under thirteen. Furthermore, the consent must be verified as coming from the parent, usually by double-checking the identifying info on a credit card number.

In addition to permission to collect information, Web sites must also post their policies for information collection and use somewhere on the site. Parents have the right to review information that has been collected on their child and to request that it be deleted.

There are, of course, exceptions. Sites may collect a child's e-mail address if it is needed to respond to a one-time request for "homework help" or other information. A Web site can also collect e-mail addresses from contest entry forms as long, as the address is used to contact the winner only once and is deleted at the end of the contest.

But in terms of how kids can be exploited, the biggest exception to COPPA is that the law only covers information submitted online. It does not say anything about information collected offline. For example, a contest that asks entrants to write an essay that must be mailed, along with the child's name and address, to a physical location is not subject to COPPA. Even though the contest may be promoted online, the fact that the identifying information submitted by the child is sent to the company using something other than the Internet relieves the company from any obligation under this law.

When it comes to protecting information in school records, two laws are most commonly cited. Perhaps the one with the most impact is the Family Educational Rights and Privacy Act (FERPA). This law gives parents (and nonminor students) the right to know about and read through all of the student's records maintained by the school. Parents have the right to request that a school correct anything that they believe is wrong or misleading. If the school elects not to change its record for some reason, the parents' rights of redress are spelled out, as is their right to add a statement to the record offering additional information, commentary, or explanation of the disputed information. In many ways, FERPA does for students what the Fair Credit Reporting Act does for consumers.

The amazing thing about FERPA is that there are two absolutely huge loopholes in it. First, schools may disclose information, without consent, to interested parties, like other schools and government officials—mostly law enforcement or the Selective Service board. In cases where a student is determined to have committed a crime of violence at school, this information can be shared with just about anyone—a good public safety measure on the face of it. But this exception to privacy, courtesy of an amendment to FERPA in 1998, unwittingly raises schools closer to the status accorded to courts—school "convictions" are now public records. As a parent, you can only hope that the "judges" are trained and unbiased.

Second, schools may disclose, without consent, "directory"-type information. Take a deep breath. Directory information includes a student's name, address, telephone number, e-mail address, photograph, date and place of birth, major field of study, dates of attendance, grade level, participation in officially recognized activities and sports, weight and height (of members of athletic teams), degrees, honors and awards received, as well as the most recent educational agency or institution attended prior to this school. Whew!

A devious identity thief could do quite nicely with this information, don't you think?

The one saving grace in the directory information loophole is that schools must tell parents what they think directory information is and what they plan to do with it. Schools must also allow parents a reasonable amount of time to opt out of any sharing. The actual means of notification, left to the discretion of each school, can be a special letter, inclusion in a PTA bulletin, student handbook, or newspaper article. Be careful, if you aren't looking for it, the notice could easily slip by.

The other law affecting school records is called No Child Left Behind. This is the law that established national testing of students and schools in 2001. In addition, it includes parental consent rights and standards for test materials. One amendment in particular requires that a parent's permission be obtained—in writing—before any student is subjected to nonemergency medical, psychological, or psychiatric examination, testing, or treatment by the school.

The new law further strengthens an older law called the Protection of Pupil Rights Amendment that stipulates that no student should be required to take any survey, analysis, or evaluation that asks them to reveal personal thoughts. In other words, research studies seeking to profile personality characteristics of kids—to predict troublemakers ahead of time, for example—are no longer okay unless the student volunteers.

One final note: private schools are not required to do any of the things above if they do not receive federal funding (which, admittedly, is relatively few of them). Students in these schools have no protection except the one that has kept most of us safe for years—the lack of coordination with other schools in a system. As the world changes, parents with children in private schools would do well to consider how the loss of practical obscurity even in these circumstances may come back to haunt you. Before you get too worked up, the Taking Action section offers some basic advice.

CHECKUP

As if there weren't enough things to worry about as a parent, here comes the guilt trip about how good you are at managing your child's blossoming information profile. The three basic areas of concern are: making sure that your kid isn't being oversold by marketers, that schools are handling personal and confidential records appropriately, and that the Internet is a positive influence on your child. The following checkups will help you understand where you need to focus your energy.

Walk Through Your Kid's School

You may have been there a million times before, but it's time to visit your kid's school again. The goal of your walk-through is to develop a subjective sense of whether or not your child is in danger of being unfairly exposed because of poor information policies or is being subjected to an overwhelming barrage of corporate advertising. As you walk around, you might want to keep an eye out for things like:

- Are there ads on the outside of the building?
- Are there banner ads in the lobby?
- Are brand-name fast foods served in the cafeteria?
- How many soda machines do you see? What brands?
- When you walk into the administrator's office, are confidential student records in plain view?
- How many computers do you see in the office?
- Are privacy notices clearly posted in the administration office?
- Are students' rights clearly noted in a handbook or a poster?
- Do lists of student's names appear on any wall in the school?
- How does the health facility/nurses office keep records? Are visits written up?
- Do team uniforms sport sponsor brands?
- Are the stadium walls covered by promotions for this and that?

- Has the roof of the school been rented out to advertisers? (The answer for some Texans is yes!)

If all feels okay, then you simply need to conduct a basic annual interview described in the Taking Action section on page 276. If you feel uncomfortable about the level of commercialism or the safety of your child's records, you will have your answer about how well the school is doing. When something feels out of balance, you might want to have a discussion with the administration and, possibly, with other parents.

Are You a Sucker for Sweepstakes?

Since contests are a popular and prominent method of convincing your kid to give up personal information, it is a good idea to make sure that he or she is equipped with the savvy to evaluate each opportunity as it arises. Answer the following questions with your child. They will help you understand how good you both are at sniffing out a fun, thought-provoking contest from a cynical marketing ploy.

1. My chances of winning a contest are:
   a. greater if more people enter it.
   b. lower if more people enter it.

2. I can find out how likely it is that I will win a sweepstakes.
   a. True
   b. False

3. It is against the law for a company to limit prizes only to contestants who:
   a. are 18 or older.
   b. live in the United States.
   c. submit an entry form by a certain date.
   d. bought the sponsor's product.

4. The purpose of a sweepstakes is generally to:
   a. make a product better known.

b. learn your name and address.

c. make you feel better about a brand or company.

d. all of the above.

5. A contest does not have to be based on luck.

a. True

b. False

6. In a contest based on skill, instead of luck, you might be judged on how well you:

a. write an essay.

b. buy a ticket.

c. guess a number.

d. fill out the entry form.

7. Skill-based contests may be easier to win because they are generally:

a. judged by softies.

b. set up to award prizes by age group.

c. take more work to enter, so fewer kids do it.

d. both b and c.

Answers: 1. B; 2. A, odds are required to be spelled out in the sweepstakes rules; 3. D; 4. D; 5. A; 6. A; 7. D.

If you and your child got more than one or two wrong, you would be advised to work through the first section in Taking Action together. If you got six or more right, congratulations! You know the difference between a luck-based sweepstakes and a skill-based contest. You know how to evaluate your odds of winning to balance the cost to you—time, or giving away personal information with the reward. And you know that something too good to be true probably is.

RED FLAGS FOR INTERNET INVASIONS

Experts all agree that you know your child best and you should trust your instincts to tell you if something is wrong. That said, there are a few warning signs that something is likely to be up. The following questions are compiled from materials prepared by noted activists seeking to protect kids from cyberpredators.

Warning Signs that Online Behavior Has Become Unhealthy and Possibly Dangerous

1. Has your child started spending a lot more time online than usual?
2. When you ask about what you child does online, does he or she seem especially evasive and unresponsive?
3. Does your child take pains to hide his or her Internet activity from you? Has he or she moved the computer to a more private location? Does he or she switch off the monitor or otherwise hide or change the screen when you enter the room?
4. Does your child become unreasonably upset when your Internet service goes down?
5. Has your child recently expressed an interest in getting a Web cam?
6. Does your child appear to have received gifts or cash from a source that you don't know about?
7. Has your child been receiving phone calls from kids or adults who are unfamiliar to you?

If you determine that your kid might be at risk, you should talk to him or her. The second section in Taking Action offers tips for this. You should probably also talk to one of the many agencies listed at the end of the chapter that can offer exceptional guidance and support.

TAKING ACTION

The good news is that it's never too late to address good information habits with your kids. Teaching your kids about how marketers work, so that they can make informed decisions of when "free" is free enough; encouraging them to understand that something as powerful as the Internet is also something that must be used with care; and working with them to assure that school administrators treat your family's information with the delicacy it deserves are the steps you need to take.

Stay Out of the Marketer's Spotlight

The most important step you can take to help your kids escape a marketing onslaught is to educate them about marketers and marketing tactics. As one educator wrote, it used to be that companies spent $100,000 to advertise to kids, and concerned parents only needed to limit their child's television time to limit their ad exposure. These days, advertising budgets for kid products have exploded to $13 billion, and kids see ads on the bus, in their textbook, on the computer, and even in their lunchbox. The assault can be savage and deafening if you haven't equipped your kid with a little perspective.

How can you do this? Have your children find some examples of contests and talk about them together. Discuss the difference between a sweepstakes and a skill-based contest. Talk about the marketing they are aware of in their school. Get them to consider the impact that this has on them. And most importantly, help them understand that there really is no such thing as a free lunch. A number of truly excellent media-awareness organizations, like The Media Channel (www.mediachannel.org), offer curricula for kids that are fun as well as effective.

Beside education, there are also a few basic things that you can do to keep your kid free from the direct-marketing assault just a little bit longer.

- Avoid giving out your child's name whenever possible. Never use his or her full name on anything unless it is a legal document and you can't avoid it. Whenever you can, simply use a first initial instead of a first name.

- Do not fill out warranty cards for kids' products. More often than not, warranty cards are nothing but a trick to get you to reveal profile information that is used to market to you. Warranty protection is generally assured if you have the blank warranty card and the dated receipt for the purchase.

- Keep your own house in order—clean up your records so that they reflect you as best they can. Marketers are going to make assumptions about your children based on your files.

- Although you can't do much about mining public records to build lists, you can opt out of the two major kids lists. Check their Web sites for up-to-date policies on name suppression.

  - Student Marketing Group, Inc. (www.studentmarketing.net)
  - American Student List LLC (www.studentlist.com)

Online Issues

Talk to Your Kids

To return to the advice offered by professionals trying to help you keep your kids safe, there is no substitute for parental involvement and supervision. The Privacy Rights Clearinghouse and The National Center for Missing and Exploited Children offer the following suggestions for how to accomplish this.

- Explain the power and value of personal information to your kids. Make sure that they understand the difference between what information is okay to share and what is not. Especially sensitive information includes last name, address, phone number, and school name. Explain the importance of passwords and set clear expectations about not sharing them, even to people who represent themselves as being from the online company. You don't need to be too heavy-handed about this either. One wonderful campaign by the University of Michigan compares passwords to underwear (they should be changed often, longer is better, don't share them with your friends, etc.).

- Teach your kids to be cautious consumers. Explain that people online may not represent themselves 100 percent truthfully, and that some information on the Web is worth just what it costs: nothing.

- Show your kids how to use tools that help them evaluate the safety and value of a site. Take the time to read through the privacy policies of sites your kids visit. For maximum effect, read the policy with your kids. As you're reading, talk to them about what to look for (what information is collected, why it's collected, and who it is shared with) and what to be wary of. Become familiar with Web seals offered by third parties that assure some oversight of Web sites your kids visit. Two common "seals of approval" come from TRUSTe and the Better Business Bureau. Teach your kids to look for and recognize these seals.

- Talk to them about potential problems they might encounter: profane or sexually explicit messages or harassment. Decide on a plan together for what to do if something uncomfortable or unfortunate occurs.

- Set reasonable and clear usage expectations. You might consider limiting the length of time and time of day that your children go online. You may want to spell out whether or not you will allow them to purchase anything online. You may want to prohibit activities like sharing pictures or downloading music files. Several organizations, including the FTC, suggest signing a contract with teens to encourage them to take responsibility for abiding by any family rules and conducting themselves appropriately.

- Establish a sense that using the Internet is a family activity. Keep the computer in a community place. All the experts agree that getting the computer out of a kid's bedroom is the single biggest step you can take to remain engaged in their online activity.

- Be curious. Get to know who your child is chatting with online. Just as you ask about his real-world friends, be curious about who he meets in cyberspace. Just as you ask your child what he saw on a field trip with school, ask about what he does online. Of course, you do yourself a huge favor if you know something about what's on the Internet yourself. If you don't have basic computer skills, you have no place putting a live computer in your house without teaching yourself about its use.

Parental Control Software

In cases where supervision isn't possible or you would simply like some help, there are bits of technology that can help you. As with all technology, a really motivated child or clever hacker will be able to get around just about anything you set up. You would be wise to think of these as aids, not substitutes for what you need to do.

Blocking software filters access to objectionable material. Objectionable may be defined as sexually explicit material, graphic violence, anything that relates to drug and alcohol use, or promotes hate groups. Sites may be blocked automatically because of keywords that appear on the sites or in picture-file names. Other software blocks sites because they appear on a list that is actively maintained by human reviewers, or because the URL suggests that the Web site falls into a category of sites, like online gaming or chat, which are deemed inappropriate. In some cases, the list of what gets blocked can be changed or added to by the parent. Software that filters material may also come with kid-centric versions of tools for Web browsing and search.

The other major class of software is monitoring software that logs what sites are visited and may or may not capture any mouse clicks or text that is typed on the keyboard. This kind of monitoring, or logger software, was discussed in the chapter on the Internet.

For more information on the most up-to-date tools available to parents, your best bet is to use one of the major Internet search engines and look up "parental-control software." There is also a good discussion of various options at www.getnetwise.org.

What to Ask Your School

It is very important that you interview your child's school each and every year about their privacy policy and record-keeping practices. New legislation and court cases keep changing what is expected of schools. The basic questions to ask are:

- What information is collected?
- Where is it stored?
- Who has access to it?
- What kind of protections are in place?
- How are staff trained who handle information?
- How is their performance reviewed?
- What does the school consider to be "directory" information?
- How do you opt out of sharing that information?
- Who is directory information shared with?

Then you want to ask to see your child's file. You are not asking for an update on his or her performance. You are looking to see what kind of information is tracked and how accurate it is. Is there a lot of subjective information? Can you find obvious errors in what is being noted? Is there a record of who nondirectory information has been shared with?

If you find a problem, you will want to write a letter stating your concerns. Eventually, you may want to raise the issue with your school board or possibly even the government agency responsible for FERPA enforcement.

RESOURCES

If you want to raise any issues with your child's school about their information practices, you will probably want to start with your local school board, found in the government blue pages. You may also try the Department of Education, which is responsible for enforcing FERPA, or for college issues, the Council on Law in Higher Education.

To educate yourself and your kids on media issues, the following media-awareness groups offer games and guides to get you started. For child safety issues, you can download a free book written by Glen Klinkhart, a police officer in Alaska with personal and professional experience in the subject, or contact any of the agencies listed below. The executive director of WiredPatrol, Parry Aftab, has also written extensively about protecting kids online.

- U.S. Department of Education Family Policy Compliance Office (www.ed.gov/policy/gen/guid/fpco/index.html)
- Council on Law in Higher Education (www.clhe.org)
- The Media Channel (www.mediachannel.org)
- Media Awareness Network (www.media-awareness.ca)
- Commercial Alert (www.commercialalert.org)
- Center for a New American Dream (www.newdream.org)
- A Cybercop's Guide to Internet Child Safety by Glen Klinkhart (www.cybercopguide.com)
- Guardian Angels Cyberangels Program (www.cyberangels.org)
- WiredSafety.org, an umbrella organization for WiredKids.org (www.wiredsafety.org)
- GetNetWise (www.getnetwise.org)
- i-SAFE America, Inc. (www.isafe.org)
- National Center for Missing and Exploited Children (www.missingkids.com)

13. The Bigger Picture

Congratulations! You've just finished learning how your personal information and the technology that gathers it, stores it, and dishes it up on command can affect you. I hope you feel you've seen a pretty broad range of ideas and have thought about things you might not have considered before. Thanks to your hard work, you are now less likely to be caught unaware by the curveballs thrown your way by malicious marketers, overzealous officials, short-sighted bankers, rigid bureaucrats, angry ex-spouses, psychotic stalkers, or brain-dead clerks.

Are you finished? No way. Although we've painted a pretty big picture of the Information Age, new developments in technology and new legislation are adding bits to that picture all the time. Now that you've had a chance to assess where things stand now, it's time to think about the even bigger picture.

THINGS THAT WON'T CHANGE

First, let's review the things that won't change. Based on the discussions we've had so far, we can identify twelve laws of information. These ideas are basic to the whole notion of what it means to collect and use data, and it is highly unlikely that they will stop being true or important anytime soon. If you can internalize these, you will go a very long way indeed in learning how to assess new situations and evaluate the risks and rewards offered by information use. You will be better at anticipating problems before they occur and better at successfully fighting your way through problems once the worst happens.

1. **Information doesn't have a nice smile.** Even with a growing reliance on "what the computer says," we are all still human. Getting to know the people who serve you at the bank or the store matters. And when you really need someone to vouch for you, as in the case of identity theft, it can matter a lot.

2. **Information is messy.** Even though it seems that putting your name and address in a database should be completely straightforward, somehow it never is. There are typos; there are bits that don't get filled in; there are search programs that assume an inexact match. Remember how credit reports will call up your file along with files that "might" be yours? If you expect information to be messy, you will never be caught unaware. You will simply be pleasantly surprised when it isn't.

3. **Asking for information is as important as the information itself.** Inquiring about someone's past has always aroused suspicion. This is no less true in a world of databases. Don't allow too many folks to nose about your files if you can help it. It may raise red flags with companies that matter, such as your bank or credit card companies.

4. **Data spreads more quickly than most colds.** Just because you think you are dealing with one company, this doesn't mean that the company is only dealing with you. They might be sharing or selling your information with affiliates and more. It is a good idea to clean up after yourself, and seek to restrict your paper trail, even if it's a digital one. Rather than dripping data wherever you go, shred papers, don't sign blanket release of information waivers, and adopt a habit of asking that use of your information be limited to the purpose and company at hand.

5. **Irritation about information use does *not* equal injustice.** Even if you don't like the decision that someone makes

based on your information, that doesn't mean that they don't have a reasonable right to make an informed decision. Some blacklists are what they are. Get over it.

6. **Information belongs to he who collects it.** Once you give your information away (or trade it for a prize or service), you've given it away. If you want any control over it, you must actively seek control. It will not happen by magic. Do-not-call lists and opt-out lists offer one way to do this. If information is taken from you, as with credit data, you may never be able to gain control, but you can still monitor what is going on.

7. **All information is not created equal.** Your Social Security number, which follows you from cradle to grave, is more important than your opinion on the movie that opened last weekend. Passwords to your bank accounts are pretty critical. Clues to those passwords are of great value, too. Think about what information needs more careful protection than the rest.

8. **You don't set the value of information.** The person holding what you want does. Even if you believe that your Social Security number is highly worth protecting, your health insurance company may disagree. Since you really want the insurance, they are probably going to win. Employers are also in a powerful position. Learn how to weigh the value placed on your information by others and determine if you have any room for negotiation. If not, figure out what you need to watch out for to determine if it's being misused.

9. **Information is subject to mission creep.** On more than one occasion, information collected for one reason has somehow been used for another. Think about supermarket loyalty cards. Wonder about airbag data. Before you volunteer *any* information, think about the other uses to which it could eventually be put.

10. **Information-privacy agreements go out the window when the cops come knocking.** Period.

11. **Even right information can be wrong.** Interpretation is a necessary component of using information. But some interpretations may be misleading. Converting to Islam does not automatically make you a terrorist. What might be true as a generalization may not be true in the particular. Low credit scores generally indicate a higher risk for car accidents, but you individually may be a very careful driver and a very poor bill payer. Decide when to challenge the status quo. Fighting misinterpretation can be a worthy cause.

12. **Ignorance offers pretty haphazard protection from information misuse.** It is worth your time to be aware of the world around you. This is especially true when it comes to government surveillance or protecting your kids. You want to stay in touch with the latest frauds and scams and trends of identity thieves by reading those articles in your local paper. You want to stay in touch with what the profilers are doing, by checking your credit report annually. Make sure that your Social Security earnings report is right. Think about insurance renewals. And stay in touch with new laws and new technology. This last one is a little more difficult to do, but an occasional visit to many of the organizations listed at the ends of the previous chapters will go a long way.

THINGS THAT WILL CHANGE

While the fundamentals of the nature of information won't change much, the technology that gathers it and uses it certainly will. It goes without saying that eager computer scientists clustered in the United States and abroad are working on some truly whizbang technology.

If computers, networks, and miniaturization were the first three successful technology waves, what will be the fourth? Some new technology such as washable fabric that reports the wearer's body temperature and heartbeat to a central computer, is beginning to feel like something that should only exist in science fiction novels. While the jury is out on what technology will prove useful enough to gain a stronghold in our day-to-day existence, there are a few trends that may set the stage.

Massive Real-Time Processing

One candidate is massive real-time processing, which is a fancy way of saying huge computers that can read video or listen intelligently to phone conversations as they are recorded. By removing the human operator, much more data can be extracted from source material than ever before.

Smarter Analysis Software

A sister component of data extraction is software that draws conclusions about data the same way that human analysts can. This software can examine a number of data points and come up with inferences and predictions. It can cross-reference data and actually make decisions—such as issuing alerts to law enforcement.

Ultra-Compressed Information Storage

Although this couldn't sound more dry and boring, being able to store gobs more information means that current housekeeping practices, such as recording over video security camera tapes every two weeks or eliminating database records after a period of time, may simply become completely unnecessary. More and more data will be stored indefinitely, making starting over a thing of the past.

New Forms of Input

Biometrics has generated a lot of excitement for the new type of data that it has created. The tone and timbre of your voice or the gait of your walk can be used to identify you. While the technology currently works inefficiently in real-world situations, we should probably expect this to change before long. In addition, the development of new things to track to uniquely identify people may open up other avenues of analysis and create still more new types of data. Imagine insurance companies determining that having a certain type of walk means that you are more prone to an accident and should be charged higher rates.

DRAWING A LINE IN THE SAND

Depending on where things go with new technology in the next few years, you may find that society is either in tune or out of step with your conclusions about what information use is productive or justifiable. If you feel that something is getting out of whack, you might just decide that you want to step up to the plate and play some role in shaping policies for yourself and future generations. Just as ignorance offers poor protection, apathy assures unfair systems.

Organizations like the American Civil Liberties Union, the Electronic Privacy Information Center, the Privacy Rights Clearinghouse, and the many others listed at the end of the previous chapters can offer experience and knowledge on how to have your voice be heard in the debate over information collection and use. A simple letter to your legislators or favorite companies can have a lot of impact, too.

Regardless of any action that you may or may not take, the most important thing is to be aware and to have an opinion.

UPDATES TO THIS BOOK AT
WWW.IDENTITYTHEFTPROTECTIONGUIDE.COM

In a world of information, it shouldn't be surprising that this book has a Web site, too. The site is packed with links to all of the resources we've discussed in this book and will offer new and updated information as big changes occur. For breaking bits on new laws, new issues and stories, as well as the latest tips and tricks, you can always visit www.identitytheftprotectionguide.com.

For now, sit back and enjoy the security and power your new knowledge has brought you. Well done!